C000242079

Explorii
Matthew's Gospel

—————◆━━●━◆━—————

**A guide to the gospel readings in
the Revised Common Lectionary**

Personality Type and Scripture Series

Exploring Luke's Gospel
Exploring Matthew's Gospel
Personality Type and Scripture: Exploring Mark's Gospel

Personality Type and Scripture Series

Exploring Matthew's Gospel

A guide to the gospel readings in the Revised Common Lectionary

LESLIE J. FRANCIS
AND
PETER ATKINS

morehouse

Morehouse
A Continuum imprint
The Tower Building, 11 York Road, London SE1 7NX
4775 Linglestown Road, Harrisburg, PA 17112

www.continuumbooks.com

© 2001 Leslie J. Francis and Peter Atkins

Myers-Briggs Type Indicator and *MBTI* are registered trademarks of
Consulting Psychologists Press, Inc.

All rights reserved. No part of this publication may be reproduced or
transmitted in any form or by any means, electronic or mechanical including
photocopying, recording or any information storage or retrieval system,
without prior permission in writing from the publishers.

Unless otherwise stated, scripture quotations are taken from the *New Revised
Standard Version* of the Bible, copyright © 1989 by the Division of Christian
Education of the National Council of the Churches of Christ in the USA, and
are used by permission. All rights reserved.

First published 2001
Reprinted 2005

British Library Cataloguing-in-Publication Data
A catalogue record for this book is available from the British Library.

ISBN 0-8192-8133-6

Designed and typeset by CentraServe Ltd, Saffron Walden, Essex.
Printed and bound in Great Britain by Biddles Ltd, www.biddles.co.uk

Contents

Preface

Psychological type theory is already being set to work by the
Christian churches in a variety of ways. It is being employed
to promote personal and professional development among
clergy during initial training and continuing ministerial education, to enhance collaborative ministry and body-building
among local congregations, and to help individual pilgrims
find their own preferred pattern of spirituality. This book sets
psychological type theory to work in the study of scripture.

There are two very practical ways in which this approach to
scripture may be of service to the Christian community. First,
this approach provides a disciplined way in which individuals
can be helped to meditate on the richness of scripture. It helps
them to transcend the more limited focus of their own
psychological preferences. Second, this approach provides a
disciplined way through which preachers can become more
aware of how different members of their congregation may
respond to their preaching. It helps them to appreciate how
different psychological types may hear and respond to different emphases within the same readings from scripture.

This approach addresses the same four questions to each
passage of scripture. How does this passage feed the sense per-
ceptions and establish contact with the reality of the situation? How does this passage feed the imagination and spark
off new ideas? What does this passage say about human values
and interpersonal relationships? What does this passage do to
stimulate the intellect and to challenge the roots of faith?
Many Christians may instinctively find one of these questions
of greater value and interest than the others. Many Christians
may well benefit from experiencing how the scriptures can
speak to the totality of their personality, to their senses and
their imagination, to their heart and their head.

Readers who are already well versed in type theory will
benefit from knowing the psychological type of the authors.
Such information may alert them to the strengths and to the

weaknesses of each author's own perspective. In the language of type theory, Leslie Francis is an INTJ. This means that he prefers *introversion* (I), *intuition* (N), *thinking* (T) and *judging* (J). Peter Atkins is an ESTJ. This means that he prefers *extraversion* (E), *sensing* (S), *thinking* (T) and *judging* (J). Readers who are not already well versed in type theory will find these concepts defined and discussed in the series introduction.

Having carefully planned this book together we decided that it would be appropriate to allow our two independent voices to be heard through the text. We divided the forty-six chapters into two sets, working in blocks of five. Leslie drafted chapters 1–5, Peter drafted chapters 6–10, and so on until 40, then each took 3 chapters in turn. While we have critiqued the content of each other's chapters, we have given variety to the text by not writing in the same style.

Index of Sundays (Year A)

Series introduction

Exploring Matthew's Gospel is part of the *Personality Type and Scripture Series* of books which reflect on scripture in a disciplined way using insights from personality psychology. Readers as yet unfamiliar with the language and theory of personality type may benefit from a brief introduction to that theory. It is for this reason that each volume carries the series introduction, written by Leslie J. Francis.

For the preacher

Looking over the edge of the pulpit into the faces of the congregation, it is not difficult to see that people differ. At the simplest level it is obvious how people differ by age and sex. Most preachers will observe the gender and age composition of their congregation and take this information into account in structuring and delivering their message. Without wishing to sort people too rigidly into categories, it seems just good common sense to recognize that one presentation might be more appropriate for the local Cubs or Brownies, another more appropriate for the Mothers' Union, and yet another more appropriate for the Pensioners' Guild. It is clear that the experience and the expectations of the specific groups have to be taken into account.

In many ways preaching to a homogeneous group like the local Cubs or Brownies may be easier than addressing a large and mixed congregation. In one presentation the preacher is required to address the needs of the ageing widow, to acknowledge the concerns of the business executive, and to capture the attention of the restless child chorister. People differ and the preacher needs to be aware of the differences.

A particularly intriguing and useful account of how people differ is provided by Carl Jung and his theory of psychological type. The theory of psychological type suggests that it is helpful for preachers to take into account not only how the members of their congregation differ in outward ways, but also how they differ in their psychological preferences. Different psychological types may hear sermons in very different ways, and this has important implications for preachers.

For personal study

When a group of people meet to study a passage of scripture, it often becomes clear very quickly how different individuals may study the same passage in very distinctive ways. One member of the group may want to focus closely on the details of the text itself. Another member of the group may want to draw the wider implications from the text and make links with other or contemporary issues. Another member of the group may concentrate on lessons for practical living and for personal relationships. Yet another member of the group may wish to explore the theological implications of the text and the problems and challenges which it raises for faith.

Bible study groups which contain such a rich mix of people can be exciting for many Christians and open their eyes to the different ways in which scripture can enrich the lives of the people of God. When individual Christians meditate on scripture in the privacy of their own home they need to have their eyes opened to the variety of perspectives which can be brought to the same passage by other Christians who see things in a different way.

Carl Jung's theory of psychological type not only opens our eyes to the ways in which people differ, but also to the rich variety of perspectives within ourselves. The theory makes us more conscious of those parts of ourselves which we may undervalue and under-exercise. Type theory concerned with the richness of our own psychological composition has important implications for how we allow ourselves to be nurtured and nourished by scripture.

The Myers-Briggs Type Indicator

It is Jung's theory of psychological type which stands at the heart of the Myers-Briggs Type Indicator, a psychological tool being increasingly used by the Christian churches. This theory identifies two main mental processes. The first process concerns the ways in which we gather information. This is the *perceiving* process. Some people prefer *sensing* (S); others prefer *intuition* (N). According to the theory, these two types look at the world in very different ways.

The second process concerns the ways in which we make decisions. This is the *judging* process. Some people prefer *thinking* (T); others prefer *feeling* (F). According to the theory, these two types come to decisions about the world in very different ways.

Jung also suggested that individuals differ in the *orientation* in which they prefer to employ these two processes. Some people prefer the outer or extraverting world (E); others prefer the inner or introverting world (I). According to the theory, these two types are energized in very different ways. Extraverts draw their energy from the outer world of people and things, while introverts draw their energy from their inner world.

Finally, individuals differ in their *attitude* to the outer world. Both introverts and extraverts need to deal with the outer world and both may prefer to do this with a *judging* (J) or a *perceiving* (P) process. According to the theory, these two types display a very different attitude to the outer world.

What the theory understands by these preferences now needs to be explained in greater detail.

Introversion and extraversion

Introversion and extraversion describe the two preferred orientations of the inner world and the outer world. Introverts prefer to focus their attention on the inner world of ideas and draw their energy from that inner world. When introverts are tired and need energizing they look to the inner world. Extraverts prefer to focus their attention on the outer world of people and things and draw their energy from that outer world. When extraverts are tired and need energizing they look to the outer world. Since this introduction is being written by an introvert, the author prefers to present this perspective first, followed by the extravert perspective.

Introverts like quiet for concentration. They want to be able to shut off the distractions of the outer world and turn inwards. They often experience trouble in remembering names and faces. They can work at one solitary project for a long time without interruption. When they are engaged in a task in the outer world they may become absorbed in the ideas behind that task.

Introverts work best alone and may resent distractions and interruptions from other people. They dislike being interrupted by the telephone, tend to think things through before acting, and may spend so long in thought that they miss the opportunity to act.

Introverts prefer to learn by reading rather than by talking with others. They may also prefer to communicate with others in writing, rather than face-to-face or over the phone; this is particularly the case if they have something unpleasant to communicate.

Introverts are oriented to the inner world. They focus on ideas, concepts and inner understanding. They are reflective, may consider deeply before acting, and they probe inwardly for stimulation.

Extraverts like variety and action. They want to be able to shut off the distractions of the inner world and turn outward. They are good at remembering faces and names and enjoy meeting people and introducing people. They can become impatient with long, slow jobs. When they are working in the company of other people they may become more interested in how others are doing the job than in the job itself.

Extraverts like to have other people around them in the working environment, and enjoy the stimulus of sudden interruptions and telephone calls. Extraverts like to act quickly and decisively, even when it is not totally appropriate to do so.

Extraverts prefer to learn a task by talking it through with other people. They prefer to communicate with other people face-to-face or over the phone, rather than in writing. They often find that their own ideas become clarified through communicating them with others.

Extraverts are oriented to the outer world. They focus on people and things. They prefer to learn by trial and error and they do so with confidence. They are active people, and they scan the outer environment for stimulation.

Sensing and intuition

Sensing and intuition describe the two preferences associated with the *perceiving process*. They describe different preferences used to acquire information. Sensing types focus on the realities of a situation as perceived by the senses. Intuitive types focus on the possibilities, meanings and relationships, the 'big picture' that goes beyond sensory information. Since this introduction is being written by an intuitive, the author prefers to present this perspective first, followed by the sensing perspective.

Individuals who prefer *intuition* develop insight into complexity. They have the ability to see abstract, symbolic and theoretical relationships, and the capacity to see future possibilities. They put their reliance on inspiration rather than on past experience. Their interest is in the new and untried. They trust their intuitive grasp of meanings and relationships.

Individuals with a preference for intuition are aware of new challenges and possibilities. They see quickly beyond the information they have been given or the materials they have to hand to the possibilities and challenges which these offer. They are often discontented with the way things are and wish to improve them. They become bored quickly and dislike doing the same thing repeatedly.

Intuitive types enjoy learning new skills. They work in bursts of energy, powered by enthusiasm, and then enjoy slack periods between activity.

Intuitive types follow their inspirations and hunches. They may reach conclusions too quickly and misconstrue the information or get the facts wrong. They dislike taking too much time to secure precision.

Intuitive types may tend to imagine that things are more complex than they really are: they tend to over-complexify things. They are curious about why things are the way they are and may prefer to raise questions than to find answers.

Intuitive types are always striving to gain an overview of the information around them. In terms of an old proverb, they may prefer to pay attention to the two birds in the bush rather than the one in the hand.

Intuitive types perceive with memory and associations. They see patterns and meanings and assess possibilities. They are good at reading between the lines and projecting possibilities for the future. They prefer to go always for the big picture. They prefer to let the mind inform the eyes.

Individuals who prefer *sensing* develop keen awareness of present experience. They have acute powers of observation, good memory for facts and details, the capacity for realism, and the ability to see the world as it is. They rely on experience rather than theory. They put their trust in what is known and in the conventional.

Individuals with a preference for sensing are aware of the uniqueness of each individual event. They develop good techniques of observation and they recognize the practical way in which things work now.

Sensing types like to develop an established way of doing

things and gain enjoyment from exercising skills which they have already learnt. Repetitive work does not bore them. They are able to work steadily with a realistic idea of how long a task will take.

Sensing types usually reach their conclusion step by step, observing each piece of information carefully. They are not easily inspired to interpret the information in front of them and they may not trust inspiration when it comes. They are very careful about getting the facts right and are good at engaging in precise work.

Sensing types may fail to recognize complexity in some situations, and consequently over-simplify tasks. They are good at accepting the current reality as the given situation in which to work. They would much rather work with the present information than speculate about future possibilities. They clearly agree with the old proverb that the bird in the hand is worth two in the bush.

Sensing types perceive clearly with the five senses. They attend to practical and factual details, and they are in touch with physical realities. They attend to the present moment and prefer to confine their attention to what is said and done. They observe the small details of everyday life and attend to step-by-step experience. They prefer to let the eyes tell the mind.

Thinking and feeling

Thinking and feeling describe the two preferences associated with the *judging process*. They describe different preferences by which decisions are reached. Individuals who prefer thinking make decisions by objective, logical analysis. Individuals who prefer feeling make decisions by subjective values based on how people will be affected. Since this introduction is being written by a thinker, the author prefers to present this perspective first, followed by the feeling perspective.

Individuals who prefer *thinking* develop clear powers of logical analysis. They develop the ability to weigh facts objectively and to predict consequences, both intended and unintended. They develop a stance of impartiality. They are characterized by a sense of fairness and justice.

Individuals with a preference for thinking are good at putting things in logical order. They are also able to put people in their place when they consider it necessary. They are able to take tough decisions and to reprimand others. They are also able to be firm and tough-minded about themselves.

Thinking types need to be treated fairly and to see that other people are treated fairly as well. They are inclined to respond more to other people's ideas than to other people's feelings. They may inadvertently hurt other people's feelings without recognizing that they are doing so.

Thinking types are able to anticipate and predict the logical outcomes of other people's choices. They can see the humour rather than the human pain in bad choices and wrong decisions taken by others. Thinking types prefer to look at life from the outside as a spectator.

Thinking types are able to develop good powers of logical analysis. They use objective and impersonal criteria in reaching decisions. They follow logically the relationships between cause and effect. They develop characteristics of being firm-minded and prizing logical order. They may appear sceptical.

Individuals who prefer *feeling* develop a personal emphasis on values and standards. They appreciate what matters most to themselves and what matters most to other people. They develop an understanding of people, a wish to affiliate with people and a desire for harmony. They are characterized by their capacity for warmth, and by qualities of empathy and compassion.

Individuals with a preference for feeling like harmony and will work hard to bring harmony about between other people. They dislike telling other people unpleasant things or reprimanding other people. They take into account other people's feelings.

Feeling types need to have their own feelings recognized as well. They need praise and affirmation. They are good at seeing the personal effects of choices on their own lives and on other people's lives as well.

Feeling types are sympathetic individuals. They take a great interest in the people behind the job and respond to other people's values as much as to their ideas. They enjoy pleasing people.

Feeling types look at life from the inside. They live life as a committed participant and find it less easy to stand back and to form an objective view of what is taking place.

Feeling types develop skills at applying personal priorities.

They are good at weighing human values and motives, both their own and other people's. They are characterized by qualities of empathy and sympathy. They prize harmony and trust.

Judging and perceiving

Judging and perceiving describe the two preferred attitudes towards the outer world. Individuals who prefer to relate to the outer world with a judging process present a planned and orderly approach to life. They prefer to have a settled system in place and display a preference for closure. Individuals who prefer to relate to the outer world with a perceiving process present a flexible and spontaneous approach to life. They prefer to keep plans and organizations to a minimum and display a preference for openness. Since this introduction is being written by a judger, the author prefers to present this perspective first, followed by the perceiving perspective.

Judging types schedule projects so that each step gets done on time. They like to get things finished and settled, and to know that the finished product is in place. They work best when they can plan their work in advance and follow that plan. Judging types use lists and agendas to structure their day and to plan their actions. They may dislike interruption from the plans they have made and are reluctant to leave the task in hand even when something more urgent arises.

Judging types tend to be satisfied once they reach a judgement or have made a decision, both about people and things. They dislike having to revise their decision and taking fresh information into account. They like to get on with a task as soon as possible once the essential things are at hand. As a consequence, judging types may decide to act too quickly.

When individuals take a judging attitude towards the outer world, they are using the preferred *judging process*, thinking or feeling, outwardly. Their attitude to life is characterized by deciding and planning, organizing and scheduling, controlling and regulating. Their life is goal-oriented. They want to move towards closure, even when the data are incomplete.

Perceiving types adapt well to changing situations. They make allowances for new information and for changes in the situation in which they are living or acting. They may have trouble making decisions, feeling that they have never quite got enough information on which to base their decision.

Perceiving types may start too many projects and consequently have difficulty in finishing them. They may tend to postpone unpleasant tasks and to give their attention to more pleasant options. Perceiving types want to know all about a new task before they begin it, and may prefer to postpone something new while they continue to explore the options.

When perceiving types use lists they do so not as a way of organizing the details of their day, but of seeing the possibilities in front of them. They may choose never to act on these possibilities. Perceiving types do not mind leaving things open for last minute changes. They work best under pressure and get a lot accomplished at the last minute under the constraints of a deadline.

When individuals take a perceiving attitude towards the outer world, they are using the preferred *perceiving process*, sensing or intuition, outwardly. They are taking in information, adapting and changing, curious and interested. They adopt an open-minded attitude towards life and resist closure to obtain more data.

Personality type and preaching

The Myers-Briggs Type Indicator provides information about the individual's orientation (introversion or extraversion), perceiving process (sensing or intuition), judging process (thinking or feeling) and attitude towards the outer world (judging or perceiving). The crucial information for the preacher, however, centres on the two processes, that is to say on the two distinctions between sensing and intuition (the perceiving process) and between thinking and feeling (the judging process).

According to the theory, every individual needs to draw on all four functions of the two processes: sensing and intuition, thinking and feeling. But at the same time one of these four functions is preferred and becomes dominant. The four functions of sensing and intuition, thinking and feeling, when dominant, approach the world in very different ways. These different approaches will be attracted by very different perspectives in preaching.

At its most basic level, the sensing type needs to respond to facts and information, to details and clearly defined images. The intuitive type needs to respond to challenges to the imagination and arresting ideas, to theories and possibilities. The feeling type needs to respond to issues of the heart and to the stuff of human relationships. The thinking type needs to respond to issues of the head and to the stuff of logical analysis.

Of course, left to their own devices preachers will emphasize their own type preference. The preacher who prefers intuition will preach a message full of fast-moving ideas and imaginative associations. The sensing types in the congregation will quickly lose the thread and accuse those preachers of having their heads in the air and their shoes high above the ground. The preacher who prefers sensing will preach a message full of detailed information and the close analysis of text. The intuitive types in the congregation will quickly tire of the detail and accuse those preachers of being dull and failing to see the wood for the trees.

The preacher who prefers feeling will preach a message full of human interest and of loving concern for people. The thinking types in the congregation will quickly become impatient with this emphasis on interpersonal matters and accuse those preachers of failing to grasp the hard intellectual issues and the pressing challenges and contradictions of the faith. The preacher who prefers thinking will preach a message full of theological erudition and carefully argued nuance of perspective. The feeling types in the congregation will quickly become impatient with this emphasis on theological abstraction and accuse those preachers of missing the very heart of the gospel which cries out for compassion, understanding and human warmth.

Responding to the challenge

The theory of psychological types helps to clarify and to sharpen one of the problems confronting the preacher. There is no one simple solution to this problem, although being aware of the problem is itself an important step towards addressing it.

One suggestion is to try to include within the majority of sermons components which will speak directly to each of the four types: sensing, intuition, thinking and feeling. The problem with this solution is that the time generally allowed for preaching makes it difficult to develop all four perspectives in any depth. Evenly distributed, a ten-minute sermon would allow two and a half minutes on each perspective. A second suggestion is to try to vary the preaching style from week to week. In this sense perhaps an ideal preaching team should include four preachers representing the four psychological types. Few churches, however, may have such a resource readily available!

Our aim in this book has been to take 46 gospel passages from Matthew included in the *Revised Common Lectionary* and to interrogate each passage from the distinctive perspectives of the four psychological types. For all 46 gospel passages we have followed the same disciplined pattern of exploring the four functions in the same fixed order: sensing, intuition, feeling and thinking. There is a logic in this order. We need the sensing function to ground us in the reality of the passage of scripture. We need the intuitive function to draw out the wider implications and to develop the links. We need the feeling function to become attuned to the issues of values and human priorities within the narrative. We need the thinking function to face the theological implications and to struggle with the intellectual issues.

We cannot imagine preachers wishing to follow this pattern slavishly week in and week out. But we can imagine preachers using this material in two main ways. On some Sundays we envisage sermons being preached which self-consciously present four different perspectives on the one gospel passage. We envisage congregations, as well as preachers, being aware of the reason for this. We envisage this process leading to a wider and better-informed discussion of the relevance of type theory for appreciating the diversity of perspectives and the diversity of gifts within the local congregation.

On other Sundays we envisage the preacher deliberately targeting one of the perspectives and developing that consistent line of presentation. We envisage individuals in the congregation representative of all four types being challenged to listen and to respond. We envisage this process leading to a deeper spiritual awareness as individuals gain closer contact with the less well-developed aspects of their inner self, and come to appreciate more deeply how the God who created us with diversity of gifts and diversity of preferences can be worshipped and adored through sensing as well as intuition, through thinking as well as feeling.

1

Matthew 1:18–25

[18]Now the birth of Jesus the Messiah took place in this way. When his mother Mary had been engaged to Joseph, but before they lived together, she was found to be with child from the Holy Spirit. [19]Her husband Joseph, being a righteous man and unwilling to expose her to public disgrace, planned to dismiss her quietly. [20]But just when he had resolved to do this, an angel of the Lord appeared to him in a dream and said, 'Joseph, son of David, do not be afraid to take Mary as your wife, for the child conceived in her is from the Holy Spirit. [21]She will bear a son, and you are to name him Jesus, for he will save his people from their sins.' [22]All this took place to fulfil what had been spoken by the Lord through the prophet:

> [23]'Look, the virgin shall conceive and bear a son,
>   and they shall name him Emmanuel',

which means, 'God is with us.' [24]When Joseph awoke from sleep, he did as the angel of the Lord commanded him; he took her as his wife, [25]but had no marital relations with her until she had borne a son; and he named him Jesus.

Context

Matthew's Gospel begins with a carefully crafted genealogy showing Jesus to be the descendant of David, the descendant of Abraham. It is Joseph, not Mary, who is crucial to the lineage. Now Matthew makes it clear that Joseph accepts and names Jesus as his own son.

Sensing

If people paid attention to Matthew, Joseph would be taken a lot more seriously by the Christian church.

According to Matthew, the whole significance of Jesus hinges on his claim to be the direct descendant of David. The promised Messiah was to be born of the house of David. Matthew spells out one by one the fourteen generations from David to the deportation to Babylon and the fourteen generations from the deportation to Babylon to the Messiah. It is Joseph who secures the link between David and Jesus. If people paid attention to Matthew, Joseph would be taken a lot more seriously by the Christian church.

According to Matthew, in the birth of Jesus God intervened in human affairs in a decisive and distinctive way. God's plans were made known by speaking directly to the chosen one through dreams and through the message of the angel. It was to Joseph that the dream came. It was to Joseph that the angel spoke. If people paid attention to Matthew, Joseph would be taken a lot more seriously by the Christian church.

According to Matthew, God's plans for the birth of the Messiah depended wholly on human obedience. It was Joseph who was obedient to the divine behest. When Joseph awoke from sleep, he did as the angel of the Lord commanded him. Joseph took Mary as his wife. Joseph legally claimed and publicly proclaimed her child as his own son when he spoke aloud his name 'Jesus' at the ceremony of circumcision and naming. If people paid attention to Matthew, Joseph would be taken a lot more seriously by the Christian church.

Intuition

Now I wonder what conclusion you would have jumped to had you stood where Joseph stood?

In accordance with Jewish custom and law, Joseph had entered into the legally binding contract of betrothal with Mary. Betrothal was much more than engagement, for only divorce could break the relationship. Yet betrothal was less than marriage, for they were not yet living under the same roof as man and wife. Then Mary was found to be pregnant. Now I wonder what conclusions you would have jumped to had you stood where Joseph stood?

In accordance with Jewish custom and law Joseph could have insisted on a public trial to determine the origin of the child whom Mary was carrying. Indeed Deuteronomy 22 sets down the legal view on three different scenarios which may befall the virgin already engaged to be married: prostitution, seduction and rape. Each has its own penalty. For prostitution and seduction the woman is to be stoned to death. Now I wonder what conclusions you would have jumped to had you stood where Joseph stood?

In accordance with Jewish custom and piety, Joseph decided to follow the path of compassion and mercy. Instead of demanding a public inquest he resolved to divorce Mary quietly. In so resolving he gave up his right to vengeance. He also remained committed to the financial cost of divorce. Now I wonder what conclusions you would have jumped to had you stood where Joseph stood?

In accordance with Jewish custom and piety, Joseph slept and in his sleep the angel of the Lord appeared to him in a dream and said, 'Joseph, son of David, do not be afraid to take Mary as your wife, for the child conceived in her is from the Holy Spirit.' The angel of the Lord appeared to him in a dream and said, 'Joseph, she will bear a son, and you are to name him Jesus, for he will save his people from their sins.' Now I wonder what conclusions you would have jumped to had you stood where Joseph stood?

Feeling

In popular piety Mary and Joseph are often referred to as the *Holy Family*. What secrets of family life lie hidden in this brief narrative?

We know nothing of what first brought the world-famous couple together. We know from Matthew that Joseph was a righteous man. We know from Luke that Mary found favour with God. We know from both Gospels that they were an obedient couple, obedient to the word of God. But we know nothing of what brought them together.

We know nothing of their hopes and dreams as they entered the legally binding state of betrothal. We know from Matthew that Joseph was a carpenter. We know from Luke that during this betrothal they lived in a town in Galilee called Nazareth. But we know nothing of the life they planned to live together there.

We know nothing of how Joseph learned about Mary's pregnancy. Scripture says boldly that Mary was found to be with child. We do not know whether Mary told Joseph, whether Joseph observed for himself, or whether the tale was brought to him by rumour and gossip. We know nothing of what Joseph felt about this news.

We know nothing of how Mary and Joseph discussed this extraordinary disruption to their lives. Matthew tells us simply

that Joseph planned to dismiss her quietly. No reference is made
to how Mary felt about this decision which would have affected
the rest of her life. We know nothing of how Mary and Joseph
communicated the one with the other.

We know nothing of how this special couple integrated their
unique religious experiences into their lives or into their relationship. From Luke we know that the angel Gabriel came to Mary
and said:

Do not be afraid, Mary, for you have found favour with God.
And now you will conceive in your womb and bear a son, and
you will name him Jesus.

From Matthew we know that an angel of the Lord appeared to
Joseph in a dream and said:

Joseph, son of David, do not be afraid to take Mary as your
wife, for the child conceived in her is from the Holy Spirit.
She will bear a son, and you are to name him Jesus.

But we do not know how this special couple shared their revela-
tions and their personal experiences of God.

In popular piety Mary and Joseph are often referred to as the
Holy Family. What secrets of family life lie hidden in their
relationship?

Thinking

Theologically speaking, names carry great power. Names can
transform individuals and whole cultures.

The child who is to be born is named Jesus. The name is
redolent with power to transform. The Greek name Jesus is the
same as the Hebrew name Joshua. Literally Jesus means 'God
saves'. Through Jesus God saves the people of God from their
sins. In the Old Testament Joshua had led the people of God to
claim their promised land. Theologically speaking, names carry
great power.

The child who is to be born is named Messiah. The name is
redolent with power to transform. The Greek name Christ is the
same as the Hebrew name Messiah. Literally Messiah means 'the
anointed one'. Jesus is anointed to lead the people of God. In the
Old Testament Jesus' great ancestor David had been anointed as
king over the people of God. Theologically speaking, names carry
great power.

The child who is to be born is named Emmanuel. The name is redolent with power to transform. Matthew translates the name Emmanuel to mean 'God is with us'. In and through this child, conceived by the Holy Spirit, God stands alongside and among the people of God. In and through this child, conceived by the Holy Spirit, God is with the people of God and not against them. God is alongside them and on their side. Theologically speaking, names carry great power.

The child who is to be born is given his name by prophecy, for it was Isaiah who said:

> Look, the virgin shall conceive and bear a son,
> and they shall name him Emmanuel.

The child who is to be born is given his name by lineage, for it was determined that the Messiah should rise up from the house of David. The child who is to be born is given his name by divine revelation, for it was the angel who said:

> She will bear a son and you are to name him Jesus.

The child who is to be born is given his name by paternal authority and religious custom, for Joseph named the boy Jesus.

Theologically speaking, names carry great power. Names can transform individuals and whole cultures.

2
Matthew 2:1–12

¹In the time of King Herod, after Jesus was born in Bethlehem of Judea, wise men from the East came to Jerusalem, ²asking, 'Where is the child who has been born king of the Jews? For we observed his star at its rising, and have come to pay him homage.' ³When King Herod heard this, he was frightened, and all Jerusalem with him; ⁴and calling together all the chief priests and scribes of the people, he inquired of them where

the Messiah was to be born. [5]They told him, 'In Bethlehem of Judea; for so it has been written by the prophet:

> [6]"And you, Bethlehem, in the land of Judah,
>   are by no means least among the rulers of
>   Judah;
>   for from you shall come a ruler
>   who is to shepherd my people Israel." '

[7]Then Herod secretly called for the wise men and learned from them the exact time when the star had appeared. [8]Then he sent them to Bethlehem, saying, 'Go and search diligently for the child; and when you have found him, bring me word so that I may also go and pay him homage.' [9]When they had heard the king, they set out; and there, ahead of them, went the star that they had seen at its rising, until it stopped over the place where the child was. [10]When they saw that the star had stopped, they were overwhelmed with joy. [11]On entering the house, they saw the child with Mary his mother; and they knelt down and paid him homage. Then, opening their treasure-chests, they offered him gifts of gold, frankincense, and myrrh. [12]And having been warned in a dream not to return to Herod, they left for their own country by another road.

Context

Matthew shows, right from the time of Jesus' birth, how the Jewish leaders reject God's Messiah and how the Gentiles come to accept Jesus as their king.

Sensing

Matthew's account of the visit of the Magi is a powerful story of adventure, danger and adoration. Share in the Magi's pilgrimage and let the details sink in.

Look up into the night sky. See a bright new star never before seen by human eye. Let that star draw you by its power and magic. Commit yourself to follow that star to the ends of the earth.

Pack up your belongings into a sack. Break away from all that holds you back and set out on a long long journey of adventure and danger. Follow that star wherever it leads, across deserts, through cities, beside flowing rivers and through scorched desert landscapes.

Keep following the star that leads you until you enter the powerful Herod's majestic palace. See the star flicker and fade as you digress from the path of your journey. See the fear and the hate in Herod's eyes as you tell him of your quest for a new-born king.

Keep following the star that leads you until you enter the humble home where the Christ child awaits you. See the star burn brighter and clearer as your gaze meets the eyes of the Son of God. See the love and the acceptance in the young child's eyes as you tell Mary and Joseph of your quest across the paths of time.

Unpack your sack as you settle in the Christ child's presence. Take out the gleaming cup of gold and run your hand across the smooth polished surface. Place the gleaming cup of gold at the Christ child's feet.

Unpack your sack as you settle in the Christ child's presence. Take out the precious bag of frankincense and breathe in deeply the haunting fragrance. Place the precious bag of incense at the Christ child's feet.

Unpack your sack as you settle in the Christ child's presence. Take out the fragile jar of myrrh and gently moisten your hand with the fragrant ointment. Place the fragile jar of myrrh at the Christ child's feet.

Matthew's account of the visit of the Magi is a powerful story of adventure, danger and adoration. Share in the Magi's pilgrimage and let the details sink in.

Intuition

Matthew's story of the wise men illustrates just how much an encounter with Jesus can disrupt and change lives. Are you really willing to follow in their footsteps?

For those wise men the religious journey began with a dim and unarticulated aspiration. Literally they set their hopes upon a star and set out in faith. Are you willing to take such a step of faith?

For those wise men the religious journey meant leaving so much behind. Literally they packed up their belongings, left their homes and set out on a new beginning. Are you willing to make such a fresh start?

For those wise men the religious journey meant living with questions and accepting uncertainty. Literally they knew that they did not have the answers to their questions. Are you willing to live with such uncertainty?

For those wise men the religious journey meant seeking and testing the wisdom of others. Literally they listened to Herod, to the chief priests and to the scribes of the people. They listened to the accumulated wisdom of scripture. Are you willing to listen to the wisdom of others?

For those wise men the religious journey meant entering the house where Jesus dwelt. Literally they went into the very place where Jesus was to be found. Are you willing to persevere with your journey until you come to that very place?

For those wise men the religious journey meant kneeling down and worshipping Jesus. Literally they discounted their own wisdom and acknowledged the wisdom of the one who was wiser than them. Are you willing to lay aside your own claims to wisdom?

For those wise men the religious journey meant giving up the wealth and treasures they had accumulated. Literally they unpacked and left with Jesus their gold, their frankincense and their myrrh. Are you willing to use your wealth in his service?

For those wise men the religious journey meant that they were ready to return to their own country when their plans changed. Literally they returned by another road. Are you willing to return by another route?

Matthew's story of the wise men illustrates just how much an encounter with Jesus can disrupt and change lives. Are you willing to follow in their footsteps?

Feeling

Look at the story through Mary's eyes. Put yourself in her shoes. Was all this fuss really in the best interests of her young child?

Times had been pretty traumatic for Mary. After all it had been touch-and-go whether Joseph would go through with the wedding after she had been found to be pregnant. Had the angel not appeared in a dream to Joseph, Mary would have been divorced before the marriage had ever been completed. Was such anxiety really in the best interests of her unborn child?

If Luke's account can be trusted, the birth itself was pretty traumatic. There was the disruptive and tiring journey from

Nazareth to Bethlehem. There was overcrowding in the inn. There was the agony of labour and childbirth in the unhygienic surroundings of the cattle shed. There was the inquisitive intrusion of the shepherds. Was such discomfort in the best interests of her new-born child?

Now when the immediate turmoil seems all something of the past, strange uninvited guests arrive from the East, hooked on a star and seeking a king in the most unregal surroundings. These uninvited guests require feeding. Their uninvited camels require stabling. Was such an invasion in the best interests of her young child?

No sooner had the foreigners arrived than they began to present gifts to the inquisitive child. They drew from their treasures not the cuddly toy camel, not the glittering star, not the Eastern delicacy, but gifts of much more puzzling nature. Were such unusual gifts really in the best interests of her young child?

According to much later tradition it was Melchior who unpacked the gift of gold, the gift for a king. It was Caspar who unpacked the gift of frankincense, the gift for a priest. It was Balthasar who unpacked the gift of myrrh, the gift for one who is to die. Were such portentous gifts really in the best interests of her young child?

Look at the story through Mary's eyes. Put yourself in her shoes. Was all this fuss really in the best interests of her young child?

Thinking

It is passages like this which are unique to Matthew's gospel that give us insights into Matthew's distinctive theology. Can you work out what Matthew is trying to say?

Matthew describes two quite different reactions to the birth of Jesus. On the one hand, there is Herod and all Jerusalem with him. On the other hand, there are wise men, foreigners from the East. Can you work out what Matthew is trying to say?

Herod and all Jerusalem with him are frightened by the prospect of the birth of God's Messiah. Here in Jerusalem is the heart of God's chosen people for whose sake the Messiah has been sent. But Herod and all Jerusalem with him are frightened. Can you work out what Matthew is trying to say?

The wise men, foreigners from the East, travel miles to

seek out the King of the Jews. Foreigners from the East are the first to recognize God's anointed Messiah. They bring gifts from their foreign land and lay them at the feet of him who is born King of the Jews. Can you work out what Matthew is trying to say?

Matthew describes two quite different reactions to the birth of Jesus. On the one hand, Herod pretends to want to go to pay homage to Jesus. On the other hand, the wise men come and kneel down before him. Can you work out what Matthew is trying to say?

Here at the time of Jesus' birth are foreshadowed events that will take place some thirty years later. Then once again all Jerusalem will set their hearts against him and lead him on the path to the cross. But then the good news of the resurrection will be proclaimed to all Gentile nations. Can you work out what Matthew is trying to say?

It is passages like this which are unique to Matthew's gospel that give us insights into Matthew's distinctive theology.

3

Matthew 2:13–23

¹³Now after they had left, an angel of the Lord appeared to Joseph in a dream and said, 'Get up, take the child and his mother, and flee to Egypt, and remain there until I tell you; for Herod is about to search for the child, to destroy him.' ¹⁴Then Joseph got up, took the child and his mother by night, and went to Egypt, ¹⁵and remained there until the death of Herod. This was to fulfil what had been spoken by the Lord through the prophet, 'Out of Egypt I have called my son.'

¹⁶When Herod saw that he had been tricked by the wise men, he was infuriated, and he sent and killed all the children in and around Bethlehem who were two years old or under, according to the time that he had learned from the wise men. ¹⁷Then was fulfilled what had been spoken through the prophet Jeremiah:

[18]'A voice was heard in Ramah,
    wailing and loud lamentation,
  Rachel weeping for her children;
    she refused to be consoled,
      because they are no more.'
[19]When Herod died, an angel of the Lord suddenly appeared in a dream to Joseph in Egypt and said, [20]'Get up, take the child and his mother, and go to the land of Israel, for those who were seeking the child's life are dead.' [21]Then Joseph got up, took the child and his mother, and went to the land of Israel. [22]But when he heard that Archelaus was ruling over Judea in place of his father Herod, he was afraid to go there. And after being warned in a dream, he went away to the district of Galilee. [23]There he made his home in a town called Nazareth, so that what had been spoken through the prophets might be fulfilled, 'He will be called a Nazorean.'

Context

After the wise men had inadvertently alerted Herod to Jesus' birth, Herod resolved to put the child to death. So as not to allow the child to escape, Herod had all the young children in and around Bethlehem executed.

Sensing

In the bible there are two stories of infants who miraculously escaped from the hand of slaughter. One is told in the Old Testament. The other is told in the New Testament. Put these two stories side by side and spot the similarities.

Step back in time to the cruel days when the Israelites were held captive in Egypt. Sense the powerful and troubled Pharaoh grow anxious for his safety. Hear the powerful and troubled Pharaoh command his soldiers, saying, 'Every boy that is born to the Hebrews you shall throw into the Nile.'

Step back in time to the cruel days when the Israelites were held captive in Egypt. Hear the mothers scream as their baby sons were torn from their arms. Feel the terror in the young children's bodies. See the heartless soldiers do their job.

Step back in time to the cruel days when the Israelites were held captive in Egypt. See the young child Moses hidden in the reeds on the bank of the river. Hear how the young child Moses was rescued by Pharaoh's daughter and how he escaped the massacre of the innocents.

Then look forward and see how God called Moses out of Egypt to lead the people of God to their promised land.

Step back in time to the cruel days when the Israelites were oppressed in their own land by Herod their king. Sense the powerful and troubled Herod grow anxious for his safety. Hear the powerful and troubled Herod command his soldiers to kill all the children under two years of age in Bethlehem.

Step back in time to the cruel days when the Israelites were oppressed in their own land by Herod their king. Hear the mothers scream as their baby sons were torn from their arms. Feel the terror in the young children's bodies. See the heartless soldiers do their job.

Step back in time to the cruel days when the Israelites were oppressed in their own land by Herod their king. See the young child Jesus smuggled out into Egypt by his mother and father. Hear how the young child Jesus was rescued through a dream and how he escaped the massacre of the innocents.

Then look forward and see how God called Jesus out of Egypt to lead the people of God to their promised land.

Put these two stories side by side and spot the similarities, as Matthew presents Jesus as the new Moses.

Intuition

Human history is littered with stories of inhuman behaviour. What examples come to your mind?

Go back to the Old Testament story of the birth of Moses. In those days Pharaoh ordered the mass destruction of all Hebrew new-born boys. The slaughter of children was great. Surely such atrocities could never happen again?

Go back to the New Testament story of the birth of Jesus. In those days King Herod ordered the mass destruction of all children under two years of age in or around Bethlehem. The slaughter of children was great. Surely such atrocities could never happen again?

Visit the Holocaust museum in present-day Jerusalem. See the pictures of the concentration camps. Consider the sophisticated gas chambers and hear the young children scream. The slaughter of children was great. Surely such atrocities could never happen again?

See the television news of war-torn countries. See the civilian casualties inflicted by missiles and by air attacks. Consider the sophisticated machinery of war in irresponsible hands. The slaughter of children is great. Surely such atrocities cannot continue to happen today?

Read the newspaper reports of missing children. Consider how individual children are abducted, abused and murdered in the heart of our civilized society. Consider how little value is placed on the life of a child. Surely such atrocities cannot continue to happen today?

Hear how some children are let down by their parents. Consider how some children are neglected, abused and mistreated in the heart of their family home. Consider how little value is placed on the life of a child. Surely such atrocities cannot continue to happen today?

Human history is littered with stories of inhuman behaviour. What can you do to make the world a better and safer place for children?

Feeling

All too often the story of Jesus' birth and early child-care is told from the perspective of Mary the mother. That, after all, is the way Luke presents the matter. But step aside from the familiar Lucan perspective and see how things look through the eyes of Joseph the father. For that is what Matthew invites us to do.

Three times during those early years Joseph the father was anxious about the welfare of Mary's child. The first occasion was long before the baby had been born. The first occasion was when Mary's pregnancy was known and the child's paternity remained in dispute. Joseph was anxious about the future of the child.

Three times during those early years the angel of the Lord steered Joseph's sound judgement. On the first occasion the angel said:

Joseph . . . do not be afraid to take Mary as your wife, for the child conceived in her is from the Holy Spirit.

Joseph listened to the angel's message and named the child as his own son. Joseph the father secured a future for the young child.

Three times during those early years Joseph the father was anxious about the welfare of Mary's child. The second occasion was immediately after the wise men had caused such a stir about the birth of a king in Bethlehem. The second occasion was when the child stirred jealousy in Herod's heart. Joseph was anxious for the life of the child.

Three times during the early years the angel of the Lord steered Joseph's sound judgement. On the second occasion the angel said:

> Get up, take the child and his mother, and flee to Egypt, and remain there until I tell you.

Joseph listened to the angel's message and went by night to Egypt. Joseph the father secured the life of the young child.

Three times during those early years Joseph the father was anxious about the welfare of Mary's child. The third occasion was while the child was growing up in the pagan land of Egypt. The third occasion was while the child was separated from his religious roots. Joseph was anxious about the development of the child.

Three times during those early years the angel of the Lord steered Joseph's sound judgement. On the third occasion the angel said:

> Get up, take the child and his mother, and go to the land of Israel, for those who were seeking the child's life are dead.

Joseph listened to the angel's message and made his home in Nazareth. Joseph the father secured an Israelite home for the child.

All too often the story of Jesus' birth and early child-care is told from the perspective of Mary the mother. Joseph the father was very involved as well.

Thinking

According to Matthew's gospel, during those early days of Jesus' life God leaves nothing to chance. Here is a highly engaged interventionist God. Here is a God who sends dreams and angels to sort things out whenever the going gets tough. Can you believe in a God just like that?

The first crisis occurred when Mary became pregnant and Joseph knew he could not have been the father. The crisis occurred when Joseph threatened not to go through with the marriage; when Joseph threatened to break the Davidic lineage of the Messiah. The angel was sent to sort matters out. Can you believe in a God just like that?

The second crisis occurred when the enraged Herod set out to kill the rival king. The crisis occurred when the young child's life stood in the balance; when the young child looked death in the face. The angel was sent to sort matters out. Can you believe in a God just like that?

The third crisis occurred when the Holy Family was about to return to Judaea after Herod's death. The crisis occurred when Archelaus was ruling over his father's territory, when Archelaus may be tempted to inherit his father's brutality. The dream was sent to sort matters out. Can you believe in a God just like that?

According to Matthew's gospel, during those early days of Jesus' life God leaves nothing to chance. Here is a highly engaged interventionist God. Here is a God who sends dreams and angels to sort things out when the going gets tough. Can you believe in a God just like that? And where was that God at the time of the crucifixion?

4
Matthew 3:1–12

¹In those days John the Baptist appeared in the wilderness of Judea, proclaiming, ²'Repent, for the kingdom of heaven has come near.' ³This is the one of whom the prophet Isaiah spoke when he said,

  'The voice of one crying out in the wilderness:
  "Prepare the way of the Lord, make his paths
      straight." '

⁴Now John wore clothing of camel's hair with a leather belt around his waist, and his food was locusts and wild honey. ⁵Then the people of Jerusalem and all Judea were going out to him, and all the region along the Jordan, ⁶and they were baptized by him in the river Jordan, confessing their sins.

⁷But when he saw many Pharisees and Sadducees coming for baptism, he said to them, 'You brood of vipers! Who

warned you to flee from the wrath to come? [8]Bear fruit worthy of repentance. [9]Do not presume to say to yourselves, "We have Abraham as our ancestor"; for I tell you, God is able from these stones to raise up children to Abraham. [10]Even now the axe is lying at the root of the trees; every tree therefore that does not bear good fruit is cut down and thrown into the fire.

[11]'I baptize you with water for repentance, but one who is more powerful than I is coming after me; I am not worthy to carry his sandals. He will baptize you with the Holy Spirit and fire. [12]His winnowing fork is in his hand, and he will clear his threshing floor and will gather his wheat into the granary; but the chaff he will burn with unquenchable fire.'

Context

John the Baptist is introduced as the forerunner whose job it is to prepare the way for Jesus the Messiah.

Sensing

John the Baptist is really an enigmatic figure until you begin to pick up the clues from the Old Testament.

Take John's taste in clothing for example. According to Matthew's account, John wore clothing of camel's hair with a leather belt around his waist. Now go and look up 2 Kings 1:8. There you will find Elijah the Tishbite described as:

A hairy man, with a leather belt around his waist.

The enigma of John the Baptist begins to unfold.

Take John's urgency in preaching for example. According to Matthew's account, John proclaimed that the kingdom of heaven has come near. Now go and look up Malachi 4:5. There you will find the prophet making it clear how God will prepare for the kingdom:

Lo I will send you the prophet Elijah before the great and terrible day of the Lord comes.

The enigma of John the Baptist continues to unfold.

Take John's choice of location for preaching for example. According to Matthew's account, John forsook the city and the temple as the obvious place for prophetic utterance. Instead he withdrew to the wilderness. Now go and look up Isaiah 40:3. There you will find God's promise for future hope, when a voice cries out:

> In the wilderness prepare the way of the Lord,
> make straight in the desert a highway for our God.

The enigma of John the Baptist continues to unfold.

Take John's distinctive ritual for example. According to Matthew's account, John was busily engaged washing people, dipping them in the river Jordan. Now go and look up Isaiah 1:16. There you will find the prophet instructing God's people to prepare for God's coming kingdom:

> Wash yourselves, make yourselves clean;
> remove the evil of your doings from before my eyes.

The enigma of John the Baptist continues to unfold.

John the Baptist is really an enigmatic figure until you have picked up the clues from the Old Testament.

Intuition

John the Baptist clearly held magnetic appeal to the ordinary people of his day. According to Matthew, the people of Jerusalem and all Judea were going out to him, and all the region along the Jordan, and they were baptized by him in the river Jordan confessing their sins. So what clues does this provide for evangelism today?

John clearly stood out in the crowd. His rough dress and his austere diet caught attention. How well would this work today?

John clearly forsook the temple and synagogues and set up his mission away in the desert. How well would this work today?

John clearly developed a new and attractive ritual conducted in the full gaze of public attention. How well would this work today?

John clearly spoke with conviction and presumed to speak in the name of God. How well would this work today?

John clearly confronted head-on the spiritual and public leaders of his age and insulted them to their faces. How well would this work today?

John clearly called men and women to repentance. With urgency he demanded that they should re-evaluate their lives. How well would this work today?

John clearly confronted men and women with the awful spectacle of divine judgement. He pointed to a God who separated the chaff from the wheat and who burnt the chaff with unquenchable fire. How well would this work today?

And having built up such a profile for himself John unambiguously pointed away from himself to the Christ. How well would this work today?

John the Baptist clearly held magnetic appeal to the ordinary people of his day. So what clues does this provide for evangelism today?

Feeling

Do you sometimes share the feeling that Matthew may have been unnecessarily unkind about the Pharisees and Sadducees? Put yourself in their shoes and see things from their perspective.

John had set himself up as a preacher and as a prophet without any real training, any real credentials. The Pharisees and Sadducees as guardians of the Jewish scriptures properly felt a responsibility to assess this new religious fanatic. Put yourself in their shoes and see things from their perspective.

John had taken to himself the authority and identity of Elijah of old, without any real authorization. The Pharisees and Sadducees as responsible religious leaders properly needed to test whether John really stood in Elijah's prophetic tradition. Put yourself in their shoes and see things from their perspective.

John had adopted the most abrasive and offensive style of preaching. He rounded on his listeners and accused them of being a brood of vipers. The Pharisees and Sadducees as individuals concerned with public order and decency had every right to feel affronted. Put yourself in their shoes and see things from their perspective.

John had perfected a highly distinctive and most attractive religious ritual down in the river Jordan. There was neither precedent nor mandate for such innovation within the scriptures. The Pharisees and Sadducees as people trained in the scriptures (although with different views on what counted as authoritative scripture) were properly suspicious of such unscriptural and unlawful ritual. Put yourself in their shoes and see things from their perspective.

John had the audacity to reinterpret the sacred traditions and to proclaim new things in the name of God. 'God', he said, 'is able from these stones to raise up children to Abraham.' The Pharisees and the Sadducees as inheritors of that sacred tradition and as the lawful children of Abraham had every right to feel protective. Put yourself in their shoes and see things from their perspective.

Thinking

Parts of the gospel message are really quite difficult to hear. So what do you make of Matthew's theology of judgement?

Listen with care to the voice of John the Baptist as Matthew heard it. John's opening words are:

> Repent, for the kingdom of heaven has come near.

The invitation seems gentle, open-ended and inclusive. Perhaps a gospel of repentance is easy enough to proclaim. But what of those who fail to repent? Is there something uncomfortable in store? Parts of the gospel message are really quite difficult to hear.

Listen with care to the voice of John the Baptist as Matthew heard it. John goes on to challenge the Pharisees and Sadducees:

> You brood of vipers! Who warned you to flee from the wrath to come? Bear fruit worthy of repentance.

The invitation seems less gentle, less open-ended, and less inclusive. Perhaps a gospel of repentance is not that easy to proclaim. Parts of the gospel message are really difficult to hear.

Listen with care to the voice of John the Baptist as Matthew heard it. John goes on to warn the Pharisees and Sadducees:

> Even now the axe is lying at the root of the trees; every tree therefore that does not bear good fruit is cut down and thrown onto the fire.

The invitation seems cruel, closed and exclusive. Perhaps the gospel of repentance is hard to proclaim. Parts of the gospel message are really very difficult to hear.

Listen with care to the voice of John the Baptist as Matthew heard it. Speaking of Jesus, John says:

> His winnowing fork is in his hand, and he will clear his threshing floor and will gather his wheat into the granary: but the chaff he will burn with unquenchable fire.

Parts of the gospel message are really extremely difficult to hear. So what do you make of Matthew's theology of judgement?

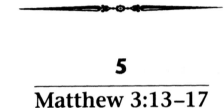

5

Matthew 3:13–17

¹³Then Jesus came from Galilee to John at the Jordan, to be baptized by him. ¹⁴John would have prevented him, saying, 'I need to be baptized by you, and do you come to me?' ¹⁵But Jesus answered him, 'Let it be so now; for it is proper for us in this way to fulfil all righteousness.' Then he consented. ¹⁶And when Jesus had been baptized, just as he came up from the water, suddenly the heavens were opened to him and he saw the Spirit of God descending like a dove and alighting on him. ¹⁷And a voice from heaven said, 'This is my Son, the Beloved, with whom I am well pleased.'

Context
After introducing John the Baptist and his teaching, Matthew presents a conversation between John and Jesus, leading to Jesus being baptized by John.

Sensing
Each of the three synoptic gospels tells the story of the baptism of Jesus in a somewhat different way. Make sure that today you are really listening to Matthew's account.

Notice first how Matthew ascribes real intentionality to Jesus' steps. According to Matthew, Jesus comes from Galilee to the Jordan specifically to be baptized by John. Mark makes the event look so much more casual and Luke avoids describing it altogether. In Matthew Jesus actually comes to be baptized.

Listen to what John says to Jesus. According to Matthew, John tries to prevent Jesus being baptized: 'I need to be baptized by you, and do you come to me?' Matthew voices the question which must have been on so many minds and about which Mark was so totally silent. In Matthew John acknowledges the problem of the lesser man baptizing the greater man.

Picture what takes place when Jesus comes up from the water of baptism. According to Matthew, suddenly the heavens were opened, and Matthew gives the impression that this theophany was there for all to see. In Mark the same event is described as if it were for Jesus' eyes only. In Matthew God's activity is proclaimed openly.

Hear what takes place when Jesus comes up from the water of baptism. According to Matthew, a voice from heaven said, 'This is my son, the Beloved, with whom I am well pleased', and Matthew gives the impression that this voice spoke for all to hear. In Mark the voice addresses only Jesus and says, 'You are my son.' In Matthew God's proclamation is for the whole world to hear.

Each of the three synoptic gospels tells the story of the baptism of Jesus in a somewhat different way. Make sure that today you are really listening to Matthew's account.

Intuition

According to Matthew, John made it none too easy for some people to get baptized. So what do you make of that?

When the Pharisees and Sadducees came seeking baptism, John rounded on them and called them 'a brood of vipers'. He put obstacles in their path and challenged their motives in coming for baptism. We do not know how many of them turned away. So what do you make of that?

When Jesus came seeking baptism, John rounded on him and said, 'Why do you come to me?' He put obstacles in Jesus' path and challenged his motives in coming for baptism. We do know that Jesus refused to be put off. So what do you make of that?

According to Matthew, John made it none too easy for some people to get baptized. Now do you hear clear echoes of Matthew's baptism policy in today's church?

When some young parents come seeking baptism for their baby, it is noticed that these parents never attend church themselves. Obstacles are put in their path and their motives for seeking baptism are challenged. We do not know how many of them turn away and never come near a church again. So what do you make of that?

Those who advocate a restrictive baptism policy argue that it is their duty to safeguard the sacrament from abuse. They argue that it is their duty to ensure that parents appreciate their responsibilities and the seriousness of the baptismal promises. They argue that such promises can never be fulfilled unless the parents sign up themselves for a proper programme of baptism preparation and a proper commitment to church attendance. Now that seems reasonable enough doesn't it?

Those who advocate an open baptism policy argue that it is their duty not to place unnecessary obstacles in the path of sacramental grace. They argue that it is their duty to ensure that parents feel welcomed and accepted by the church. They argue that once baptized, children know that they have real Christian roots. Now that sounds reasonable enough doesn't it?

So where should we go from there?

Feeling

There are certain times when religious rituals feel just right. There are certain times when the outward rites unlock the door to the deepest and innermost heart-felt religious experience.

Put yourself in Jesus' shoes as he walks across the rough path from Galilee towards the Jordan. His soul is stirred by that famous river valley coming into sight for the first time in the distance. Jesus knows it is to that water that he is called.

Put yourself in Jesus' shoes as he merges with a whole crowd of people converging on the Jordan valley. His soul is stirred by people coming from Jerusalem, from all Judaea and from all the region along the Jordan, people making pilgrimage together to the self-same point in the Jordan valley. Jesus knows it is to that point that he is called.

Put yourself in Jesus' shoes as he hears for the first time the stern voice of John the Baptist rise clearly above the roar of the crowds. His soul is stirred by the constant refrain, 'Repent . . . brood of vipers . . . repent . . . the kingdom of heaven has come near . . . repent . . . the axe is lying at the root of the trees . . . repent . . . the chaff he will burn with unquenchable fire . . . repent.' Jesus knows it is to that voice that he is called.

Put yourself in Jesus' shoes as he sees for the first time the austere appearance of John the Baptist standing out clearly in the crowd. His soul is stirred by the prophetic coat of camel's hair and by the prophetic leather belt. Jesus knows it is to that man that he is called.

Put yourself in Jesus' shoes as he submits to the flowing waters of baptism. His soul is stirred when he sees the heavens torn open, when he sees the dove descending, when he hears the voice proclaiming, 'This is my son, the Beloved, with whom I am well pleased.' Jesus knows that this marks the start of a new beginning.

There are certain times when religious rituals feel just right. There are certain times when the outward rites unlock the door to the deepest and innermost heart-felt religious experience. Perhaps the baptism of Jesus was something like that.

Thinking

What do you make of Jesus being baptized by John?

Surely John was the forerunner and Jesus was the Messiah. So what do you make of Jesus being baptized by John?

Surely John proclaimed baptism for the forgiveness of sins and Jesus was born the sinless one. So what do you make of Jesus being baptized by John?

The apocryphal *Gospel according to the Hebrews* tried to sort the matter out by suggesting that Jesus only came to be baptized to please his mother who wanted the family done *en masse*. Jesus protests, 'What sin have I committed that I should go and be baptized?' Then Jesus submits to maternal pressure? But surely that is no solution?

Matthew takes an altogether more subtle line by working hard on his text. Matthew changes John's fundamental call to baptism. In Mark John 'proclaimed a baptism of repentance for the forgive-ness of sins'. In Matthew John's message is, 'Repent for the kingdom of heaven is come near', and John baptizes 'with water for repentance'. Significantly the baptism of John and the forgive-ness of sins are uncoupled. So what do you make of Jesus being baptized by John?

Matthew takes an altogether more subtle line by working hard on his text. In Matthew's scheme of things, God had sent John to prepare Israel for a new exodus, not through the Red Sea but through the water of baptism. In Matthew's shape of things Jesus, the Moses called out of Egypt, passes through the waters of baptism together with the people of Jerusalem, all Judaea and all the region along the Jordan. So what do you make of Jesus being baptized by John?

Matthew takes an altogether more subtle line by working hard on his text. In Matthew's scheme of things, Jesus refuses to debate John's question of who is greater. Jesus simply reminds John that at the present time it is John who is commissioned to baptize in water. Jesus' baptism in the spirit is for a later time. Now to fulfil all righteousness is to submit to God's will in the present time. So what do you make of Jesus being baptized by John?

Perhaps when the heavens opened, when the dove descended and when the voice spoke, both John and Jesus knew that they had got it right. Then the Messiah had been properly anointed. So what do you make of Jesus being baptized by John?

6
Matthew 4:1–11

[1]Then Jesus was led up by the Spirit into the wilderness to be tempted by the devil. [2]He fasted for forty days and forty nights, and afterwards he was famished. [3]The tempter came and said to him, 'If you are the Son of God, command these stones to become loaves of bread.' [4]But he answered, 'It is written,

> "One does not live by bread alone,
>   but by every word that comes from the
>   mouth of God."'

[5]Then the devil took him to the holy city and placed him on the pinnacle of the temple, [6]saying to him, 'If you are the Son of God, throw yourself down; for it is written,

> "He will command his angels concerning you",
>   and "On their hands they will bear you up,
> so that you will not dash your foot against a
>   stone."'

[7]Jesus said to him, 'Again it is written, "Do not put the Lord your God to the test."'

⁸Again, the devil took him to a very high mountain and showed him all the kingdoms of the world and their splendour; ⁹and he said to him, 'All these I will give you, if you will fall down and worship me.' ¹⁰Jesus said to him, 'Away with you, Satan! for it is written,

"Worship the Lord your God, and serve only him." '

¹¹Then the devil left him, and suddenly angels came and waited on him.

Context

Matthew records how Jesus sees his role as Son of God. In a time of testing in the wilderness Jesus sorts out his priorities in mission, and decides how he will use his powers in obedience to the will of God. Scripture from the Book of Deuteronomy is his guide.

Sensing

This Lent reconsider your priorities in life. Find in this passage a pattern for your own reflections. Jesus is led by the Spirit to consider deeply life's priorities. Pray for the Spirit's guidance as you set your own. Jesus uses a period of fasting to concentrate on seeking to do the will of God. Follow his pattern of fasting to sharpen your hunger to do the will of God. Jesus considers the means by which to use the power God has given him as Son. Follow his pattern of examining the evidence of what makes for good.

So go with Jesus into the wilderness and face hunger. Touch a loaf of bread. Feel its warmth. Taste its sustenance. Smell its tempting aroma. Hear your tummy rumble in anticipation of the joy eating will bring. Modern society presents food in such a tempting way. People eat and overeat to compensate for the lack of satisfaction in other things. It is tempting to give food top priority in life. As a Christian also feel the pangs of hunger to live off the word of God.

Stand on the edge of the Temple wall and look down to the street below. See the people look up to you. Hear God's promise to keep you safe in all circumstances. Maybe this allows you to take extraordinary risks for God: to give up your job; cash up all your savings; rush off and heal someone as a daring Christian. Get a sense of perspective, following the pattern of Jesus. Be realistic about what God does for us and what we are asked to do for God.

Take a look at the world from the top of the highest mountain you know. See the people with every kind of need. Hear God's guidance as to what would make this world a better place. You know the ends can never justify the means. History shows us that there are no short cuts to the kingdom of God. There is only one way to a better world – putting God's ways first. Affirm with Jesus that you will 'worship the Lord your God, and serve only him'.

Follow the pattern Jesus set. Pray with his Spirit and sharpen your focus through fasting. This word of God gives us realistic guidance.

Intuition

All of us struggle to find the right way to spread the gospel. Let this passage fire your imagination and make connections with your situation. In the mission of the church in the world today the tussle continues between meeting people's material needs and meeting their spiritual needs.

Hunger is a major issue for millions in the world. For hungry people good news is a loaf of bread and a drink of clean water. Surely the church's mission is to eradicate poverty and disease. Listen to the scripture's warning: 'One does not live by bread alone.' People are more than their stomachs. Food is not the ultimate satisfaction. So what is the gospel for the hungry? Obedience to God is a struggle of decisions.

Signs and wonders are part of the church's mission. They may demonstrate the power of God to people today. What sort of miracles can we expect from God? The God of healing should cure the sick. The God of care should protect us from harm. God should not let bad things happen to good people. Jesus struggled with the same issues as we do. He told us miracles could never be used as a proof or otherwise of God's love for us. They are no 'test' of God. What are the right ways to show the power of God to others? Obedience to God is a struggle of decisions.

We need to find appropriate means for mission today. Should we employ expensive advertising agents to make the gospel attractive? Can we use gambling money to build our places of worship? How much entertainment should we use to hype up our worship? Obedience to God is a struggle of decisions.

Out of his struggle Jesus focuses sharply on this one truth:

worship of God takes top priority. Only what honours God can be included in the mission of the church. It is God who is the focus, not humanity. And what that means in practice is still a struggle to decide. Let the spirit of this passage inspire your decisions.

Feeling

As you read this passage you feel sorry for Jesus. As Son of God everyone had such high expectations of what he could do. Everyone wanted their needs made top priority in the 'must do' list.

You feel for Jesus when he looks at the dreadful plight of the poor. Giving up his paid job to become an itinerant preacher, he shared their lot: dependent on others for his daily food. As Son of God it would be right to satisfy his own needs and those of the poor without bread. You feel for Jesus and you feel for the poor. Compassion is the hallmark of the Christian. Provision of the essentials of life should be given priority in God's rule. Yet there is suffering passion in all compassion.

You feel for Jesus when everyone expected his presence to comfort them, and give them what they wanted. People expected God to protect the Son from all dangers and difficulties. But you know the story of the opposition and the cross. With the readers of Matthew's gospel we feeling people ask how God could let such hard things happen to Jesus. Yet the gospel does not hide the truth. God's compassion takes seriously the need for humanity to change. Harmony can only be achieved through justice and truth. Care for others means challenge as well as comfort. Look into your heart and recognize its need for change. Hating has to be turned into loving. Only the cross provided the shocking revolution for such a change. Feel Jesus' compassion for you. It is challenge as well as comfort.

You feel glad for Jesus when his inner struggle is resolved. The struggle of devilish temptation left him, and the comfort of the angels attended him. He has worked through his struggle and found inner peace. He knew the will of God, and was ready to carry out his mission – however tough it was.

This Lent be in touch with your own feelings. Use your compassion to discover again the will of God for yourself and others. Then experience the peace of God in your own heart.

Thinking

Matthew and Luke both expand Mark's brief mention of Jesus' time 'in the wilderness' between the baptismal affirmation of his role as Son of God and the beginning of his ministry. Matthew's gospel builds the incident around three quotations from the Book of Deuteronomy. In this way scripture is used as the basis of the plan for mission.

In this passage Jesus is shown as emerging in triumph from the testing time. Unlike the failure of the Children of Israel in the Sinai desert on their way to the Promised Land, Jesus resists all false paths to mission. He comes out of the desert focused on obedience and worship of God. God alone is the reason for service, and God's way of love is the only means of service.

The passage also shows that verses of scripture cannot be blindly used as guidance for action. One passage of scripture must be measured against its context and other parts of scripture. It is important to grasp this truth as we search the scriptures for confirmation of a right course of action. The devil is also clever at quoting scripture accurately.

Matthew's inclusion of verse 6 may reflect its use by those who argued against the authenticity of a Messiah who had suffered death on a cross. The verse can be linked with the cries of the scoffers in 27:43. They expect any Saviour to be delivered by God from suffering.

The message Matthew gives to his readers is clear. Jesus is Son of God because he lived his life in focused obedience to God. He committed himself to serve God alone without being diverted into unreasonable attempts to satisfy the physical needs of all or acting as a miracle maker who would substitute miracles for faith and trust in the goodness of God. The explanation as to why such pathways fall short of the will of God is made clear. Humanity needs more than food. Humanity will not find faith in God through miracles. Evil means cannot ever achieve good ends. It is a message we too can learn as we journey through Lent.

7
Matthew 4:12–23

¹²Now when Jesus heard that John had been arrested, he withdrew to Galilee. ¹³He left Nazareth and made his home in Capernaum by the sea, in the territory of Zebulun and Naphtali, ¹⁴so that what had been spoken through the prophet Isaiah might be fulfilled:
>   ¹⁵'Land of Zebulun, land of Naphtali,
>   on the road by the sea, across the Jordan,
>   Galilee of the Gentiles –
>   ¹⁶the people who sat in darkness have seen a
>   great light,
>   and for those who sat in the region and shadow
>   of death light has dawned.'

¹⁷From that time Jesus began to proclaim, 'Repent, for the kingdom of heaven has come near.'

¹⁸As he walked by the Sea of Galilee, he saw two brothers, Simon, who is called Peter, and Andrew his brother, casting a net into the sea – for they were fishermen. ¹⁹And he said to them, 'Follow me, and I will make you fish for people.' ²⁰Immediately they left their nets and followed him. ²¹As he went from there, he saw two other brothers, James son of Zebedee and his brother John, in the boat with their father Zebedee, mending their nets, and he called them. ²²Immediately they left the boat and their father, and followed him.

²³Jesus went throughout Galilee, teaching in their synagogues and proclaiming the good news of the kingdom and curing every disease and every sickness among the people.

Context

Once Jesus had determined the priorities for mission, Matthew shows it had to begin. John the Baptist had been arrested. His work must be taken forward. Jesus chose Galilee as the centre for mission; four fishermen as the first agents of mission; and teaching, preaching and healing as the means of mission.

Sensing

Beside the lake in Galilee archaeologists have uncovered from the silt the foundations of a house in Capernaum. They believe it could be the house of Simon Peter. Sit at the table there and share the news. Jesus from Nazareth is in town and has taken up residence. This town is Jewish, but stands on the edge of Gentile territory. Here a mixture of races and religions mingle. It stands at the crossroads of sea and land routes.

Sit at the table and hear people asking what Jesus is doing in town. Listen to the explanation: John the Baptist has been arrested but the truth cannot be silenced. Jesus has taken up his cousin's message: 'God's rule on earth is in our midst, and we must have a change of heart and follow God's way.'

People are asking what that will mean for each person in practice. Maybe it will bring a change in occupation or a change in life-style; maybe it will bring healing to the sick and enlightenment to those in confusion and darkness. The gospel writer is keen to provide some answers.

Sense the excitement in Peter's house as you hear how he and others have become followers of the new teacher. Share the expectancy that some great new event has occurred. Look at the signs of anxiety on the faces of his wife and family about his change of occupation. From now on Peter and his brother Andrew will be immersed in the mission of Jesus, not in the waters of the lake. They will be creating a new family.

Hear the talk of the town that Jesus has been teaching in their synagogue and providing a new sense of fulfilling the old scriptures. A new light has chased away the darkness of confusion about how to obey God. Obedience will mean putting our religion before business, the community of God before our natural family, compassion for the sick before our own comfort.

Here in this cross-roads town of Capernaum listen to the excitement about this new beginning. Hear the talk and then make your decision. You too are called to be an agent of mission, sharing its excitement and its commitment like the apostles of old. It will mean a new set of priorities within a new community.

Intuition

Can you see the connection between the activity of the two sets of brothers and the missionary activity of the kingdom of God?

Peter and Andrew were the explorers and initiators. They cast their nets into the lake. They looked for new areas in which to catch fish. They were quick to push out to new boundaries. They would form the vanguard for the mission of spreading the kingdom of God.

James and John were the compassionate and careful ones. They spent time in mending their nets. All the details needed to be in place. Care must be taken to look after everything. No fish must be allowed to get away through lack of attention. Their mission would highlight pastoral care as their means of evangelism.

Which sort of ministry do you prefer – casting nets or mending nets?

Are you best at casting nets, pushing the boundaries to move on to new areas to proclaim the gospel? Do you highlight conversion as the basic necessity for making new disciples? Does your ministry call for repentance as the reality of the kingdom is realized through the challenge Jesus brings?

Or are you one of those whose ministry works most effectively through pastoral care? Are you good at 'mending the nets' among your fellow worshippers and in your community? Do you consider that the essentials for mission lie in healing for the sick, care for those whose lives have been broken through tragedy, and the mending of broken relationships in families and in communities?

This passage concludes with the summary of the total activity of the mission of Jesus. There was education. There was proclamation. There was medication. Jesus called people into a team which could carry on all the aspects of the work of mission. It is the same today. We are all called to participate in mission, but mission is a multi-faceted venture. Each person is called to use his or her particular talents for the sake of the kingdom. Which gift is yours? Are you using it in co-operation with the other members of the congregation? Casting nets, or mending nets, we are all part of God's mission team.

Feeling

Jesus said to Andrew and Peter, 'Follow me.'

Take the place of Andrew and share his feelings. Jesus has stepped into your life in dramatic fashion and demanded that you leave your work and follow him. Feel the pride at being chosen to be in his company and do such vital work to help others. Out of pride you want to respond eagerly. Take the place of Andrew and feel the sense of anxiety holding you back. Surely there should be time to consider the request and to consult others involved in such a major change in your life. Take the place of Andrew and try to relate to Jesus as he calls you to 'Follow me.'

Take the place of Peter and hear the same call. Jesus is hardly being fair in making such a demand. Peter has a wife and family. Take the place of James and hear the same call. James and his brother John have responsibilities towards their parents. Jesus appears as rather a tough task master. He knows those whom he wants to help him with the task of mission and makes no bones about it. Take the place of Peter and James and ask Jesus to be more considerate and think of all the issues involved.

Take the place of John. The call came so suddenly and demanded an immediate answer. Feel the urgency in the call to mission. Jesus must have thought that the closing moments of the world's history were about to happen. The sense of urgency is still with us, even though we live in a different age. The good news of the gospel must be shared. People are dying out of need of it.

Take your place before Jesus. Feel the attraction of his dynamic personality, feel the compulsion of his call. To be a disciple means obedience as well as benefit. Jesus is Lord as well as Saviour. Do you feel like running after him or away from him?

Thinking

In this passage Matthew puts forward some key statements about the ministry of Jesus. He gives the priority to Jesus' work of teaching. In verse 23 teaching, proclamation and healing are placed in that order. In Mark's gospel proclamation of the kingdom takes pride of place. In Luke's gospel healing is highlighted. Here in Matthew's gospel teaching heads the list. For Matthew, Jesus came to clarify and teach the will of God. The activities of proclamation and healing are present, but teaching receives the spotlight. Jesus, the new Moses, would reveal the law of God and put it into practice.

For teaching to take place you not only need a teacher but learners. These fall into two categories: the students (disciples), who in turn would be qualified to teach, and the wider crowd of listeners, who in turn would learn wisdom and live by it in their daily lives. The call of the first group of disciples took place in Galilee. Among them there were students with initiative, the quick thinkers, and students with diligence, the consolidators. All types of people would respond to learn the ways of God.

Matthew gives his reasons why Jesus the teacher was able to attract such a large group of listeners. Jesus' first teaching was in the synagogues. There the hearers would be regularly gathered expecting to hear teaching about God's ways and God's purpose. To reach beyond this circle of religious people Jesus would have to take his message outdoors. There the larger crowd could gather. The enquirers could float along the edges. Of them there would be no questions asked about race or religion. All could learn wisdom.

Here was a teacher who put his message into practice in his outpouring of love for others. He proved himself a carer as well as a teacher. In wonder and in gratitude the people would return to listen to him again. The kingdom of God was at hand. The will of God was being taught. The good news of the kingdom was spreading. The sick were being restored to fullness of life. This is Matthew's message to those who would listen and learn.

<hr>

8

Matthew 5:1–12

¹When Jesus saw the crowds, he went up the mountain; and after he sat down, his disciples came to him. ²Then he began to speak, and taught them, saying:

³'Blessed are the poor in spirit, for theirs is the kingdom of heaven.

⁴'Blessed are those who mourn, for they will be comforted.
⁵'Blessed are the meek, for they will inherit the earth.
⁶'Blessed are those who hunger and thirst for righteousness, for they will be filled.
⁷'Blessed are the merciful, for they will receive mercy.
⁸'Blessed are the pure in heart, for they will see God.
⁹'Blessed are the peacemakers, for they will be called children of God.
¹⁰'Blessed are those who are persecuted for righteousness' sake, for theirs is the kingdom of heaven.
¹¹'Blessed are you when people revile you and persecute you and utter all kinds of evil against you falsely on my account. ¹²Rejoice and be glad, for your reward is great in heaven, for in the same way they persecuted the prophets who were before you.'

Context

Like Moses, Jesus the teacher instructs the crowds and the disciples on a mountain side. His 'sermon' begins with an affirmation of the attitudes and actions of the people who obey God's law. These are the attributes of the saints of every age.

Sensing

Hills rise steeply from the shores of Lake Galilee. There are a number of spurs on these hillsides which form natural amphitheatres. These are ideal places where crowds of people can hear the teacher's words.

Sit on the grassy bank and listen to the voice of Jesus. Open your ears to catch the words which tell you of those who are in tune with God's will. God calls blessed those who in need put their whole trust in God; those who in sorrow cry for the hurts and sins of humanity; those who with patient humility serve others first; those who with commitment to God long for justice and truth. These are the ones whom God calls blessed.

Sit on the grassy bank and listen to the voice of Jesus. Open your ears to catch the words which tell you of those who act as God's followers. The true disciples are those who show mercy, and so receive God's mercy; those who show sincerity, and so find God's presence; those who show how to make peace, and so form part of God's reconciled family; those who show steadfastness under persecution, and so discover how God's kingdom grows.

Sit on the grassy bank and listen to the voice of Jesus. Open your ears to catch the words which tell you how to suffer under persecution. When people put you down, rejoice. When people threaten you, rejoice. When people defame you as evil, rejoice. When people tell lies about you, rejoice. Such are those whom God will reward with true joy, the joy of God's presence and power. These are the ones who can claim to be like the prophets of old, who told the truth and suffered for it. These are the ones whose treatment shows that they are worthy of the title 'The blessed of God'.

Sit on the grassy bank and listen to the voice of Jesus. Open your ears to the truth. Open your heart and through your actions of faithfulness to Christ's teaching you too can earn the title of saint.

Intuition

The church has its various lists of saints whom it holds in honour. Some are local to a particular area. Some are more widely recognized. Some are from our generation. Some are saints of long ago, but their mighty deeds and examples have been an inspiration across the generations. But the list should not be so limited. We need to name those who have inspired us and turned the teaching of Christ into reality for us.

So who are the people you would call a hero or a heroine of the faith? Who would be included as saints in your calendar?

Who are the people you know who depend on God alone and who give top priority to spiritual goals; who weep for Jerusalem as the fabric of society disintegrates; who turn the other cheek in the struggle of competition; who fast for justice and truth amid the lies and corruption of corporate life? Those are the people God calls blessed. Include them in your list of saints.

Who are the people you would call a hero or a heroine of the faith? Who else would be included as saints in your calendar?

Who are the people you know who forgive others as they seek to be forgiven; who show sincerity rather than deception; who create peace and cause reconciliation; who endure persecution for speaking and acting for what is right? God names them as blessed. Let us name them with honour as our saints.

Who are the people you would call a hero or a heroine of the faith? Who else would be included as saints in your calendar?

Who are the people you know who rejoice in persecution; who can absorb injury without hating in return; who can share Christ's cross and turn it into a symbol of glory and redemption? These are also saints whom we should honour today. These are our heroes and heroines in the faith. These are the ones who show us in their lives what the teaching of Jesus means for us all.

Feeling

Sympathize with the first disciples. They made a total commitment to the teaching of Jesus. They proclaimed the message of total reliance on God. They gave up their jobs, sold their possessions, left family support behind and lived on the generosity of those with whom they shared the gospel.

Sympathize with the first disciples. They wept over the stubbornness of those who believed they alone knew God. They wept over the sins and failures of those who made a mess of their Christian witness – sometimes themselves. They wept for the martyrs, many their own colleagues and friends, who were murdered for being Christian.

Sympathize with the first disciples who patiently waited for the seeds of faith to grow, who refused to meet violence with violence, who turned the other cheek, who allowed people the option of refusing to believe the good news they brought.

Sympathize with the first disciples who were starving because they would not steal or cheat to gain a meal when famine struck, who fasted voluntarily as a sign of revulsion at the unjust distribution of food, whose desire to bring the truth to others exposed them to many dangers as they crossed the seas and the deserts.

Sympathize with the first disciples who withstood persecution in all its forms – physical, verbal, spiritual and mental. It was tough being a first disciple. Putting the teaching into practice made you rely totally on God and on the care of your fellow disciples.

Feel what it is like to be a first disciple. Feel the pain. Feel the trust in God and others. Feel also in your heart the glow of the rewards. See the rule of God grow in the lives of others. Hear people tell the truth and stand up for justice. Be part of a community that gives and receives mercy. Share in the process of making peace. Know the presence and guidance of God in your life. There is joy in being a follower of Jesus. There is joy in being a saint.

In your heart rejoice to be called a disciple, a saint, God's truly blessed one.

Thinking

Finding true happiness is the key to human existence. That had been the wisdom of many generations of thinkers. Matthew in his gospel patterns Jesus' teaching about happiness on its First Testament roots. There the various Psalmists describe those whom God delights to call 'happy'. They are –

> Those who do not follow the advice of the wicked . . .
> but their delight is in the law of the Lord.   (Psalm 1:1–2)
> Those who consider the poor,
> the Lord delivers them in the day of trouble.   (Psalm 41:1)
> Those who live in your courts;
> we shall be satisfied with the goodness of your house.
> (Psalm 65:4)
> Those whose strength is in you,
> in whose heart are the highways of Zion.   (Psalm 84:5)
> Those who observe justice,
> who do righteousness at all times.   (Psalm 106:3)
> Those who fear the Lord,
> who greatly delight in his commandments.   (Psalm 112:1)
> Everyone who fears the Lord,
> who walks in his ways.   (Psalm 128:1)

Compare these verses with those from the sermon on the mount and you see some obvious similarities and some sharp divergence. The experience of the community to which Matthew wrote gives them a fuller understanding of the happiness that the first disciples discovered from the teaching of Jesus. But the sermon also includes the mark of suffering and persecution, it foreshadows the cross as the pathway to heaven.

It is in verses 7 to 11 that the contrast is most striking. Here Jesus' teaching focuses on forgiveness and mercy, and the need to be merciful. The teaching is revealed in greater depth in the verses yet to come. Revenge is forbidden (Matthew 5:38–42); purity must be found in the inner mind as well as the outward actions (Matthew 5:27–30); in making peace, even our enemies are to be loved (Matthew 5:43–48). Persecution is seen as part of discipleship. It is that test which shows the true nature of the disciple. Only those who put their full trust in God can know true happiness (Matthew 6:19–34).

Such careful comparisons show how the whole sermon on the mount is linked together. These first verses produce a succinct introduction. They are the template for the lives of all the saints who strive for happiness. Thoughtful comparison and reflection will see the truth of that. Thoughtful action will find ways of making happiness a reality, for us and for others.

9

Matthew 5:13–20

¹³'You are the salt of the earth; but if salt has lost its taste, how can its saltiness be restored? It is no longer good for anything, but is thrown out and trampled under foot.

¹⁴'You are the light of the world. A city built on a hill cannot be hidden. ¹⁵No one after lighting a lamp puts it under the bushel basket, but on the lampstand, and it gives light to all in the house. ¹⁶In the same way, let your light shine before others, so that they may see your good works and give glory to your Father in heaven.

¹⁷'Do not think that I have come to abolish the law or the prophets; I have come not to abolish but to fulfil. ¹⁸For truly I tell you, until heaven and earth pass away, not one letter, not one stroke of a letter, will pass from the law until all is accomplished. ¹⁹Therefore, whoever breaks one of the least of these commandments, and teaches others to do the same, will be called least in the kingdom of heaven; but whoever does them and teaches them will be called great in the kingdom of heaven. ²⁰For I tell you, unless your righteousness exceeds that of the scribes and Pharisees, you will never enter the kingdom of heaven.'

Context

As the next part of the 'sermon on the mount' Matthew includes two parable-like sayings of Jesus. The second of these, about light, leads into a section on keeping the teaching of the law and the prophets. This was considered to be the light of guidance for God's true community.

Sensing

This passage is about tasting, seeing and doing. These are activities to which we can easily relate.

Taste the salt in your favourite vegetables. As a cook use the jar of salt by the stove. Put in the salt to bring out the flavours in the food. Put in the salt to act as a preservative. Without salt there are few flavours in the daily round of life. Without salt food soon turns bad. Without the salt of the Christian faith life lacks full flavour. Without the salt of the Christian faith life lacks a true zest. Without the salt of the Christian faith life soon turns sour.

See the light in the darkness. Turn on the lamp, watch it fill the room with light and warmth. In the light of the lamp everything can be seen and utilized. Bring in a large cardboard box and put it over the light. Watch the room turn into darkness. Hear the curses as people in the room stumble into things and break them. Listen as they demand that the light be clearly displayed so that everything can be clearly seen. Hear them curse you for being so stupid as to light a lamp and then put it under a box.

Hear the command to let the gospel shine out in your life. You cannot hide the good news about Jesus' teaching from others. It is just like a light for you. It illuminates the darkness of the confusion about what you should do with life. You cannot hide the fact that you are a Christian. Your actions will make it clear for all to see. You must make the gospel known to all.

Act on the teaching of Jesus as the Old Israel acted on the commands of the law and the prophets. They called that their light. By that they tasted the goodness in life. Only as we practise what Jesus teaches can we participate in the kingdom of God. Those are the facts. Those are the actions required. It is plain for all to see.

Taste the salt. See the light. Carry out the deeds of righteousness.

Intuition

When you think of salt what springs to mind?

For years salt has been used as a preservative. It keeps meat and fish fresh. It maintains the flavours in food. Do you see the connection between salt and faith? Faith acts to preserve all that is best in life. Faith keeps fresh the corporate memory of what is best in life. Faith holds firm to certain truths about the consequences of behaviour. Faith is a source of wisdom and encouragement to every generation. When salt is considered stale it is discarded. If you have thrown out your faith because it has lost its freshness, what has been lost in the process? When you see corporate faith trampled underfoot, how do you react? How can you keep faith fresh?

When you think of lamplight, what springs to mind?

For years such light has been used to allow us to make more use of the day. It enables us to keep relating, reading and working. Life would be very restricted without the light of lamps. Do you see the connection between lamplight and faith? Life would be very restricted without our faith. Faith enlarges our horizons, gives us guidance about new situations, helps us explore the boundaries while being supported by the love of God.

When you think of the law what springs to mind?

For many the law is the framework within which society can operate. It sets out choices and their consequences. It draws on best practice built up over many generations. The law could be hard and rigid but it maintained order. In what ways does the teaching of Jesus act like a law for you? For years set guidelines were enforced in society. Then many rules were abandoned, old structures rejected in the name of new freedoms. How do you consider the laws set down by past authorities? Do you see them as enabling or restricting 'freedom'?

Salt, light, law – Jesus used them to help us see faith from a new perspective. Can you make the connections?

Feeling

A feeling person is often torn over the clash between love and the law. For us the stroke of the letter of the law kills the warmth of love. Put yourself into the position of caring for another person. Surely you want to love them no matter what the law decrees. Maybe you will react with some confusion or even anger when Matthew records that Jesus told his disciples that the law must be kept, even down to the last letter. From your point of view love has always taken precedence over the law. Does not the scripture say that love is the fulfilling of the law?

The Scribes and Pharisees prided themselves on the way they carefully carried out the law. Jesus says we have to share the kingdom of God with such types of people. We may criticize them for being all show and for lacking sincerity. We want to be free to respond to each new situation in love without being restricted by laws and past ways of doing things. We want to treat people as people, not as objects of the law's demands. It is hard to be a feeling type and listen to Jesus telling his disciples that they must keep the law. Hold your anger and disappointment. Relate to Jesus as he puts the law as he interprets it into practice.

Jesus puts the law to work in a new way. He shows compassion without indulgence. He shows mercy by taking sin seriously. He shows kindness through challenge for change as well as care. On the lips of a loving Saviour the law takes on a new light. It becomes a set of principles to guide our emotions and turn them into proper 'good works'. Without the discipline of the law our loving might be soft, lacking the wisdom of tradition and the framework of experience. In the teaching of Jesus the law of righteousness becomes the law of love. As a feeling person you can relate to that!

Thinking

Scholars have seen in this passage an example of the various ways the Christian faith took root among people of different cultures and traditions. Verses 17-20 are seen as an affirmation by Matthew of the group of Christians who were former Jews. They wanted to keep their strong traditions which were reflected in the books of the Law and the Prophets. This group saw the Christian way as the fulfilment of the old law. For them there was no clash between a proper interpretation of the law and the teaching of Jesus. For them Jesus was a Jew who kept the law in its true form as an expression of the will of God. The law produced right conduct and therefore access to the very heart of God. For them the law was the light of their lives. It was like salt which preserved the best of the past traditions and wisdom. All that was needed was a teacher of the law who could expound the way to put it into practice.

For Matthew Jesus was just such a teacher. His interpretation of the law gave it new strength. His teaching made clear how to practise the law. His instructions gave it full meaning, so that his disciples could learn it and be an example to others. Jesus in his teaching could clear up false interpretations and cast out corruption. For Matthew the law was not a static system but a living instrument for righteousness, truth and love.

It was the duty of every disciple to learn the teaching of Jesus – the commandments – and pass them on correctly. This was one of the key purposes for writing the gospels. The teaching of Jesus would be preserved. The truth would be set on a lampstand for all to see. The new Jerusalem would be a city set on a hill whose reputation would be there for all to admire.

When you think about this passage it makes good sense to set out the teaching of Jesus so clearly and to call on the ongoing group of disciples to obey 'these commands'. We too would be wise to heed the warning that such teaching cannot be ignored without the breakdown of the fabric of our society that the law aims to uphold.

10

Matthew 5:21–37

21'You have heard that it was said to those of ancient times, "You shall not murder"; and "whoever murders shall be liable to judgement." 22But I say to you that if you are angry with a brother or sister, you will be liable to judgement; and if you insult a brother or sister, you will be liable to the council; and if you say, "You fool", you will be liable to the hell of fire. 23So when you are offering your gift at the altar, if you remember that your brother or sister has something against you, 24leave your gift there before the altar and go; first be reconciled to your brother or sister, and then come and offer your gift. 25Come to terms quickly with your accuser while you are on the way to court with him, or your accuser may hand you over to the judge, and the judge to the guard, and you will be thrown into prison. [26]Truly I tell you, you will never get out until you have paid the last penny.

[27]'You have heard that it was said, "You shall not commit adultery." [28]But I say to you that everyone who looks at a woman with lust has already committed adultery with her in his heart. [29]If your right eye causes you to sin, tear it out and throw it away; it is better for you to lose one of your members than for your whole body to be thrown into hell. [30]And if your right hand causes you to sin, cut it off and throw it away; it is better for you to lose one of your members than for your whole body to go into hell.

[31]'It was also said, "Whoever divorces his wife, let him give her a certificate of divorce." [32]But I say to you that anyone who divorces his wife, except on the ground of unchastity, causes her to commit adultery; and whoever marries a divorced woman commits adultery.

[33]'Again, you have heard that it was said to those of ancient times, "You shall not swear falsely, but carry out the vows you have made to the Lord." [34]But I say to you, Do not swear at all, either by heaven, for it is the throne of God, [35]or by the earth, for it is his footstool, or by Jerusalem, for it is the city of the great King. [36]And do not swear by your head, for you cannot make one hair white or black. [37]Let your word be "Yes, Yes" or "No, No"; anything more than this comes from the evil one.'

Context

Jesus' teaching demands a greater righteousness than that shown by the keepers of the Mosaic law. Matthew here gives six examples contrasting the old law with the new law as set down by Jesus. The contrasts lie between the attitudes of the outward observance and of the inner soul.

Sensing

Your accusers have brought you to court. Take your place in the dock. Your defence counsel points out to the judge that you have done nothing wrong.

Listen with amazement as the prosecution brings forward

charges about your inner thoughts. It is true that you have never killed anyone, but how many times have you harboured anger against another person? How do you plead? It is true that you have never killed anyone, but how many times have you flattened them with insults? How do you plead?

You have to admit the truth. You start to tell the judge it is quite unfair. You cannot be judged by your inner thoughts. You begin to make excuses. Listen to the judge say, 'What have you done to repair the damage? Don't make excuses that you have asked for God's forgiveness in church. The priority is to be reconciled with those you have hurt, and even those who have hurt you.'

Remember the words of Christ, 'Come to terms quickly with your accuser.' Do not wait to be forced into it by a judge. Act now for reconciliation.

Take your place in the dock at your trial. Hear your defence counsel point out that you are a self-controlled person. You have never committed an act of adultery. Listen with amazement as the prosecution brings forward charges about your hidden thoughts. It is true that you have never committed adultery in deed, but what about your eyes? Have they never committed adultery and led your thoughts to sexual delights? Hear yourself saying in admission of the truth, 'What should I do?'

Take Jesus' advice, do whatever radical steps are required to regain your wholeness. Purity is essential for wellbeing. The teaching of Jesus strikes at the root of our problems. His teaching about divorce and honesty is just as demanding. The fact is that only a heart renewed by God's Spirit can obey teaching like this. Forgiveness makes you a new person with a new start and a new spirit.

Intuition

When you listen to people swearing with a 'Christ' or an 'O God', what comes into your mind? Do you cringe at the insult to God or at the degrading of human nature? What are your rules about swearing? When you listen to people swearing on the bible in court, what comes into your mind? Do you think it helps them be more honest, afraid of offending the Almighty as well as their human integrity? When you listen to Christians in society giving their word on something, do you expect them to be more honest than their unbelieving neighbours?

When other people listen to your 'Yes' or your 'No', can they fully rely on you because you are a Christian? When you listen to yourself backing up your statements with a 'God help me' or a 'By God', do you see this as evil? Do you make the connection with Christ's words that anything more than yes or no comes from the evil one?

You can imagine all these examples taking place. When you make the connection you can see how Jesus challenges some of our deepest assumptions about proper behaviour.

When you listen to people declaring that they are seeking a divorce, what comes to mind? Do you ask the reasons, or do you declare that divorce is not an option? With the breakdown of relationships all around us is this teaching of Jesus to be taken as an ideal or as a reality? How do you combine law and compassion in your attitude to others, and to yourself?

When you listen to people talking about their breakdown in relationships, how can you help them make reconciliation the rule rather than the exception? How can you help people rebuild their lives and find renewed relationships with God and with others that will last?

Yes, there are many connections we can make with the teaching of Jesus. It challenges some of the deepest assumptions about our own and others' behaviour. Only a heart renewed by God's Spirit can obey teaching like this. A Christian needs a remake in character to be a disciple.

Feeling

Recall how you felt when someone last called you a fool or a blockhead or just plain stupid.

Remember the anger that erupted when you were insulted by that cutting remark or that false accusation. Feel the fire of anger and recall how hard it was to put it out.

Recall how you felt when someone last physically assaulted you. Remember the anger that sought revenge. An eye for an eye and a tooth for a tooth was hardly enough to satisfy your thirst for retaliation. Two blows were fired back for every one suffered. Feel the anger again burning in your heart.

Recall how you felt when someone last made a verbal assault on you. Remember the anger that stirred the tongue to fury in return. Verbal abuse was traded, phrase on phrase, until the shouting grew loud enough to shock the neighbours. Feel the anger again burning on the end of your tongue.

Recall how you felt when anger burned like fire within you. A real surge of energy rises in the body, the eyes flash and the hair stands on end. You are ready to hit out in every direction. Feel the anger again burning in your heart.

Recall now the shame you felt when the anger subsided. Remember how you wished that you had acted differently. Feel again the bitterness that was left behind and the wounded pride that found it hard to forgive and to forget. Recall how hard it was to put out the fires of anger.

Recall now the consequences of your anger and that will restrain you from lighting fires of revenge next time. Recall the forgiveness offered by Christ and his command to forgive one another. Recall that in the family of humanity to hurt another is to hurt oneself. Learn from your feelings. Jesus also knew what is was like to be provoked to anger. He knew the feelings. Learn from his experience about a better way to respond.

Jesus warns us that reconciliation must be sought quickly, that anger must be overcome by true feelings of compassion, that the law courts are not the place to sort out the problems of a violent society.

Thinking

For many these teachings of Jesus are very emotive, but they make little sense. These teachings of Jesus seem to be aimed at angels. Human beings can never achieve such heights of perfection. Matthew must have known about the facts of human nature, that it is sinful. The Christians to whom Matthew wrote must have been aware of their own behaviour. These teachings would have caused consternation and embarrassment within the group. There were sure to be those who had shown anger, and who had hidden behind religious observance to excuse their argument with a fellow Christian. There were sure to be those who knew their lustful thoughts. There were sure to be those who had already divorced their wives or married a woman who had been divorced. There were sure to be those who had used an oath.

When you think about it, Matthew was taking a risk by recording these teachings in such stark uncompromising terms. Why did he then take this risk?

The reason appears to be that the goal of perfection must always be set before us or we will believe that any wrong is all right. We will tolerate dishonesty as normal behaviour. We will allow anger to build into violence, unchecked. We will consider adultery as a normal way of accommodating lust. We will make divorce the only way out for every broken relationship. We will turn evil into the only possible option for sinful humanity.

When you think about it, this is what is happening in the world today. People say that human frailty means that the world will always be in a mess. In this philosophy there is no hope for anything better than the lowest level of behaviour. But surely Jesus was right to teach us 'the better way'. Matthew was right to record it faithfully. The church to whom this gospel was written was right to treasure it as good news.

God promises that a heart can be renewed by the Spirit to obey teaching like this. That is Christ's message of hope for the world. Surely it makes sense to aim for more than a mess.

11

Matthew 5:38-48

38'You have heard that it was said, "An eye for an eye and a tooth for a tooth." 39But I say to you, Do not resist an evildoer. But if anyone strikes you on the right cheek, turn the other also; 40and if anyone wants to sue you and take your coat, give your cloak as well; 41and if anyone forces you to go one mile, go also the second mile. 42Give to everyone who begs from you, and do not refuse anyone who wants to borrow from you.

43'You have heard that it was said, "You shall love your neighbor and hate your enemy." 44But I say to you, Love your enemies and pray for those who persecute you, 45so that you may be children of your Father in heaven; for he makes his sun rise on the evil and on the good, and sends rain on the righteous and on the unrighteous. 46For if you love those who love you, what reward do you have? Do not even the tax-collectors do the same? 47And if you greet only your brothers and sisters, what more are you doing than others? Do not even the Gentiles do the same? [48]Be perfect, therefore, as your heavenly Father is perfect.'

Context

In the sermon on the mount Jesus continues to contrast the old law given to Moses on Mount Sinai with the new law of life in the kingdom of God.

Sensing

Come away to the mountain and listen carefully as Jesus carries on instructing the disciples. Be prepared for the surprises to continue as all you ever learnt before is turned upside down.

What have you learnt in the past about the law of retribution? Did not Exodus 21:24 make it quite clear that, when harm has been inflicted, the recompense is an eye for an eye, a tooth for a tooth, a hand for a hand, and a foot for a foot? The law of retribution seems both clear and equitable. Now listen to the new teaching.

The new teaching says that, if anyone strikes you on the right cheek, then you should offer the left cheek also. Now that is quite revolutionary.

The new teaching says that, if anyone sues you for your coat, then you should give your cloak as well. Now that is quite revolutionary.

The new teaching says that, if anyone requisitions your service to go with them one mile, then you should go the second mile as well. Now that is quite revolutionary.

Come away to the mountain and listen carefully as Jesus carries on instructing his disciples. Be prepared for the surprises to continue as all you ever learnt before is turned upside down.

What have you learnt in the past about the law of love? Did not Leviticus 19:18 make it quite clear that you shall love your neighbour; and is not your neighbour your fellow Israelite who treats you well? The law of love seems quite clear and equitable. Now listen to the new teaching.

The new teaching says that you should love not only your neighbour, but your enemy as well. Now that is quite revolutionary.

The new teaching says that you should love not only those

who treat you kindly, but those who persecute you as well. Now that is quite revolutionary.

Come away to the mountain and listen carefully as Jesus carries on instructing his disciples. You never know what he is going to say next.

Intuition

It takes an agile mind and a bold conviction to turn established teaching upside down. But that is what Jesus did and that may be what Jesus calls us, his people, to do today. So where do you want to start?

You have heard that it was said, 'The Catholic church is the only true church and no true salvation exists outside its walls.' You have heard that it was said by the Protestant reformers, 'True salvation exists within the reformed traditions.' You know that men and women have died for both traditions. I wonder what Jesus will proclaim when he returns to preach from the mountain top?

You have heard that it was said, 'The only way to salvation is through Jesus Christ.' You have heard that it was said, 'The other religious faiths of the world are but illusions and lies.' You know that committed Christians have fought and killed for these beliefs. I wonder what Jesus will proclaim when he returns to preach from the mountain top?

You have heard that it was said, 'The husband is the head of the household and the wife shall obey her husband.' You have heard that it was said, 'Women shall take no leadership in the church.' You know that families and churches have been divided and split for such beliefs. I wonder what Jesus will proclaim when he returns to preach from the mountain top?

You have heard that it was said, 'Cohabitation before marriage is a sin in the eyes of God.' You have heard that it was said, 'There is no place in the kingdom of God for same-sex partnerships.' You know that individuals have been excommunicated, disfellowshipped and ostracized in the name of such beliefs. I wonder what Jesus will proclaim when he returns to preach from the mountain top?

It takes an agile mind and a bold conviction to turn established teaching upside down. But that is what Jesus did and that may be what Jesus calls us, his people, to do today. So where do you want to start?

Feeling

The followers of Jesus are called to have big hearts, very big hearts indeed; for Jesus said, 'Love your enemies and pray for those who persecute you.' Let your hearts be inspired by the example of Jesus himself.

Take the example of Jesus when he came face to face with his captors in the Garden of Gethsemane. There he addressed Judas his betrayer with the greeting 'friend'. There he counselled those who would have inflicted injury on his enemies to sheathe their swords. There he refused to fight back with twelve legions of angels. Take the example of Jesus who showed love for his enemies in the Garden of Gethsemane.

Take the example of Jesus when he came face to face with his executors at the place of his crucifixion. There he stretched out his arms. There he prayed for those who took his life, 'Father forgive them, for they know not what they do.' Take the example of Jesus who showed love for his enemies on the cross of Calvary.

The followers of Jesus are called to have big hearts, very big hearts indeed; for Jesus said, 'Love your enemies and pray for those who persecute you.' Let your hearts be inspired by the example of those who have followed in Jesus' footsteps.

Take the example of Stephen, the first Christian martyr, when he looked into the faces of those who were stoning him. There he knelt down in prayer. There he prayed, 'Lord, do not hold this sin against them' and these were his dying words. Take the example of Stephen who showed love for his enemies who stoned him to death.

The followers of Jesus are called to have big hearts, very big hearts indeed. Pray that your heart may grow in the love of Jesus.

Thinking

Sometimes the teaching of Jesus appears to be so totally unrealistic, so totally contrary to the laws of human justice. Can you really build a fair and just society founded on the precept, 'Do not resist the evildoer'?

If someone steals your car, do you not have a right, do you not have a duty to report the offence? If someone steals your car, do you not have a right, do you not have a duty to press charges? If someone steals your car, do you not have a right, do you not have a duty to expect that the thief will be prosecuted, sentenced and fined?

If someone steals your car, is not punishment necessary simply to settle the score? And if retribution itself is not sufficient grounds, is not punishment necessary to protect the rest of society from the consequences of repeated crimes on property? And if the protection of society is not sufficient grounds, is not punishment necessary to reform and to rehabilitate the thief?

Sometimes the teaching of Jesus appears to be so totally unrealistic, so totally contrary to the laws of human justice.

If someone beats up your brother within inches of his life, do you not have a right, do you not have a duty to report the offence? If someone beats up your brother within inches of his life, do you not have a right, do you not have a duty to press charges? If someone beats up your brother within inches of his life, do you not have a right, do you not have a duty to expect that the thug will be prosecuted, fined and imprisoned?

If someone beats up your brother within inches of his life, is not punishment necessary simply to settle the score? And if retribution itself is not sufficient grounds, is not punishment necessary to protect the rest of society from the consequences of repeated crimes on people? And if the protection of society is not sufficient grounds, is not punishment necessary to reform and to rehabilitate the thug?

Sometimes the teaching of Jesus appears to be so totally unrealistic, so totally contrary to the laws of human justice. Can you really build a fair and just society founded on the precept, 'Do not resist the evildoer'?

12

Matthew 6:25-34

[25]'Therefore I tell you, do not worry about your life, what you will eat or what you will drink, or about your body, what you will wear. Is not life more than food, and the body more than clothing? [26]Look at the birds of the air; they neither sow nor

reap nor gather into barns, and yet your heavenly Father feeds them. Are you not of more value than they? [27]And can any of you by worrying add a single hour to your span of life? [28]And why do you worry about clothing? Consider the lilies of the field, how they grow; they neither toil nor spin, [29]yet I tell you, even Solomon in all his glory was not clothed like one of these. [30]But if God so clothes the grass of the field, which is alive today and tomorrow is thrown into the oven, will he not much more clothe you – you of little faith? [31]Therefore do not worry, saying, "What will we eat?" or "What will we drink?" or "What will we wear?" [32]For it is the Gentiles who strive for all these things; and indeed your heavenly Father knows that you need all these things. [33]But strive first for the kingdom of God and his righteousness, and all these things will be given to you as well.

[34]'So do not worry about tomorrow, for tomorrow will bring worries of its own. Today's trouble is enough for today.'

Context

In the sermon on the mount, Jesus teaches his followers to trust in the provision which God makes for them and not to worry over unnecessary matters.

Sensing

Sometimes it helps to open our eyes to the world around us and to put our individual lives into a wider perspective.

Open your eyes, says Jesus, to the lilies of the field. See them grow in haphazard places and in random ways. See their intricate flowers. See their wonderfully crafted leaves. See their magnificent colours. God created those flowers and God's love sustains them in life. Open your eyes, says Jesus, to the lilies of the field. If God invests so much in them, how much more will God invest in you?

Sometimes it helps to open our ears to the world around us and to put our individual lives into a wider perspective.

Open your ears, says Jesus, to the birds of the air. Hear them sing in the tree tops and along the hedgerows. Hear their well-tuned voices. Hear their wonderfully crafted melodies. Hear their magnificent tunes. God created those creatures and God's love sustains them in life. Open your ears, says Jesus, to the birds of the air. If God invests so much in them, how much more will God invest in you?

Sometimes it helps to open our nostrils to the world around us and to put our individual lives into a wider perspective.

Open your nostrils, says Jesus, to the plants growing in the garden. Smell the fragrant perfume of the roses. Smell the refreshing odour of the lavender. Smell the welcoming scent of the honeysuckle. God created those flowers and herbs and God's love sustains them in life. Open your nostrils, says Jesus, to the plants growing in the garden. If God invests so much in them, how much more will God invest in you?

Sometimes it helps to become aware of God's world around us and to put our individual lives into a wider perspective.

Intuition

In today's world it is often very very difficult not to be anxious, not to be anxious about the past, not to be anxious about the present, not to be anxious about the future.

When you are really honest with yourself, what is there in your life that makes you anxious about the past? What memories do you carry of childhood? What memories do you carry of your parents? What memories do you carry of your teachers? What memories do you carry from the past that make you anxious? But do you not hear the voice of Jesus whisper from the mountain tops? Hear Jesus proclaim the message of the kingdom, 'Do not be anxious about yesterday, for anxiety cannot change the past.' What you cannot change God can forgive and God can heal.

When you are really honest with yourself, what is there in your life that makes you anxious about the present? What worries you today about your health? What worries you today about your work? What worries you today about your relationship with other people? What worries you today about your relationship with God? But do you not hear the voice of Jesus whisper from the mountain tops? Hear Jesus proclaim the message of the kingdom, 'Do not be anxious about today, for anxiety cannot change the present.' What you cannot change God can help you to accept and God can heal.

When you are really honest with yourself, what is there in your life that makes you anxious about the future? What fears haunt your heart for the future welfare of your family? What fears haunt your heart for the future welfare of your nation?

What fears haunt your heart for the future welfare of the earth? What fears haunt your heart for the future welfare of your own life? But do you not hear the voice of Jesus whisper from the mountain tops? Hear Jesus proclaim the message of the kingdom, 'Do not be anxious about tomorrow, for anxiety cannot change the future.' What you cannot change God can embrace and God can heal.

In today's world it is often very very difficult not to be anxious, not to be anxious about the past, not to be anxious about the present, not to be anxious about the future.

Feeling

Anxiety destabilizes, incapacitates and immobilizes thousands of people every day. Step into their shoes and feel what it is like from the inside.

Step into the shoes of the child made anxious by irascible parents. Experience life when parental anger is unpredictable and uncontrollable. Experience life when it is all too easy to step out of line for no good reason. Grasp how such anxiety destabilizes, incapacitates and immobilizes such a child. Does not the heart of Jesus go out to such as these? And are we not challenged to make their world a better place?

Step into the shoes of the young woman made anxious by an unreasonable and intolerant partner. Experience life when family violence is unpredictable and uncontrollable. Experience life when emotional and physical brutality becomes the norm. Grasp how such anxiety destabilizes, incapacitates and immobilizes such a woman. Does not the heart of Jesus go out to such as these? And are we not challenged to make their world a better place?

Step into the shoes of the young man made anxious by a management regime of bullying at work. Experience life when workplace victimization and intimidation are unpredictable and uncontrollable. Experience life when each new day at work is accompanied by dread and fear. Grasp how such anxiety destabilizes, incapacitates and immobilizes such a man. Does not the heart of Jesus go out to such as these? And are we not challenged to make their world a better place?

Step into the shoes of the frail elderly man made anxious by the insensitive staff within the residential home. Experience life when the basic needs of love and care are never met. Experience life when the failing body ceases to be in command and when others fail to provide the essential support for well-being. Grasp how such anxiety destabilizes, incapacitates and immobilizes such a man. Does not the heart of Jesus go out to such as these? And are we not challenged to make their world a better place?

Anxiety destabilizes, incapacitates and immobilizes thousands of people every day. Are we not called to do something about it?

Thinking

For some the lilies of the field theology might seem to promote an irresponsible view of life. If the lilies of the field do not go out to spin, should we not, too, abandon our mills, our factories, our places of toil? Is not work an over-rated and misplaced activity in the kingdom of God?

For some the lilies of the field theology might seem to promote an irresponsible view of life. If the lilies of the field do not build up a wardrobe of warm winter clothes, should we not, too, rely on God to weave our clothing and to take care of our appearance? Are not smartness and good dress sense over-rated and misplaced in the kingdom of God?

It is all too easy to misunderstand the lilies of the field theology. For the Jesus who drew our attention to the lilies of the field also taught:

> But strive first for the kingdom of God and for God's right-eousness, and all things will be given to you as well.

Here is a theology not of irresponsibilities but of priorities.

For some the birds of the air theology might seem to promote an irresponsible view of life. If the birds of the air neither sow nor reap nor gather into barns, should we not, too, withdraw from the superannuation schemes and abandon our insurance policies? Is not prudential providence an over-rated and mis-placed principle in the kingdom of God?

For some the birds of the air theology might seem to promote an irresponsible view of life. If the birds of the air do not build fine temples for the worship of God, but eternally sing the praises of God as they flutter through the sky, should we not, too, abandon our cathedrals, churches and chapels? Is not the very notion of building places of worship an over-rated and misplaced objective in the kingdom of God?

It is all too easy to misunderstand the birds of the air theology.

For the Jesus who drew our attention to the birds of the air also taught:

> But strive first for the kingdom of God and for God's right-eousness, and all things will be given to you as well.

Here is a theology not of irresponsibilities but of priorities.

13
Matthew 7:21–29

21'Not everyone who says to me, "Lord, Lord" will enter the kingdom of heaven, but only the one who does the will of my Father in heaven. 22On that day many will say to me, "Lord, Lord, did we not prophesy in your name, and cast out demons in your name, and do many deeds of power in your name?" 23Then I will declare to them, "I never knew you; go away from me, you evildoers."

24'Everyone then who hears these words of mine and acts on them will be like a wise man who built his house on rock. 25The rain fell, the floods came, and the winds blew and beat on that house, but it did not fall, because it had been founded on rock. 26And everyone who hears these words of mine and does not act on them will be like a foolish man who built his house on sand. 27The rain fell, and the floods came, and the winds blew and beat against that house, and it fell – and great was its fall!'

28Now when Jesus had finished saying these things, the crowds were astounded at his teaching, 29for he taught them as one having authority, and not as their scribes.

Context

In chapter 5 Jesus went up the mountain and began to teach. This teaching, known as the sermon on the mount, is concluded with the parable of the two houses and with the astonishment of the crowd.

Sensing

It was quite early in the day, when you saw the crowd following Jesus onwards and upwards along the mountain pass. The sun was still fixed in the east when you sat down to listen to the teaching. Like the rest of the crowd, your mind was open and you were waiting to be convinced.

It was quite early in the day, when you heard Jesus begin to turn the world upside down. In his teaching the poor in spirit were given the kingdom of heaven, the mourners were promised comfort, the meek became inheritors of the earth, those who hunger and thirst for righteousness were filled, and those who were persecuted for righteousness' sake claimed the kingdom of heaven as their possession. Such outrageous teaching carried the note of authority.

It was no longer quite so early in the day, when you heard Jesus begin to turn the law upside down. In his teaching the command against murder was extended to an injunction against anger; the command against adultery was extended to an injunction against the wandering and lustful eye; and the command to love your neighbour was extended to an injunction to love your enemy. Such outrageous teaching carried the note of authority.

It was clearly no longer early in the day, when you heard Jesus begin to turn the religious practices upside down. In his teaching, alms-giving was taken from the public gaze into the realm of privacy, praying was removed from the synagogue into your private room behind closed doors, and fasting was stripped of its outward ritual. Such outrageous teaching carried the note of authority.

It was now clearly getting late in the day, when you heard Jesus begin to turn human anxiety upside down. In his teaching, the lilies of the field dispelled human concern for fine clothes, and the birds of the air dispelled human concern for food and drink. Such outrageous teaching carried the note of authority.

Now the sun is setting in the west, the day is over and the teacher is returning home. Like the rest of the crowd, your mind has been convinced. Here is a man who teaches with authority.

Intuition

When you dig right down below the surface of your life, what do you find there? Right down at rock bottom, what are the fundamental values and truths on which you have built your life? When the rain falls and the flood comes and the wind blows, will all be safe and secure? Right down at the rock bottom what is there?

In the sermon on the mount Jesus challenged you to be merciful. What evidence is there that you have built the value of mercy into the foundations of your life?

In the sermon on the mount Jesus challenged you to be pure in heart. What evidence is there that you have built the value of purity into the foundations of your life?

In the sermon on the mount Jesus challenged you to be peacemakers. What evidence is there that you have built the value of peacemaking into the foundations of your life?

In the sermon on the mount Jesus challenged you to accept persecution for righteousness' sake. What evidence is there that you have built the value of accepting suffering for the sake of the gospel into your life?

In the sermon on the mount Jesus challenged you to show love even to your enemies. What evidence is there that you have built the value of unquestioning love into the foundations of your life?

In the sermon on the mount Jesus challenged you to give to everyone who begs from you and not to refuse anyone who wants to borrow from you. What evidence is there that you have built the value of generosity into the foundations of your life?

When you dig right down below the surface of your life, what do you find there? Right down at the rock bottom do you find fundamental values like mercy, purity, peacemaking, acceptance of suffering for the sake of the gospel, love even for your enemies, and generosity to all? When the rain falls and the flood comes and the wind blows, will all be safe and secure? Right down at rock bottom what is there?

Feeling

There is a lot of teaching in Matthew's gospel which many of us would rather not hear. There is a lot of teaching in Matthew's gospel which seems to fly in the face of the message of love, harmony and peace. So how do you feel about that?

According to Matthew's teaching, there are many who call upon the name of the Lord Jesus who will never enter the kingdom of heaven. Instead they will hear the master proclaim,

'I never knew you: go away from me, you evil-doers.' How can such rejection fit with the gospel of love, harmony and peace?

According to Matthew's teaching, there are many who prophesy in the name of the Lord Jesus who will never enter the kingdom of heaven. Instead they will hear the master proclaim, 'I never knew you; go away from me, you evil-doers.' How can such rejection fit with the gospel of love, harmony and peace?

According to Matthew's teaching, there are many who cast out demons in the name of the Lord Jesus who will never enter the kingdom of heaven. Instead they will hear the master proclaim, 'I never knew you; go away from me, you evil-doers.' How can such rejection fit with the gospel of love, harmony and peace?

According to Matthew's teaching, there are many who perform deeds of power in the name of the Lord Jesus who will never enter the kingdom of heaven. Instead they will hear the master proclaim, 'I never knew you; go away from me, you evildoers.' How can such rejection fit with the gospel of love, harmony and peace?

There is a lot of teaching in Matthew's gospel which many of us would rather not hear. There is a lot of teaching in Matthew's gospel which seems to fly in the face of the message of love, harmony and peace. So how do you feel about that?

Thinking

By the time that Jesus had finished his teaching on the mountain the people were impressed. 'This man', they said, 'teaches as someone having authority.' True authority impresses. The problem is that false authority and authoritarianism often impress as well.

At the beginning of his ministry Jesus examined a range of leadership styles. There in the wilderness he gazed on the scattered stones and knew that in his hand they could become bread. This he rejected as impressive but false authority.

At the beginning of his ministry Jesus examined a range of leadership styles. There in the wilderness he gazed at the pinnacle of the temple and knew that in God's hands he would be safe to float to the ground. This he rejected as impressive but false authority.

At the beginning of his ministry Jesus examined a range of leadership styles. There in the wilderness he gazed at all the kingdoms of the world and knew that in Satan's hands all this power would be his. This he rejected as impressive but false authority.

At the beginning of his ministry Jesus examined a range of leadership styles. There on the mountainside he challenged the religious teaching of his generation and fed the spiritual hunger of the people of God. This the people saw as true authority.

At the beginning of his ministry Jesus examined a range of leadership styles. There in the country of the Gadarenes he confronted two demoniacs and cast out their demons into the herd of swine. This the people saw as true authority.

At the beginning of his ministry Jesus examined a range of leadership styles. There in the deserted place he responded to the hunger of the crowd and fed five thousand men, plus women and children, from five loaves and two fish. This the people saw as true authority.

True authority impresses. The problem is that false authority and authoritarianism often impress as well. Are you sure that you can really tell the difference?

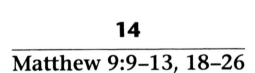

14

Matthew 9:9–13, 18–26

⁹As Jesus was walking along, he saw a man called Matthew sitting at the tax booth; and he said to him, 'Follow me.' And he got up and followed him.

¹⁰And as he sat at dinner in the house, many tax-collectors and sinners came and were sitting with him and his disciples. ¹¹When the Pharisees saw this, they said to his disciples, 'Why does your teacher eat with tax-collectors and sinners?' ¹²But when he heard this, he said, 'Those who are well have no need of a physician, but those who are sick. ¹³Go and learn what this means, "I desire mercy, not sacrifice." For I have come to call not the righteous but sinners.'

¹⁸While he was saying these things to them, suddenly a leader of the synagogue came in and knelt before him, saying,

'My daughter has just died; but come and lay your hand on her, and she will live.' ¹⁹And Jesus got up and followed him, with his disciples. ²⁰Then suddenly a woman who had been suffering from haemorrhages for twelve years came up behind him and touched the fringe of his cloak, ²¹for she said to herself, 'If I only touch his cloak, I will be made well.' ²²Jesus turned, and seeing her he said, 'Take heart, daughter; your faith has made you well.' And instantly the woman was made well. ²³When Jesus came to the leader's house and saw the flute-players and the crowd making a commotion, ²⁴he said, 'Go away; for the girl is not dead but sleeping.' And they laughed at him. ²⁵But when the crowd had been put outside, he went in and took her by the hand, and the girl got up. ²⁶And the report of this spread throughout that district.

Context

Matthew announces the theme of chapter 9 when Jesus addresses the paralytic, 'Take heart, son, your sins are forgiven.' This theme is then illustrated by the call of Matthew, by healing the woman and by raising the dead girl to life.

Sensing

Watch and hear. Today Jesus is bringing salvation, health and life itself to those whom society marginalizes.

Watch and hear as Jesus approaches Matthew sitting at the tax booth. Watch and hear as Jesus comes face to face with the man whose very work put him outside the pale of religious acceptance. Here is the man who had turned his back on his Jewish heritage to serve the occupying Roman authority. See the smile of acceptance in Jesus' face. Hear the accent of acceptance in Jesus' voice. Jesus' hand is already outstretched to restore God's fallen son to his rightful place. 'Take heart,' says Jesus, 'come and follow me.'

Watch and hear as Jesus approaches the woman who had been suffering from haemorrhages for twelve years. Watch and hear as Jesus comes face to face with the woman whose very illness puts her outside the pale of religious acceptance. Here is the woman who remains ritually unclean and who contaminates all who touch her.

See the smile of acceptance in Jesus' face. Hear the accent of acceptance in Jesus' voice. Jesus' hand is already outstretched to restore God's fallen daughter to her rightful place. 'Take heart,' says Jesus, 'your faith has made you well.'

Watch and hear as Jesus approaches the young girl who had given up on life and lay dead in her father's home. Watch and hear as Jesus comes face to face with the girl whose very death puts her outside the pale of religious acceptance. Here is the corpse that remains ritually unclean and that contaminates all who touch it. See the smile of acceptance on Jesus' face. Hear the accent of acceptance in Jesus' voice. Jesus' hand is already outstretched to restore God's fallen child to her rightful place. 'Take heart,' says Jesus, 'rise up and live.'

Watch and hear. Today Jesus is bringing salvation, health and life itself to those whom society marginalizes.

Intuition

For twelve long years that woman had longed to hear one thing, and today she heard it. Jesus spoke to her and said, 'Take heart, daughter; your faith has made you well.'

Let your mind roam and bring to the feet of Jesus all those men and women who cry out from physical pain and long to be released from their suffering. Pray that they may hear the voice of Jesus say, 'Your faith has made you well.'

Let your mind roam and bring to the feet of Jesus all those men and women who cry out from mental torment and long to be released from their suffering. Pray that they may hear the voice of Jesus say, 'Your faith has made you well.'

Let your mind roam and bring to the feet of Jesus all those men and women who cry out from spiritual anguish and long to be released from their suffering. Pray that they may hear the voice of Jesus say, 'Your faith has made you well.'

Let your mind roam and bring to the feet of Jesus all those nations of the world which cry out from economic depression and long to be released from their suffering. Pray that they may hear the voice of Jesus say, 'Your faith has made you well.'

Let your mind roam and bring to the feet of Jesus all those nations of the world which cry out from political oppression and long to be released from their suffering. Pray that they may hear the voice of Jesus say, 'Your faith has made you well.'

Let your mind roam and bring to the feet of Jesus all those nations of the world which cry out from ethnic or religious conflict and long to be released from their suffering. Pray that they may hear the voice of Jesus say, 'Your faith has made you well.'

For twelve long years that woman had longed to hear one thing, and today she heard it. Jesus spoke to her and said, 'Take heart, daughter; your faith has made you well.'

Feeling

Here are two stories of profound faith, profound faith in the love and in the power of Jesus. Let those stories of faith touch your own hearts and transform your own lives.

Feel the profound faith of the woman who had been suffering from haemorrhages for twelve full years. Walk alongside her as she shadows Jesus so hesitantly through the crowds. Share her deep-seated longing for wholeness, for health and for salvation. Identify with her apprehension as she anticipates the healing and life-giving power of Jesus.

Feel the profound faith of the woman who had been suffering from haemorrhages for twelve long years. Walk alongside her as she touches Jesus' cloak so hesitantly through the crowds. Let the joy run through your own mind as Jesus turns and catches her eye. Let the relief run through your own heart as Jesus stretches out his hand toward her. Let the praise run through your soul as Jesus proclaims, 'Take heart, daughter; your faith has made you well.'

Here are two stories of profound faith, profound faith in the love and in the power of Jesus.

Feel the profound faith of the leader of the synagogue whose young daughter had so recently died. Walk alongside him as he approaches to interrupt the teaching. Share his deep-seated longing for his daughter's salvation, health and restoration to life. Identify with his apprehension as he anticipates the healing and life-giving power of Jesus.

Feel the profound faith of the leader of the synagogue whose young daughter had so recently died. Walk alongside him as he leads Jesus to his house. Let the joy run through your mind as Jesus turns to face the dead girl. Let the relief run through your heart as Jesus stretches out his hand and touches her. Let the praise run through your soul as Jesus proclaims, 'Little girl, get up!'

Here are two stories of profound faith, profound faith in the love and in the power of Jesus. Let these stories of faith teach your own hearts and transform your own lives.

Thinking

Have you noticed just how tactile Jesus could be? And I wonder what that teaches us about a theology of touch?

Have you noticed just how tactile Jesus could be? In Matthew 8 a leper came to Jesus and knelt before him, saying, 'Lord, if you choose, you can make me clean.' Jesus stretched out his hand, touched him, and immediately his leprosy was cleansed. By touching the leper Jesus himself became unclean. What does that teach us about a theology of touch?

Have you noticed just how tactile Jesus could be? In Matthew 8 Jesus entered Peter's house, and saw Peter's mother-in-law lying in bed with a fever. Jesus touched her hand and the fever left her. What does that teach us about a theology of touch?

Have you noticed just how tactile Jesus could be? In Matthew 9 Jesus was approached by the leader of the synagogue whose daughter had just died. The leader of the synagogue said to Jesus, 'Come and lay your hand on her, and she will live.' Jesus went and took the girl by the hand, and the girl got up. What does that teach us about the theology of touch?

Have you noticed just how tactile Jesus could be? In Matthew 9 Jesus was approached from behind by a woman who had been suffering from haemorrhages for twelve years. The woman said, 'If only I touch his cloak, I will be made well.' The woman touched Jesus' cloak, Jesus spoke to her, and instantly she was made well. What does that teach us about a theology of touch?

Have you noticed just how tactile Jesus could be? In Matthew 9 Jesus was followed by two blind men, crying loudly, 'Have mercy on us, Son of David!' When Jesus entered the house the blind men came right up to him. Jesus touched their eyes and spoke to them, and their eyes were opened. What does that teach us about a theology of touch?

Have you noticed just how tactile Jesus could be? So I wonder why the church today keeps so silent regarding the theology of touch?

15

Matthew 9:35 to 10:8

35Then Jesus went about all the cities and villages, teaching in their synagogues, and proclaiming the good news of the kingdom, and curing every disease and every sickness. 36When he saw the crowds, he had compassion for them, because they were harassed and helpless, like sheep without a shepherd. 37Then he said to his disciples, 'The harvest is plentiful, but the labourers are few; 38therefore ask the Lord of the harvest to send out labourers into his harvest.'

1Then Jesus summoned his twelve disciples and gave them authority over unclean spirits, to cast them out, and to cure every disease and every sickness. 2These are the names of the twelve apostles: first, Simon, also known as Peter, and his brother Andrew; James son of Zebedee, and his brother John; 3Philip and Bartholomew; Thomas and Matthew the tax-collector; James son of Alphaeus, and Thaddaeus; 4Simon the Cananaean, and Judas Iscariot, the one who betrayed him.

5These twelve Jesus sent out with the following instructions: 'Go nowhere among the Gentiles, and enter no town of the Samaritans, 6but go rather to the lost sheep of the house of Israel. 7As you go, proclaim the good news, "The kingdom of heaven has come near." 8Cure the sick, raise the dead, cleanse the lepers, cast out demons. You received without payment; give without payment.'

Context

After recording Jesus' teaching in the sermon on the mount, Matthew devoted two chapters to Jesus' proclamation of the kingdom through healing. Now Jesus authorizes the twelve disciples to share in the work of proclaiming that 'the kingdom of heaven has come near'.

Sensing

Before showing us how Jesus commissioned the twelve disciples to share in his work, Matthew wants to make sure that we have properly identified the three basic strands in what Jesus set out to do.

Jesus set out to teach. Matthew 4:23 tells us that Jesus went through Galilee, teaching in their synagogues. Then Matthew 9:35 tells us again that Jesus went about all the cities and villages, teaching in their synagogues. While as yet we have not been allowed into the synagogues to hear this teaching we have been privileged to listen to the open-air sermon on the mount.

According to Matthew the crowds were astonished at Jesus' teaching, for he taught them as one having authority, and not as their scribes.

Jesus set out to proclaim the good news of the kingdom. In chapter 9 Matthew shows us how the good news of the kingdom is proclaimed both through words and through experience. Good news was proclaimed to the paralysed man through words when Jesus said, 'Take heart, son; your sins are forgiven.' Good news was proclaimed to the paralysed man through experience when he stood up and went to his home.

According to Matthew when the crowds witnessed such proclamation they were filled with awe, and they glorified God.

Jesus set out to cure every disease and every sickness. In Matthew 8 and 9 the leper was cleansed, the centurion's servant was healed, Peter's mother-in-law's fever left her, two demons were exorcized, the paralysed man walked, the woman who had been suffering from haemorrhages grew well, the young girl was raised to life, sight was restored to two blind men, and speech was given to the man who had been mute.

According to Matthew when the crowds witnessed such healings, they said, 'Never has anything like this been seen in Israel.'

Matthew wants to make sure that we have identified the three basic strands in what Jesus set out to do.

Intuition

Names are important; names mean a lot. What springs to your mind when you hear the names of Jesus' chosen twelve?

Take Peter. The Greek name Petros means rock. Jesus makes full use of the name and says to Peter, 'You are the rock on which I will build my church.' Pray that you may share Peter's rock-like qualities in the service of Jesus.

Take Thomas. The name Thomas has become a byword for doubting. After the resurrection Thomas refused to believe until he had been given proof. When Thomas eventually saw, then he believed. Pray that you may face your doubts boldly as Thomas did and like Thomas come face to face with the living proof.

Take Matthew. Matthew is known the world over as the man who raised taxes for the occupying army. Yet when he came face to face with Jesus, Matthew found permanent acceptance and changed his way of life. Pray that you may have the courage to repent and to follow Jesus' call.

Take James and John. These two brothers have been known through the gospels as Boanerges, the Sons of Thunder. Tales are told of their quick temper and of their personal ambition, and yet they were loved, accepted and forgiven by Jesus. Pray that you may have grace to accept Jesus' forgiveness for your lapses of temper and excesses of self-interest.

Take Thaddaeus. What do you know of Thaddaeus' ministry and mission? Where are his deeds recorded? What traits of character single him out for notoriety or for celebration? Pray that you may rejoice in anonymity in the service of him to whom no one is anonymous.

Take Judas and reflect on his place among the twelve.

Names are important; names mean a lot. What springs to your mind when you hear the names of Jesus' chosen twelve?

Feeling

The gospels show Jesus as a man of true and deep compassion. Open your hearts to share Jesus' concern.

The gospels show Jesus as a man of true and deep compassion. According to Matthew 9, when Jesus saw the crowds, he had compassion for them because they were harassed and helpless, like sheep without a shepherd. Jesus' heart continues to go out to those who are harassed and helpless. Open your hearts to share Jesus' concern.

The gospels show Jesus as a man of true and deep compassion. According to Matthew 14, when Jesus saw the crowds bring to him those who were suffering, he had compassion for them and cured their sick. Jesus' heart continues to go out to those who are sick and suffering. Open your heart to share Jesus' concern.

The gospels show Jesus as a man of true and deep compassion. According to Matthew 15, Jesus called his disciples and said to them, 'I have compassion for the crowd, because they have been with me now for three days and have nothing to eat; and I do not want to send them away hungry, for they might faint on the way.' Jesus' heart continues to go out to those who are starving and hungry. Open your hearts to share Jesus' concern.

The gospels show Jesus as a man of true and deep compassion. According to Matthew 20, two blind men cried out to Jesus to have mercy on them. Moved with compassion, Jesus touched their eyes and immediately they regained their sight and followed him. Jesus' heart continues to go out to those who inhabit a world of darkness. Open your heart to share in Jesus' concern.

The gospels show Jesus as a man of true and deep compassion. According to Luke 7, when Jesus visited Nain he met a funeral procession in which a widow was mourning the death of her only son. When Jesus saw the widow he had compassion for her and said, 'Do not weep.' Jesus touched the bier and restored the young man to life. Jesus' heart continues to go out to the bereaved and to those who mourn. Open your hearts to share in Jesus' concern.

The gospels show Jesus as a man of true and deep compassion. Open your hearts to share Jesus' concern.

Thinking

If you were setting out to build a team would you have gone about it in the way that Jesus did?

Would you have started by calling Simon Peter, knowing now all that you know about the man? Would you have selected someone so obviously able but unstable? Would you have selected someone who so obviously misunderstood the nature of his call that he would rebuke you for accepting the path of suffering, that he would disgrace you by attacking your captors with a sword, and that he would disown you three times in your hour of need?

Would you have called Simon Peter's brother Andrew as well, knowing now all that you know about the bonds both of affection and of rivalry that exist between sons of the same father? Would you have selected a pair of brothers who might generate division within the team?

Would you have repeated such a dangerous experiment by calling another pair of brothers, James and John, knowing all you know about potential rivalries between two family firms of fishermen? Would you have selected a pair of brothers who had been nicknamed 'Sons of Thunder', who were so ambitious that they sought the chief seats beside Jesus in his kingdom, and who would so readily call down fire from heaven?

Would you have called Matthew, such a traitor against his fellow countrymen and such an ally of the Roman occupation, to lead the new people of God? Then having recruited a republican into your team would you have gone out of your way to call Simon the Cananaean, a member of the Zealot party so committed to overthrowing Roman rule?

Would you have called Judas Iscariot, the man capable of betraying you with a kiss?

If you were setting out to build a team would you have gone about it the way that Jesus did? Perhaps you would if you were committed to showing that the kingdom of heaven was open to all and you wanted to start something that would really last.

16

Matthew 10:24–39

24'A disciple is not above the teacher, nor a slave above the master; 25it is enough for the disciple to be like the teacher, and the slave like the master. If they have called the master of the house Beelzebul, how much more will they malign those of his household!

26'So have no fear of them; for nothing is covered up that will not be uncovered, and nothing secret that will not become known. 27What I say to you in the dark, tell in the light; and what you hear whispered, proclaim from the housetops. 28Do not fear those who kill the body but cannot kill the soul; rather fear him who can destroy both soul and body in hell. 29Are not two sparrows sold for a penny? Yet not one of them will fall to the ground apart from your Father. 30And even the hairs of your head are all counted. 31So do not be afraid; you are of more value than many sparrows.

32'Everyone therefore who acknowledges me before others, I also will acknowledge before my Father in heaven; 33but

whoever denies me before others, I also will deny before my
Father in heaven.

> ³⁴'Do not think that I have come to bring peace to the
>   earth; I have not come to bring peace, but a
>   sword.
> ³⁵For I have come to set a man against his father,
>   and a daughter against her mother,
>   and a daughter-in-law against her mother-in-law;
> ³⁶and one's foes will be members of one's own
>   household.

³⁷Whoever loves father or mother more than me is not worthy
of me; and whoever loves son or daughter more than me is
not worthy of me; ³⁸and whoever does not take up the cross
and follow me is not worthy of me. ³⁹Those who find their life
will lose it, and those who lose their life for my sake will find
it.'

Context

Matthew brings to a close Jesus' instructions to the disciples with
warnings about the persecutions and divisions that his followers
will suffer. These are matched with words of strength and comfort
for those who remain faithful to his teaching.

Sensing

Listen to Jesus' instructions to his disciples to equip them for
their mission to the world.

As a faithful disciple pack your bag and listen to Jesus. First
hear his words of warning about the situation you will find: 'If
they treated me with insults, so it will be for you. If you think all
will work for harmony and peace, then think again, there will be
divisions, even within the family. If they put me on a cross and
kill me, you may have to suffer like that also.' Feel your heart
beating rapidly as the words of Jesus sink into your conscious-
ness. Sense the taste of fear in your mouth. Stare in stunned
amazement at such straight talking. It is very tough being a
disciple.

As a faithful disciple pack your bag and listen to Jesus. Now
hear his words of encouragement about the situation you will
find: 'Have no fear of those who try to put a covering blanket
over the good news and straight talking of the Gospel, such

exciting truth cannot be kept in the dark. Have no fear of those who make physical attacks on you, they cannot destroy your relationship with God. Have no fear that you will count for nothing, you are precious in every way to God.' Feel Christ's hand of support on your shoulder. Sense the bones in your back pulling you up straight. With such encouragement nothing will stop you being a disciple.

As a faithful disciple pack your bag and listen to Jesus. Now hear his words of challenge about the situation you will find: 'If you stand up for me before others, I will declare you faithful before God. If you let me down and deny that you are my disciple, I will declare you faithless before God. If you seek for a life of ease, you will have nothing to give away. If you give your life away, I will give you everything you ever sought.'

As a faithful disciple pack your bag and commit yourself to follow Jesus: 'Lord, with your encouragement, I am ready to go, whatever the cost.'

Intuition

Those who lived in the times of persecution in the early church would have found it easy to relate to these instructions from Jesus. Risks, hardships, lies, division within and without, even death, were familiar experiences. Even in more settled times these words still speak to our situation. Can you make the connection?

You can still hear people say, 'Those are good Christian people, surely God should have protected them from hardship and vicious attack. Those are good Christian people, surely they should not have family divisions. Those are good Christian people, surely they should find life easy. Those are good Christian young people, surely God should not allow such churchgoers to die in accidents at such a young age.' People today still complain that God does not give special favour to those who give their all to God.

Use the teaching of Jesus to help you give an answer to such complaints. 'The disciple should be like the teacher. Whoever loves father or mother more than me is not worthy of me. Those who find their life will lose it; those who lose their life for my sake will find it. Whoever does not take up the cross is not worthy of me.' What Jesus found to be true, must be true as well for every disciple. The connection is clear for us all to see.

Use the record of the life and death of Jesus to help you give an answer to such complaints. Matthew's gospel records the following: 'They called the master of the house "A Spirit of Evil"' (10:25), 'While he was still speaking to the crowds his mother and brothers were standing outside, waiting to speak to him' (12:46), 'This is the heir, come, let us kill him and get his inheritance' (21:38). What is good enough for the master is good enough for every disciple. The connection is clear for all to see.

God's love had to be expressed and lived out whatever the cost. That is what Jesus taught and that is what Jesus lived to do. The cross is God's glory for even there God's love is most obvious. If we are true to our mission and faithful to God's call we will apply such teaching to our own lives and be able to make the connection for all to see.

Feeling

Fear is a natural human emotion we all feel when we are faced with dire warnings. It fills us with foreboding for ourselves and empathy for others.

When we hear of persecutions we feel afraid for those who suffer. When we hear of fellow Christians in many parts of the world being persecuted for sharing their faith with their non-Christian neighbours, we feel for them, upholding them in prayer that they 'will not be put to the test'. When we hear of divisions within families caused by firm stands on religious principles, we feel for those in such tensions, praying for better understanding and just peace.

Fear is a natural human emotion we all feel when we are faced with dire warnings. Jesus knew this. Matthew's gospel acknowledges this. Christ's teaching about a disciple's proper behaviour in the face of persecution is matched by words of comfort and strength. Jesus knows that the task he has given the disciples causes fear in their hearts, so he also encourages them with the assurance that they are valued by God.

When it is really tough being a disciple, we are afraid that there may be little worth in what we do. When being a missionary for Christ is a struggle, we find it difficult to feel valued. When others place little value on our work for Jesus, we feel a loss of our self-esteem. When the going is rough, we feel our efforts for God are not worth the cost. We are afraid it is all worthless.

In the face of such fears, feel in your heart the assurance of Jesus: 'Do not fear those who can destroy the body but not the soul. Even the hairs of your head are counted. Everyone who acknowledges me before others, I will acknowledge before God.' In the midst of honest apprehension about the difficulties and dangers of being a disciple, feel the assurances of Jesus: 'Those who lose their life for my sake, will find it.'

We all have feelings of fear, but put your fears behind you for the joy of living life to the full with Jesus, in this life and in the life of resurrection.

Thinking

Some commentators see these verses as a collection of sayings of Jesus which were circulating in the early church to provide realism and encouragement in times of persecution. These verses mirror what we know were the conditions under which the mission of the church had to be undertaken. The church struggled with why this task was so tough. Considering this evidence we need to think deeply about our methods and plans for mission.

In the reality of the facts, what is our strategy for mission? How do we continue with proclamation even when it arouses strong opposition and causes dissension? How do we make the sort of demands that are seen as absolutes and are sure to put some people off the journey into discipleship? What do we consider successes and what do we see as failures in mission?

In the reality of the facts, what is our strategy for mission? What is the proper balance between words of warning and words of comfort? Do we explain to enquirers the costs as well as the rewards of discipleship? Have we grown soft on the challenges of the gospel and only stressed the love and care of God for each person?

In the reality of the facts, what is our strategy for mission? When we emphasize the harmony and unity that the Christian faith can bring to all our relationships, how do we also warn that giving God top priority will mean rearranging all our other priorities, yes even those to our family? How do we explain those difficult words, 'Those who find their life will lose it. Those who lose their life for my sake will find it'?

When putting those sayings in order in a consecutive passage, Matthew must have had a purpose behind his scheme. What do you think that purpose was? Your answer will help you draw up plans for a mission strategy today, proclaiming the good news with its true cutting edge.

17

Matthew 10:40–42

⁴⁰'Whoever welcomes you welcomes me, and whoever welcomes me welcomes the one who sent me. ⁴¹Whoever welcomes a prophet in the name of a prophet will receive a prophet's reward; and whoever welcomes a righteous person in the name of a righteous person will receive the reward of the righteous; ⁴²and whoever gives even a cup of cold water to one of these little ones in the name of a disciple – truly I tell you, none of these will lose their reward.'

Context

Jesus' instruction to his disciples ends with a strong message about rewards. He explains the role of the disciple in God's plan and the value of the mission of the church. His words of encouragement counterbalance the warnings about the difficulties of mission that he has already given.

Sensing

Stand on the doorstep of a house and knock on the door. Watch the door open slowly. Explain that you have come to share the gospel. Hear the words of warm welcome, 'Do come in.' Sense the warm glow of satisfaction that someone wants to hear your story of faith. Share with them something of your relationship with God and what it means for your life.

Stand on the doorstep of a house and knock on the door. Watch the door open slowly. Explain that you are a Christian with a message of hope about the future. Hear the words of warm welcome, 'Any Christian teacher is welcome here. Do come in.' Sense the warm glow of satisfaction that you are recognized as a Christian with words of hope to share. Tell them how God's will is unfolding for the future as people seek to fulfil God's purpose.

Stand on the doorstep of a house and knock on the door. Watch the door open slowly. Explain that you are a Christian in business with an experience of fair dealing. Hear the words of warm welcome, 'A person with a moral code in business dealings is warmly welcome here. Do come in.' Sense the warm glow of satisfaction that your actions in business are seen as fair and moral. Help them understand how you establish your principles and how they work out in practice.

Stand on the doorstep of a house and knock on the door. Watch the door open slowly. Explain that you have given a sum of money to a charity to provide fresh water to a village which previously suffered from disease. Ask the householder for a donation. Hear the words of warm welcome, 'Do come in while I fetch my cheque book. In the name of Christ I want to share your joy in making people whole.' Sense the warm glow of satisfaction in seeing Christ's mission in action. Show them photographs of the people at the well who now enjoy so much better health.

'Truly I tell you none of these will lose their reward!'

Intuition

Rewards, everyone in modern society offers rewards. There are rewards for finding lost articles. There are rewards for loyal customers. There are rewards for catching criminals. There are rewards for good behaviour. Rewards, everyone in modern society likes receiving rewards!

What sort of reward do you expect for serving as a Christian? Do you expect high praise on some public occasion from your fellow Christians for your faithful service? Do you expect special seats of honour in the church for those with long years of service? Do you expect a special place at God's table for bringing others to know Christ? What sort of reward do you expect for being a faithful disciple?

One of the prized rewards for being a disciple of Christ is the welcome received from those with whom the gospel is shared. However, modern society is cautious about welcoming others into their houses and lives. The door of a house is mostly kept firmly locked. A chained bolt may be fitted to keep folk out.

When the doorbell rings it often causes resentment or fear. Everyone in modern society is cautious about welcoming others.

When someone knocks on your door and claims to be a Christian, what sort of welcome do you offer? When someone shares with you the joy of the gospel, what sort of welcome do you give? When someone brings you a word of God relevant to your situation, what sort of welcome do you offer? When someone shares with you the experience of the right thing to do as a Christian, what sort of welcome do you give? When someone does something practical to help you in a crisis, what sort of welcome do you offer? When someone invites you to share in raising money for a charity, what sort of welcome do you give?

When someone knocks on your door and claims to be a Christian, do you see that person as a representative of Jesus inviting you to share in the work of discipleship or just as another person interrupting your life? Jesus said, 'Whoever welcomes you, welcomes me.' A warm welcome is the true reward for being a disciple.

Rewards and welcomes, it is not hard to see how they are connected.

Feeling

The experience of being a Christian is often a satisfying one. We feel good when we have the opportunity to share the gospel message with others. They and we feel glad as we break open the word and see how it speaks to us of God's love and calls for our response. We feel good when we have the opportunity to speak an appropriate word of hope or challenge to a person at the crossroads of decision making. We are happy to pray and search for God's will for that person. We feel good when we have the opportunity to do something practical to help others in their time of need. We love the kiss of thanks and the obvious difference we have made to their lives. The experience of being a Christian is often a satisfying one.

The experience of being a Christian makes you feel you are representing Christ to other people. When you see the welcome in their eyes, you see why Christ was so warm about his relationship with others. When you see people welcome your words of hope, you see why Christ was so happy to be called a prophet. When you see people appreciate the practical help you offer in times of crisis, you see why Christ was full of joy as he washed

his disciples' feet. Like Mother Theresa of Calcutta we see Christ
in those whom we serve and they see Christ in those who care
for them. The experience of being a Christian is often a satisfying
one.

The experience of being a Christian brings many moments of
joy and fulfilment. When you welcome Christ into your heart,
you feel life taking on a new meaning and you enter into a loving
mutual relationship. When you welcome Christ's moral teaching
into your heart, you sense the working of the Holy Spirit to guide
you and give you courage to pursue the right path. When you
welcome Christ's loving touch into your heart, it is like balm in
your sorrow or sickness; it soothes the trouble, heals the wounds
and brings deep peace.

Enter into the experience of being a Christian with its true
joys and rich rewards.

Thinking

Mark and Luke both have parallel wording to that found in
Matthew 10:40 and 42. The representatives of Christ are worthy
of receiving Christ's own reward, that of sharing the kingdom of
God with the Father in heaven. As Christ had been the 'model'
for their suffering, so Christ will be the 'model' of their resurrection to glory. The resurrection and ascension of Christ were seen
as the declaration of God's approval of the life and mission of
Jesus. The disciples as they faithfully carry out the mission with
which they have been charged will be rewarded both by the
human welcome they receive and by the welcome extended to
them by the Father in heaven.

Matthew 10:41 has no parallels in Mark and Luke. The verse
picks up key themes in Matthew's exposition of who Jesus is. He
is the true prophet like Moses. He is the righteous servant of God
who knows God's law and does it. His disciples are to become the
prophets and the righteous people. This novel saying leaves open
the meaning as to what kind of reward is due to the prophet, and
what kind of reward is due to the righteous person. In Matthew
13:17 the prophets and righteous people long to see what the
first disciples saw, 'the secrets of the kingdom of heaven'. So is
the reward promised here the joy of seeing the kingdom coming
to fruition in the lives of real people? What do you think? How
do you interpret this verse?

These verses bring to a conclusion the section of Matthew's

gospel (9:35 to 10:42) which contains Jesus' choice of the first disciples and his instructions to all disciples as to the content and conditions for mission. They are to be ambassadors for Christ. They are to be prophets for Christ. They are to be loving examples of Christ's ethical teaching. They are to be servants of compassion for Christ.

These are the tasks of mission. The reward for faithful discipleship will be to see the kingdom of God come to fruition in the lives of people and in the working of the community. Seeing this harvest of the gospel, all disciples will share in the joy of the master.

18
Matthew 11:2–11

²When John heard in prison what the Messiah was doing, he sent word by his disciples ³and said to him, 'Are you the one who is to come, or are we to wait for another?' ⁴Jesus answered them, 'Go and tell John what you hear and see: ⁵the blind receive their sight, the lame walk, the lepers are cleansed, the deaf hear, the dead are raised, and the poor have good news brought to them. ⁶And blessed is anyone who takes no offence at me.'

⁷As they went away, Jesus began to speak to the crowds about John: 'What did you go out into the wilderness to look at? A reed shaken by the wind? ⁸What then did you go out to see? Someone dressed in soft robes? Look, those who wear soft robes are in royal palaces. ⁹What then did you go out to see? A prophet? Yes, I tell you, and more than a prophet. ¹⁰This is the one about whom it is written,

"See, I am sending my messenger ahead of you,
who will prepare your way before you."
¹¹Truly I tell you, among those born of women no one has arisen greater than John the Baptist; yet the least in the kingdom of heaven is greater than he.'

Context

At this point Matthew begins a new section of his gospel which proclaims Jesus as Messiah and John the Baptist as the herald of this good news. Both provide through word and deed ample evidence of the fulfilment of their role. The reader is challenged to see them for who they truly are.

Sensing

Stand on the roadside with Jesus as some messengers arrive. Hear the words of those who identify themselves as the disciples of John the Baptist. They put this crucial question to Jesus: 'Your cousin is now in prison. He has heard what you are doing: teaching, preaching and healing. He wants to be certain that you are the Messiah everyone longs for. If not, are we still looking for the coming of the Messiah some time in the future?'

Stand on the roadside with Jesus and listen as he makes his reply to the disciples of John the Baptist: 'Look about you in this crowd. Ask them what they have experienced of my teaching and healing. Ask that one in the front, for he has heard my words and grasped the truth about God and himself. Ask that one over there, for he was blind and now he has sight. Ask that one at the back, for she was crippled and now she can walk. See that group over there, they are cleansed lepers. See that man near the front, he can hear every word now, although before he was deaf. See that man and his daughter, she was raised to life, even though she was taken to be dead. All this crowd has longed to see such things happening. Ask them what has been good news for them.'

Stand on the roadside with Jesus and add your evidence. You have heard his teaching, it makes sense to you. You have watched his care of the sick, they have been made whole. You have seen his actions to bring hope to the despairing, they have new life. For you there can be no other explanation. His actions and his words show that Jesus is the long awaited Messiah.

Stand on the roadside with Jesus and watch the messengers depart. What will they make of the evidence? What will they make of your evidence? Surely John, surely every enquirer, will come to see the truth that clearly Jesus is the Messiah. We have no need to wait for the coming of God's kingdom, it is here in our midst.

Intuition

Can you identify with John the Baptist as you proclaim the truth about Jesus and human relationships?

John was firm and strong. He stood up for a clear code of moral behaviour. That is why he was in prison. You too must stand up for the principles of a proper code of moral ethics in human relationships.

John was firm and strong. He did not sway like a reed that could be blown about by every wind of common opinion and change. That is why he was in prison. You too must remain firmly committed to your beliefs and principles.

John was firm and strong. He knew the truth and lived by it. He did not sell his soul for money. That is why he was in prison. You too must resist the temptation to sell the truth for an easy life. You must be prepared to be isolated if that is the outcome of your stand.

John was humble and strong. John was a prophet. He proclaimed what God had spoken to him. That is why he was in prison. You too must be humble enough to listen to God, and strong enough to tell others what God is saying.

John was humble and strong. He did not point to himself. He pointed only to Jesus. He did not keep his relationship with Jesus to himself. He shared the truth with all who would listen. You too must be strong enough to prepare the way for Christ, the Messiah, and to share the good news of his coming.

John was humble and strong. He sent his disciples to clarify the role Jesus had in the kingdom of God. You too must have an answer to the question John's disciples asked about Jesus. It is a question many people ask today: 'Is Jesus the Messiah who comes from God to bring God's kingdom to earth?' This is the Advent question for every generation.

Feeling

Share in Jesus' feelings as he is questioned again about who he is. He had due cause to be frustrated and annoyed. He had poured out his love for others in word and deed. He had used every method he could find to teach the truth about God. He had used every illustration to draw parallels between earthly things and heavenly things. He had used his powers of love to care for people to bring them life, warmth and healing.

Share in Jesus' feelings as he is questioned again about who he is. He had due cause to be frustrated and annoyed. He had shared in the despair of the people. He had shared with people his hope and faith in God's goodness. And still they questioned who he was. Share in Jesus' feelings as he finds the words with which to give an answer to the messengers from his cousin John.

Be in touch with your own feelings as people ask you why you are a Christian; why you go on believing in the goodness of God when there is so much suffering around; why people are in prison or on trial even though they have done the right thing by God's law. Be in touch with your own feelings as people put the hard questions to you. Acknowledge how frustrated and annoyed you can become.

Share in Jesus' feelings when various groups in the church claim to be disciples of this modern prophet and that popular preacher; when groups in the church fight with one another as to who is in the kingdom and who is less than that. Share in Jesus' feelings when that kind of behaviour is seen among so-called Christians.

Share in Jesus' feelings when, in the face of all these situations, he proclaims, 'Blessed is anyone who takes no offence at me.' Here are feelings of hope as well as feelings of frustration. Here is a call to future disciples as well as to the crowd around him. Here is an affirmation of all those who will see him as Messiah.

Be in touch with your own feelings as you look to answer those who question you about Jesus and your discipleship. Share in his love, his patience, his humility, his gentleness with others' questions. Feel secure enough to use questions as an opportunity to tell others that for you Jesus *is* the Messiah, whose actions for us, in us, and through us, are good news for all.

Share in Jesus' feelings. Be in touch with your own feelings as his disciple.

Thinking

It is not difficult to work out the reasons why Matthew wants to clarify at this point in the gospel who Jesus is and who John the Baptist is.

In the first part of his gospel Matthew has given evidence on the three main activities of Jesus: his teaching, his preaching and his healing. In the light of this evidence his gospel must now challenge the hearer to identify what this proves Jesus to be. Is Jesus a prophet, in the line of earlier prophets like Isaiah? Or is Jesus a prophet in line with the new prophet John, who has called for repentance and moral uprightness?

Matthew wants to make very clear that the evidence shows that there can be no doubt that Jesus is the Messiah, the long-expected anointed of God who inaugurates the rule of God on earth. The evidence is plain but the responses to it are varied. Some people greet the news with joy. Some people hear the news with disbelief. Some people are openly hostile.

Matthew also wants to clarify the role that John the Baptist plays. He too has disciples. There is reason to believe that they were a group that continued even to the days when the gospels were being written (see Acts 19:1-7). The question must have arisen among this group and among the disciples of Christ as to whether John was equal with Jesus. Was it a valid option to join the group of John's disciples? Was John a key witness to the truth or the truth himself?

Matthew makes clear in this passage that John should be honoured as a necessary forerunner of Jesus, but was not equal to Jesus. It was Jesus himself who inaugurated the kingdom. The evidence Matthew points out has been plainly laid before us. The way we accept or refute that evidence will judge us as believers or doubters. It is no wonder that the liturgical season of Advent is traditionally a time of judgement of the truth about Jesus and about ourselves.

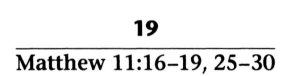

19
Matthew 11:16-19, 25-30

[16]'But to what will I compare this generation? It is like children sitting in the market-places and calling to one another,
[17]"We played the flute for you, and you did not
dance;
we wailed, and you did not mourn."

¹⁸For John came neither eating nor drinking, and they say, "He has a demon"; ¹⁹the Son of Man came eating and drinking, and they say, "Look, a glutton and a drunkard, a friend of tax-collectors and sinners!" Yet wisdom is vindicated by her deeds.'

²⁵At that time Jesus said, 'I thank you, Father, Lord of heaven and earth, because you have hidden these things from the wise and the intelligent and have revealed them to infants; ²⁶yes, Father, for such was your gracious will. ²⁷All things have been handed over to me by my Father; and no one knows the Son except the Father, and no one knows the Father except the Son and anyone to whom the Son chooses to reveal him.

²⁸'Come to me, all you that are weary and are carrying heavy burdens, and I will give you rest. ²⁹Take my yoke upon you, and learn from me; for I am gentle and humble in heart, and you will find rest for your souls. ³⁰For my yoke is easy, and my burden is light.'

Context

Claiming that Jesus is the wisdom of God and that Jesus reveals that wisdom in a new law, Matthew shows the difference between those who 'play with the idea' and those who take it seriously. The wise will find refreshment in doing God's will and in making mature reflection on their faith.

Sensing

Take the place of a young boy and play at weddings. Become the bridegroom and listen as you are piped to the altar. Walk there with your betrothed. After the wedding hear the music and dance with your bride. Let your heart twirl with joy. Invite the other boys, your circle of friends, to enter into the fun and games. Look with amazement and then despair as they hold back and refuse to join you in the game. 'Come on,' you pipe, but it is useless, for they sit in stony silence.

Take the place of a young girl and play at funerals. Become a mourner and raise your voice, cry, wail and screech with grief. Plunge into the depths of sadness. Feel your handkerchief; it is wet with tears. Invite the other girls to join you in the game and cry with you. Look with amazement and then despair as they walk away and refuse to join in. 'Come on,' you cry, but it is useless, for they have turned their backs on you.

Now be yourself. Acknowledge the experience of living life to the full as a Christian. Raise your voice in thanksgiving and joy for all the benefits and wonder of creation: for sunshine and flowers, for a song of joy in being alive, for relationships with others and with God. Remember that Jesus promises us abundant life, life lived to the full. Sense your disappointment that others will not join in your song of thanksgiving and joy.

Now be yourself. Acknowledge the experience of living a life of restraint, mourning over your sins, dying to selfish desires, and weeping over the tragedy of humanity divided by greed and violence. Remember that Jesus promises us forgiveness and calls for discipline. Sense your disappointment that others will not join in your tears of repentance and shame.

In the face of such experiences Jesus declares, 'I thank you Father, Lord of heaven and earth, because you have hidden these things from the wise and the intelligent, and revealed them to the young at heart, open to the games of life through which they see the will of God.' Such are the words of Jesus who invites us to participate fully in the game of life.

Intuition

John the Baptist was known as someone who was austere and ascetic. He withdrew from society so that he could challenge its concepts. He fasted to focus his mind on God and his lips on God's message. What place do you see for such principles in your Christian discipleship and in the life of the church? How do we withdraw today in order to gain a true perspective on modern life? How do we fast today to focus on the priority of God? How do you express the spirit of self-control?

When you withdraw from the outward pleasures of life, do people say, 'You must be crazy'? If so, how do you answer them? Do you invite them to try it, to practise discipline, and to join your 'game'?

Make your connection with the way that John the Baptist lived his life in obedience to God.

Jesus Christ was known as someone full of life and full of fun. He called people into engagement with society. He mixed with all types of people, the so-called good and the so-called bad. He welcomed the opportunity to share in dinner feasts with both groups. He could be found in the pub or the wine bar. His motto was 'Live life to the full' in harmony with one another and with God. What place do you see for such principles in your Christian discipleship and in the life of the church? How do we engage with society in order to gain a true perspective on modern life? How can we 'feast' today to focus on the priority of God's welcome? How do you express the spirit of joy?

When you engage fully with life and have fun, do people say, 'You don't take things seriously enough. You keep bad company'? If so, how do you answer them? Do you invite them to see for themselves, to enter fully into life and join your 'game'?

Make your connections with the way that Jesus lived his life in obedience to God.

Feeling

Jesus said, 'Come to me, all you that are weary and are carrying heavy burdens, and I will give you rest.'

For many people these comfortable words have been a source of solace in times of trial and struggle. These words of Jesus touch the heartstrings and help us feel consoled. When we feel that the pilgrimage to God is an uphill task and the struggle to obey God is an intolerable burden, these words of Jesus are like balm to our wounded selves. They soothe and heal and allow us to rest for a while. Enter into that experience now.

Jesus said, 'Take my yoke upon you, and learn from me; for I am gentle and humble in heart, and you will find rest for your souls.'

For many people these comfortable words of Jesus have been a source of solace in times of trying to do God's will in difficult circumstances. When they hear these words many people feel that God will support them with tenderness as they struggle on in their pilgrimage. They gain strength from Christ's words of understanding for their difficulties. They gain hope from Christ's humility. They allow themselves to rest in Christ's love on their journey towards God's perfection. Enter into that experience now.

For many people these comfortable words of Jesus have been a solace in times of trying to discern God's will: 'For my yoke is easy, and my burden is light.' Hearing this they feel that God does not make intolerable demands on them. They feel that God does not ask them to do the impossible. They feel that even the sorrows they suffer are not too heavy for them to bear. Share this experience of comfort and care.

For many people these comfortable words of Jesus convey the warmth of Christ's embrace. They sense the sympathy and understanding of their Saviour. They receive Christ's welcome. Refreshed in the presence of Christ they are ready to take up the yoke and be partners with Christ on the journey through life. Share this experience of Christ's warm invitation.

With these experiences in mind, thank God for Christ's comfortable words!

Thinking

Verse 27 sounds very much like words taken from St John's Gospel. It is a verse that shows mature reflection on Christ's authority and mission. Read it again and think through the meaning in each of its four statements.

First, Jesus claims to have been given authority in all matters. The word to 'hand over' means to receive the tradition of truth. Maybe the word 'entrusted' is a better translation in English. Jesus indicates that he has received full knowledge about the created order and how it does and should work best. Second, Jesus claims that his relationship with God the Father is so perfect that the Father trusts him fully and he knows everything the Father intends to do. Third, Jesus claims that his relationship with God the Father is so perfect that he can interpret fully the mind and heart of God, and knows exactly the purpose of God for all things. Finally, Jesus claims that those chosen to be his disciples will share the same relationship with God, so they in turn will be able to interpret the mind and heart of God.

When you consider them carefully these four claims are fundamental. They stand at the very centre of the Gospel message. The purpose of Christ's coming was to reveal the nature and the intentions of the Godhead. Christ came to make clear to humanity the answer to our deepest questions about our existence: Who am I and what is the nature of this world about me? Who is this God who created the world in which I find myself, and how do I relate to that God and the world in which I live?

We need a Messiah to help us discover the answers to our questions. We want intelligent answers. Yet Christ teaches us that our wisdom must be 'child-like'. Like children we must be eager to learn rather than to condemn; to search for new truth rather than hide away from it under old clichés. To answer our questions we need a teacher to trust who comes with the Maker's authority and confidence. Mature reflection leads us to thoughtful answers.

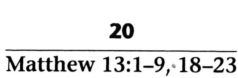

20

Matthew 13:1–9, 18–23

¹That same day Jesus went out of the house and sat beside the sea. ²Such great crowds gathered around him that he got into a boat and sat there, while the whole crowd stood on the beach. ³And he told them many things in parables, saying: 'Listen! A sower went out to sow. ⁴And as he sowed, some seeds fell on the path, and the birds came and ate them up. ⁵Other seeds fell on rocky ground, where they did not have much soil, and they sprang up quickly, since they had no depth of soil. ⁶But when the sun rose, they were scorched; and since they had no root, they withered away. ⁷Other seeds fell among thorns, and the thorns grew up and choked them. ⁸Other seeds fell on good soil and brought forth grain, some a hundredfold, some sixty, some thirty. ⁹Let anyone with ears listen!'

¹⁸'Hear then the parable of the sower. ¹⁹When anyone hears the word of the kingdom and does not understand it, the evil one comes and snatches away what is sown in the heart; this is what was sown on the path. ²⁰As for what was sown on rocky ground, this is the one who hears the word and immediately receives it with joy; ²¹yet such a person has no root, but endures only for a while, and when trouble or persecution arises on account of the word, that person immediately falls away. ²²As for what was sown among thorns, this is the one who hears the word, but the cares of the world and the lure of wealth choke the word, and it yields nothing. ²³But as for what was sown on good soil, this is the one who

hears the word and understands it, who indeed bears fruit and yields, in one case a hundredfold, in another sixty, and in another thirty.'

Context

Jesus told the parable of the farmer sowing seeds to illustrate the way the gospel is proclaimed and how different people respond to it. The parable is followed by an explanation of its application based on experiences in the early church.

Sensing

Stand with Jesus on the edge of a ploughed field on one of the slopes that run down to the Sea of Galilee. Watch a farmer at work sowing seeds. Record the data in your mind. The ground is ready. Now is the time for sowing. The farmer takes the seed into his pouch. All seed comes from the same big bag. There is no difference in quality.

Watch the farmer walk over the field, scattering the seed to right and left. Some seeds fall on the ploughed earth; then comes a pathway trodden hard by trampling feet. See some seed fall onto the path. Hear the sounds of the sparrows chirping in delight. As soon as the farmer moves on they swoop and snatch the seed from the path. What a waste! Watch the farmer ignore the birds and walk on. In the next patch of ground the rocks show through. There is little chance of seed growing here. The roots will not be deep enough to withstand the heat of the sun. Still he sows. What a waste! Watch some seed fall near the boundary. The thistles have not been cleared along the hedge line. Their seed will choke the grain. Still he sows. What a waste! But most seed falls into well-prepared ground. It will grow up strongly. In due time it will ripen. What a harvest!

Stand with the crowd on the beach below the fields. Hear Jesus relate the data about the farmer sowing his seed. Listen to the crowd. For them the facts are obvious. Some is wasted; most produces a fine harvest. See the point of the data.

Stand with the disciples in the early church. Listen as they tell the story of the spread of the gospel. Some people started the journey of faith and never finished it. Some people were enticed away by trials. Some people collapsed under persecution. Some people gave it away when they grew rich. Most disciples remained constant and true. When you look at the record of the church, what a waste! What a harvest!

The facts are obvious. There is no fault in the seed, only in its reception according to the state of the ground. The facts are obvious. There is no fault in the gospel, only in its reception by the hearer. There is a waste, but the harvest is much greater.

Intuition

Where do you see yourself in this parable? There is the farmer and there are the various seeds. Where do you place yourself? There is the seed that falls on good ground, and that which falls on the path; there is the seed that falls on good ground, and that which falls on the soil without depth, or on areas infested with weeds. Where do you see yourself in this parable? There is the seed that produces a harvest of 100 times the initial grain, and some seed that produces 60 times, and some 30 times. When you make the connections, where do you see yourself in this parable?

Where do you see yourself in the explanation of the parable? There is the preacher and there are various listeners. There is the person that cannot understand the message, and the person who is overwhelmed by evil. Do you identify with any of these? There is the person who gets burnt out and gives up being a disciple; and there is the person who is overburdened by the troubles of life and gives up on God. Do you identify with either of these? There is the person who under persecution finds that the faith withers away within; and the person whose faith has continued to grow and grow. Do you identify with either of these? There is the person whose faith so spills over that it is gladly shared with others. When you make the connections, where do you see yourself in the explanation of the parable?

Where do you see yourself in the harvest of the faith? How can you grow from 30 fold to 100 fold? How can you sustain your faith under persecution? How can you prevent your cares choking out your opportunities for faith development? How can you maintain a simple lifestyle that leaves space to develop your faith? When you make the connections, where do you see yourself in the harvest of the faith?

Feeling

Some people find this parable full of heartache. It makes them depressed. The way it is presented causes guilt or despondency.

They feel guilty because they see themselves as failures of the faith. They feel that they are part of a group that cannot live up to the gospel's potential. They feel angry at being a failure, and project the blame onto other factors. There seems little chance of maintaining the faith when you are attacked by evil influences. There seems little chance of maintaining the faith when troubles absorb all the energies available. There seems little chance of maintaining the faith when the culture of wealth swamps the value of spiritual things. Share some of these feelings. It could make you feel despondent and make you try to find excuses why your faith has stopped growing.

Some people feel dispirited by the explanation. The focus seems to be on the rejection of the gospel. The failure of good Christians under persecution, ridicule, cultural clashes and personal neglect of faith causes a general loss of nerve among Christians. The whole enterprise of evangelism seems to lose heart. It is hard to feel that the fields could ever be said to be ripe for harvest again. Share some of these feelings. It could make you wonder at times if the church will maintain its growth.

But such feelings focus on the negative points in the parable. The punch-line at the end must not be overlooked. The outcome of the work is an abundant harvest, despite some wastage. This is the cause for harvest joy. The experience of the early church was overall positive. Share their positive feelings. For them this parable proved that it was well worth spreading the gospel message. The rejection by some people was more than matched by the growth in faith by others. Be positive!

In this parable Jesus is sharing his realism about the response to the gospel. He knows its successes and its failures. Share his joy and sorrow, match his inner assurance that God feels it is still worth the wastage for the bumper size of the harvest of the faith. Let your feelings share Christ's optimism. Be positive!

Thinking

Usually a parable is told within a context but without an explanation as to its meaning.

Commentators have tried to separate the two elements which are found in this passage. They see the parable in its basic outline as appropriate to the context of Jesus responding to the rejection as well as to the reception of his message; he needs to reassure his followers and possible critics. Both these groups can share the question from the disciples of John whether the harvest shows that Jesus is the right sower. Jesus points out that every farmer goes out to sow seed knowing that there will be some wastage in a really good harvest. Every preacher knows what it is to be understood and to be misunderstood. When you think about it, this parable fits clearly into the context of Jesus' ministry at this point.

However, like all good parables, this one can be applied in many different contexts. It was important for the early church to identify the causes for the rejection of, and the falling away from, the gospel message. The explanation echoes the new context. The Acts of the Apostles and the Epistles of Paul give us ample examples.

Do you think that we should then declare the explanation as beyond the words of Jesus, introduced by Matthew to apply the original parable to the new situation for his readers? Maybe, but this misses the point that the words of Jesus in scripture have lasting meaning, not only in their first context, which cannot be retained, but also in each new context. In this way the word of God goes on speaking. That is the work of the Holy Spirit.

So let Jesus' parable speak to your situation. Over many generations people have listened to this parable and found encouragement to go on sharing the gospel, knowing that it will be rejected by some, but many more will let it grow in their hearts until it reaches maturity. Have you 'ears' to listen and lips to act, sharing the good news of Jesus Christ, God's preacher and our teacher?

———————◆◈◆———————

21

Matthew 13:24-30, 36-43

24He put before them another parable: 'The kingdom of heaven may be compared to someone who sowed good seed in his field; 25but while everybody was asleep, an enemy came and sowed weeds among the wheat, and then went away. 26So when the plants came up and bore grain, then the weeds

appeared as well. [27]And the slaves of the householder came
and said to him, "Master, did you not sow good seed in your
field? Where, then, did these weeds come from?" [28]He
answered, "An enemy has done this." The slaves said to him,
"Then do you want us to go and gather them?" [29]But he
replied, "No; for in gathering the weeds you would uproot
the wheat along with them. [30]Let both of them grow together
until the harvest; and at harvest time I will tell the reapers,
Collect the weeds first and bind them in bundles to be burned,
but gather the wheat into my barn." '

[36]Then he left the crowds and went into the house. And
his disciples approached him, saying, 'Explain to us the parable of the weeds of the field.' [37]He answered, 'The one who
sows the good seed is the Son of Man; [38]the field is the world,
and the good seed are the children of the kingdom; the weeds
are the children of the evil one, [39]and the enemy who sowed
them is the devil; the harvest is the end of the age, and the
reapers are angels. [40]Just as the weeds are collected and
burned up with fire, so will it be at the end of the age. [41]The
Son of Man will send his angels, and they will collect out of
his kingdom all causes of sin and all evildoers, [42]and they will
throw them into the furnace of fire, where there will be
weeping and gnashing of teeth. [43]Then the righteous will
shine like the sun in the kingdom of their Father. Let anyone
with ears listen!'

Context

The third section of Jesus' teaching presented by Matthew
(13:3–52) is a collection of parables and the explanation of
parables. Jesus is speaking to the crowds and to the disciples, but
only the disciples begin to understand.

Sensing

Sometimes in Matthew's gospel Jesus' teaching sounds so very
black and white. Take the parable of the weeds growing in the
field as a classic example.

Take a close look at that field. Look at the two key crops that
are growing there. On the one hand, see the good-quality wheat
growing there. See the tall strong stems and the rich golden ears.
Look and admire all that has grown from the good seed. On the

other hand, see the poor-quality weeds growing there. See the tall strong stems of the darnel and the useless crop which it is producing. Look and despise all that has grown from the bad seed. Sometimes in Matthew's gospel Jesus' teaching sounds so very black and white.

Take a close look at that field. Look at the two key characters who have been busy sowing seed there. On the one hand, see the owner of the field come out in broad daylight to scatter good seed across the field. See the smile on his face and the goodness in his eyes. Sense his good intentions. On the other hand, see the enemy of the field come out in the shades of night to scatter bad seed across the field. See the frown on his face and the evil glint in his eyes. Sense his evil intentions. Sometimes in Matthew's gospel Jesus' teaching sounds so very black and white.

Take a close look at that field. Listen to the key conversation between the workmen and the master. On the one hand, hear the workmen press for the weeds to be pulled out long before the harvest. On the other hand, hear the master press for the crop to be left intact until harvest time. Sometimes in Matthew's gospel Jesus' teaching sounds so very black and white.

Take a close look at that field. Look at the two key destinies that await all that is growing there. On the one hand, see the good wheat being harvested and gathered into the barn. Look at the satisfaction on the farmer's face. On the other hand, see the bad darnel being bound into bundles and cast into the fire. Look at the disdain on the farmer's face. Sometimes in Matthew's gospel Jesus' teaching sounds so very black and white.

Intuition

It is a very human tendency to want to uproot the weeds as early as possible, and the church can be a very human institution.

Take the example of Christian doctrine. Throughout the ages there have been church leaders who have been very clear about their ability to distinguish between true doctrine and false doctrine. The true doctrine has been allowed to flourish and the false doctrine has been plucked out. The books of false doctrine have been burnt in the fire. Remember, too, that Jesus was crucified for teaching false doctrine.

Take the example of Christian ministry. Throughout the ages there have been church leaders who have been very clear about their ability to distinguish between true leaders and false leaders.

The true leaders have been allowed to flourish and the false leaders have been plucked out. The false leaders have been burnt in the fire. Remember, too, that Jesus was crucified for being a false leader.

Take the example of Christian worship. Throughout the ages there have been church leaders who have been very clear about their ability to distinguish between true worship and false worship. The true worship has been allowed to flourish and the false worship has been plucked out. The false altars have been burnt in the fire. Remember, too, that Jesus was crucified for practising false worship.

Take the example of Christian lifestyle. Throughout the ages there have been church leaders who have been very clear about their ability to distinguish between true lifestyles and false lifestyles. The true lifestyles have been allowed to flourish and the false lifestyles have been plucked out. Those who have exemplified false lifestyles have been burnt in the fire. Remember, too, that Jesus died to save sinners, not to condemn them.

It is a very human tendency to want to uproot the weeds as early as possible, and the church can be a very human institution.

Feeling

The parable of the weeds growing in the field distinguishes clearly between harmony and justice. Justice is for God to deal with at the end of the ages. Harmony is for the people of God to practise here and now. Now that should make some feel better about their Christian vocation.

Listen carefully to the people of God in the parable. They notice immediately that all is not well in the field. They notice that harmony is being threatened. They notice that weeds are growing silently, surreptitiously but violently alongside and interspersed with the wheat. They remain, however, reluctant to judge. They go to their Lord God to check whether they are reading things correctly. 'Lord', they ask, 'did you not sow good seed in your field? Where then did these weeds come from?'

Listen carefully to the people of God in the parable. They hear their Lord tell them that an enemy has been at work in the field. They recognize that the problem is deep and profound. But they decide not to act precipitously on their own initiative. They remain reluctant to judge. They go to their Lord God to check whether they should really take matters into their own hands. 'Lord', they ask, 'do you want us to go and gather the weeds?'

Listen carefully to the people of God in the parable. They hear their Lord tell them to leave well alone. They recognize that in dealing with the weeds they might well harm the wheat. In the interests of the good they leave unchallenged the bad. For the present at least they are content to let the weeds and the wheat grow together. They know that God will deal with the situation at the end of the ages.

The parable of the weeds growing in the field distinguishes clearly between harmony and justice. Justice is for God to deal with at the end of the ages. Harmony is for the people of God to promote here and now. Now that should make some feel better about their Christian vocation.

Thinking

The parable of the weeds growing in the field provides a clear mandate for Christian tolerance. But just how far can tolerance go? What do you think?

What do you think about the youths who colonize the shopping arcade as evening comes and the shops close? What do you think about the youths who use the benches to eat and drink their way into the night and use the pavement as a race track? These are the young people who have nowhere else to go, who have nothing else to do in the town centre. Because of their very presence the liberty of many to enter the shopping arcade is infringed. Just how far can your tolerance go?

What do you think about the people living at the end of the road who play loud music well into the night? What do you think about people who turn up the sound and open wide the windows? These are the adults who have worked hard for years in order to afford their own home where they can do as they please. Because of the music tired and weary neighbours are deprived of their well-earned sleep. Just how far can your tolerance go?

What do you think about the company which opens an adult sex shop at the corner of your street? What do you think about the adult sex shop which arranges erotic displays in its windows? Here are people going about their lawful business meeting a real demand in the market. Because of their trade the sensibilities of many in the neighbourhood are offended. Just how far can your tolerance go?

What do you think about the political party which espouses and propagates extreme racist beliefs? What do you think about the political party which encourages attacks on minority groups? Here are people who have every right to their own beliefs and convictions. Because of their views the rights of others can be infringed and the lives of others endangered. Just how far can your tolerance go?

The parable of the weeds growing in the field provides a clear mandate for Christian tolerance. But is it Christian to tolerate the intolerance of others?

22
Matthew 13:31–33, 44–52

[31]He put before them another parable: 'The kingdom of heaven is like a mustard seed that someone took and sowed in his field; [32]it is the smallest of all the seeds, but when it has grown it is the greatest of shrubs and becomes a tree, so that the birds of the air come and make nests in its branches.'

[33]He told them another parable: 'The kingdom of heaven is like yeast that a woman took and mixed in with three measures of flour until all of it was leavened.'

[44]'The kingdom of heaven is like treasure hidden in a field, which someone found and hid; then in his joy he goes and sells all that he has and buys that field.

[45]'Again, the kingdom of heaven is like a merchant in search of fine pearls; [46]on finding one pearl of great value, he went and sold all that he had and bought it.

[47]'Again, the kingdom of heaven is like a net that was thrown into the sea and caught fish of every kind; [48]when it was full, they drew it ashore, sat down, and put the good into baskets but threw out the bad. [49]So it will be at the end of the age. The angels will come out and separate the evil from the

righteous ⁵⁰and throw them into the furnace of fire, where there will be weeping and gnashing of teeth.

⁵¹'Have you understood all this?' They answered, 'Yes.' ⁵²And he said to them, 'Therefore every scribe who has been trained for the kingdom of heaven is like the master of a household who brings out of his treasure what is new and what is old.'

Context

In chapter 13 Matthew presents a collection of Jesus' parables about the kingdom of heaven. In this section two parables of growth are followed by two parables of worth and one of judgement.

Sensing

In Jesus' mind the most profound theological insights are triggered by the ordinary details of life. Open your eyes to see life as it is, and see there the kingdom of heaven.

Step outside into the herb garden and take a long cool look at everything growing there. Then pause and look with care and with curiosity at the tiny seeds produced by the mustard plant. See there one of the smallest seeds in the garden. Then look up at the mustard plants which have grown to tree-like proportions, almost twice as tall as you are. See there how the birds make nests in the branches. In Jesus' mind the most profound theological insights are triggered by the herb garden. Open your eyes and see in the mustard seed insights into the kingdom of heaven.

Step inside into the kitchen and take a long cool look at everything happening there. Then pause and look with care and with curiosity at the tiny lump of yeast. See how this yeast is mixed with flour many times its own volume. Then look up and see how much has been leavened by so little yeast. See the loaves taken from the oven. In Jesus' mind the most profound theological insights are triggered by the kitchen. Open your eyes and see in the yeast insights into the kingdom of heaven.

Step into the courtyard and listen to the labourer talk about his remarkable find. There digging in the field he stumbled across the most glorious find of hidden treasure. Selling everything he possessed that man raised just enough cash to purchase the field and to claim the treasure as his own. In Jesus' mind the most profound theological insights are triggered by listening to workmen going about their business. Open your ears and hear in the tale of hidden treasure insights into the kingdom of heaven.

Step into the dining room and listen to the jeweller talk about his trade. There in the market he spotted one pearl of enormous value. Selling the whole of his stock he invested in that one precious pearl. In Jesus' mind the most profound theological insights are triggered by listening to jewellers discussing their affairs. Open your ears and hear in the tale of the pearl of great price insights into the kingdom of heaven.

Intuition

Here is a sample of Jesus' parables about the kingdom of heaven. All of them make the same fundamental point that the kingdom of heaven follows the same natural laws as our world of daily work and experience. Go now to your world and write parables for today out of your experience of life.

To understand the kingdom of heaven, says Jesus, you need to know about its unlimited power to grow. Think of the exponential growth of the mustard seed. The smallest seed grows into the biggest shrub. Think of the remarkable activity of the yeast. The smallest piece of yeast leavens a huge amount of flour. Now go to your world and brainstorm the images of growth that fire your imagination. For therein lies the secret to the kingdom of heaven.

To understand the kingdom of heaven, says Jesus, you need to know about its priceless value and about its power to capture and to take over the imagination of all who see its true worth. Think of the full potential in a field laden with buried treasure; think of what a workman would do to purchase just such a field. Now go to your world and brainstorm the images of priceless value that fire your imagination. For therein lies the secret to the kingdom of heaven.

To understand the kingdom of heaven, says Jesus, you need to know about the coming judgement and how God will sort out the good from the bad. Think of how the fisherman casts his net into the sea and lands every kind of fish, good and bad. The good fish he keeps and the bad fish he throws away. Now go to your world and brainstorm the images of judgement that fire your imagination. For therein lies the secret to the kingdom of heaven.

Here is a sample of Jesus' parables about the kingdom of heaven. All of them make the fundamental point that the kingdom of heaven follows the same natural laws as our world of daily work and experience.

Feeling

The parable of the yeast is a parable to appeal to people who prefer feeling. Here is a story about human transforming power. Today the people of God continue to be sent into the world to transform the face of society. See how that is happening all around you.

See how Jane, a young Christian mother, freely gives of her time to transform the lives of young children. See how she invests her energy in helping to run the Cubs and the Brownies. See how young lives respond to her openness and to her generosity. See how they recognize that her motivation stems from commitment to Christ. The parable of the yeast is a story about human transforming power.

See how Derek, a retired Christian businessman, freely gives of his time to transform the lives of the handicapped. See how he invests his energy in helping to drive the minibus for the disabled society. See how human lives respond to his openness and to his generosity. See how they recognize that his motivation stems from commitment to Christ. The parable of the yeast is a story about human transforming power.

See how Judith, a busy self-employed Christian mother who works from home, freely gives of her time to transform the lives of the elderly. See how she invests her energy in organizing the local luncheon club for senior citizens. See how elderly lives respond to her openness and to her generosity. See how they recognize that her motivation stems from commitment to Christ. The parable of the yeast is a story about human transforming power.

See how Philip, a young Christian graduate, freely gives of his time to transform the lives of families struggling to survive in the developing world. See how he invests his energy on a world development project in one of the poorest places on the globe.

See how human lives respond to his openness and to his generosity. See how they recognize that his motivation stems from commitment to Christ. The parable of the yeast is a story about human transforming power.

Here is a parable to appeal to people who prefer feeling.

Thinking

The parable of the pearl of great price is a parable to appeal to people who prefer thinking. Here is a story about decisive action and clear commitment. Today the people of God continue to be challenged to single-minded commitment in the service of Christ.

For some the call to priesthood may typify the pearl of great price. Take the example of Matthew the civil servant who decided to give up his career, sacrifice his salary and go to theological college to train. Here was a decision that changed his life, and changed the lifestyle of his wife and children. The parable of the pearl of great price is a story about decisive action and clear commitment.

For some the call to the priesthood may typify the pearl of great price. Take the example of Pamela the general practitioner who decided to give up her career, sacrifice her salary and go to theological college to train. Here was a decision that changed her life, and changed the lifestyle of her husband and children. The parable of the pearl of great price is a story about decisive action and clear commitment.

For some the call to Christian commitment in the secular world may typify the pearl of great price. Take the example of Ronald the investment banker who becomes uneasy with the unethical policies of his corporation. His decision to accept a less highly paid post in an ethically managed charity changed his life, and changed the lifestyle of his wife and children. The parable of the pearl of great price is a story about decisive action and clear commitment.

For some the call to Christian commitment in the secular world may typify the pearl of great price. Take the example of Stephanie the businesswoman who becomes uneasy with the way in which her company exploits its employees in the developing world. Her decision to accept a less highly paid post in a world development agency changed her life, and changed the lifestyle of her husband and children. The parable of the pearl of great price is a story about decisive action and clear commitment.

Here is a parable to appeal to people who prefer thinking.

23
Matthew 14:13–21

¹³Now when Jesus heard this, he withdrew from there in a boat to a deserted place by himself. But when the crowds heard it, they followed him on foot from the towns. ¹⁴When he went ashore, he saw a great crowd; and he had compassion for them and cured their sick. ¹⁵When it was evening, the disciples came to him and said, 'This is a deserted place, and the hour is now late; send the crowds away so that they may go into the villages and buy food for themselves.' ¹⁶Jesus said to them, 'They need not go away; you give them something to eat.' ¹⁷They replied, 'We have nothing here but five loaves and two fish.' ¹⁸And he said, 'Bring them here to me.' ¹⁹Then he ordered the crowds to sit down on the grass. Taking the five loaves and the two fish, he looked up to heaven, and blessed and broke the loaves, and gave them to the disciples, and the disciples gave them to the crowds. ²⁰And all ate and were filled; and they took up what was left over of the broken pieces, twelve baskets full. ²¹And those who ate were about five thousand men, besides women and children.

Context

The feeding of the five thousand is not only included in all three synoptic gospels, but in John as well. As Matthew presents the narrative the interest of the story is clearly focused on Jesus.

Sensing

To be effective and well-developed human beings we need to be able to use all four of the key functions of the human psyche in an appropriate way, although we do not expect all four functions to be equally well developed. There are some stories in the gospels which show Jesus drawing on all four functions. The feeding of the five thousand is one such story. So focus now on Jesus the sensor.

People who prefer sensing are realistic people. They have a good appreciation of the here and now. They act in the present moment. Now the feeding of the five thousand shows Jesus as someone very aware of the present moment. The story begins with Jesus recognizing that he and his companions are tired and exhausted by their ministry of healing, teaching and suffering. Jesus the realistic person seeks out a deserted place for rest. The story proceeds with Jesus recognizing that the crowds have followed him, pressing all around. He accepts this new reality and works with it. Jesus the realistic person exchanges solitude for public ministry.

People who prefer sensing are practical people. They have a good appreciation of what needs doing and how to get it done. They act in response to the needs. Now the feeding of the five thousand shows Jesus as someone who is very practical. The story begins with Jesus wanting to get away and he has the need for transport. Jesus the practical person has very quickly arranged a boat. The story proceeds with Jesus meeting the crowds and identifying their needs. Jesus the practical person heals their sick. Jesus the practical person fills their hungry stomachs.

People who prefer sensing have a fine eye for detail. They are concerned about precise information and a clear description of the environment. Now the feeding of the five thousand shows Jesus as someone who is concerned with the facts and the figures. Surely it is no accident that the story records so precisely that there were *five* loaves, *two* fishes, *five thousand* men and *twelve* baskets of leftovers.

In the feeding of the five thousand we meet Jesus the person who is comfortable with the sensing function.

Intuition

To be effective and well-developed human beings we need to be able to use all four of the key functions of the human psyche in an appropriate way, although we do not expect all four functions to be equally well developed. There are some stories in the gospels which show Jesus drawing on all four functions. The feeding of the five thousand is one such story. So focus now on Jesus the intuitive.

People who prefer intuition are people who can see their way out of difficulties. They can dream into the future and generate imaginative solutions to present problems. Now the feeding of the five thousand shows Jesus as someone who can see his way out of difficulties. The story begins with Jesus solving the problem of his own and his disciples' exhaustion. Jesus the intuitive is planning an escape to the desert. The story proceeds with Jesus facing the problem of apparent lack of food in the desert. Jesus the intuitive is planning to feed the crowds.

People who prefer intuition are people who can see the range of possibilities in a situation. They can somehow leap over the practical obstacles in their path. Now the feeding of the five thousand shows Jesus as someone who can see the possibilities in the situation. The story begins with Jesus' plans for a quiet retreat being wrecked by an uninvited crowd. Instead of turning back in despair, Jesus the intuitive immediately sees the possibilities in the new situation. The story proceeds with the disciples lamenting the lack of resources. Instead of accepting the situation at face value, Jesus the intuitive sees the possibilities in the new situation.

People who prefer intuition are people who trust their own inspiration and who act on their intuition. They have the confidence to lead the way even when the path is none too clear. Now the feeding of the five thousand shows Jesus as someone who has total confidence in his vision of the outcome. Surely it must have taken a lot of confidence in the vision to get five thousand men to sit down to be fed when the cupboard only held five loaves and two fishes.

In the feeding of the five thousand we meet Jesus the person who is comfortable with the intuitive function.

Feeling

To be effective and well-developed human beings we need to be able to use all four of the key functions of the human psyche in an appropriate way, although we do not expect all four functions to be equally well developed. There are some stories in the gospels which show Jesus drawing on all four functions. The feeding of the five thousand is one such story. So focus now on Jesus the feeler.

People who prefer feeling are people of compassion. Their hearts go out to others and they put themselves out to make others feel better. Now the feeding of the five thousand shows Jesus as someone who is full of compassion. The story begins with Jesus taking his disciples away for a rest to recuperate after weeks of intensive ministry. Jesus the compassionate person cares for the disciples. The story proceeds with Jesus having compassion on the crowd and healing their sick. Jesus the compassionate person cares for those who are ill.

People who prefer feeling are people of empathy. They are able to put themselves in others' shoes and to know how others feel about things. Now the feeding of the five thousand shows Jesus as someone who is full of empathy. The story begins with Jesus feeling how hungry the people are growing. Jesus the empathic person feels for the hunger of the crowd. The story proceeds with Jesus feeling how disappointed and how vulnerable the people would be if they were sent away hungry. Jesus the empathic person feels for the plight of the crowd.

People who prefer feeling are people who really care about others. They put others' well-being at the top of their list of human values. Now the feeding of the five thousand shows Jesus as someone who really cares about others. Surely it is no accident that the story emphasizes how everyone was fed and how everyone was filled.

In the feeding of the five thousand we meet Jesus the person who is comfortable with the feeling function.

Thinking

To be effective and well-developed human beings we need to be able to use all four of the key functions of the human psyche in an appropriate way, although we do not expect all four functions to be equally well developed. There are some stories in the gospels which show Jesus drawing on all four functions. The feeding of the five thousand is one such story. So focus now on Jesus the thinker.

People who prefer thinking are people of order and precision. They like a well thought through structure and pattern to their way of doing things. Now the feeding of the five thousand shows Jesus as someone who communicates through structure and pattern. Here in the desert place Jesus established a pattern which is seen throughout his ministry. Here, once the bread had been brought to him, Jesus did four things: he took the loaves; he looked up to heaven to say the blessing; he broke the loaves; he gave the loaves to the disciples. These same actions were repeated at the Last Supper. These same actions were repeated on the Emmaus road. Jesus the thinker communicates through structure and pattern.

People who prefer thinking are people of logic and analysis. They like to think through how things will work and ensure their efficiency. Now the feeding of the five thousand shows Jesus as someone who takes a logical and thought through approach to the task in hand. Here in the desert place Jesus runs no risk of rioting once the food arrives. Here Jesus asks everyone to sit down in ordered rows and puts his most trusted disciples in charge of distribution. Jesus the thinker takes a logical approach to feeding the crowd.

People who prefer thinking are people who really care about fairness. They do not like to feel that other people suffer from lack of fairness, injustice or inequality. Now the feeding of the five thousand shows Jesus as someone who really cares about fairness. Surely it is no accident that the story emphasizes how the feeding included women and children as well as men.

In the feeding of the five thousand we meet Jesus the person who is comfortable with the thinking function.

<hr />

24

Matthew 14:22-33

²²Immediately he made the disciples get into the boat and go on ahead to the other side, while he dismissed the crowds. ²³And after he had dismissed the crowds, he went up the mountain by himself to pray. When evening came, he was there alone, ²⁴but by this time the boat, battered by the waves, was far from the land, for the wind was against them. ²⁵And early in the morning he came walking toward them on the sea. ²⁶But when the disciples saw him walking on the sea, they were terrified, saying, 'It is a ghost!' And they cried out

in fear. [27]But immediately Jesus spoke to them and said, 'Take heart, it is I; do not be afraid.'

[28]Peter answered him, 'Lord, if it is you, command me to come to you on the water.' [29]He said, 'Come.' So Peter got out of the boat, started walking on the water, and came toward Jesus. [30]But when he noticed the strong wind, he became frightened, and beginning to sink, he cried out, 'Lord, save me!' [31]Jesus immediately reached out his hand and caught him, saying to him, 'You of little faith, why did you doubt?' [32]When they got into the boat, the wind ceased. [33]And those in the boat worshipped him, saying, 'Truly you are the Son of God.'

Context

Immediately after feeding the five thousand, Jesus sends the disciples away and withdraws to pray. Their journey is interrupted by the storm until Jesus comes to their rescue.

Sensing

You have just lived through the most eventful of days, and now you are about to experience the most disturbed of nights.

Just remember all that has been packed into the last twelve hours. Remember how you thought that you were heading for peace and quiet, but instead were confronted by a crowd of five thousand men, plus women and children. Remember how you thought that you were due for a rest from ministry, but instead were plunged headlong into a fresh round of teaching and healing. Remember how at the end of the day you thought you could send the crowd away, but instead were caught up in the unprecedented and tiring distribution of food. Remember how you thought that at last around the evening fire you could enjoy Jesus' company, but instead were packed off in the boat to leave him alone. You have just lived through the most eventful of days.

Now you are adrift on the lake in the fourth watch of the night. Feel the boat buffeted by the rising storm. Hear the timbers creek and groan against the tumultuous waves. Peer through the oppressive darkness to see the white eyes of your fellow travellers. Sense the fear rising in your stomach. You have just lived through the most eventful of days, and now you are experiencing the most disturbed of nights.

Now the storm has reached its height. Now your fear has plumbed its depths. How you wish you had stayed at home. How you wish you had brought your life-jacket. How you wish you had more faith. You have just lived through the most eventful of days, and now you are experiencing the most disturbed of nights.

Now you see a distant figure looming through the storm, walking on the surface of the lake. Now you sense a presence drawing ever closer through the darkness. Now you feel the wind suddenly drop, and the waves suddenly still. Now you open your eyes and see Jesus sitting safely in the boat and Peter dripping wet. You have just lived through the most eventful of days, and now you have lived through the most disturbed of nights.

Intuition

Here is the classic story of Christian discipleship. Listen with care as faith is nurtured.

The disciples' faith had been nurtured by listening as Jesus taught the crowd. Their hearts were fired by the good news of the kingdom of God. Do you recognize anything of your own spiritual pilgrimage here?

The disciples' belief had been strengthened by watching as Jesus healed the sick. Their imagination was stirred by the miracles of the kingdom of God. Do you recognize anything of your own spiritual pilgrimage here?

The disciples' souls had been nourished by sharing in the loaves which Jesus broke for the crowds. Their commitment was deepened by the food of the kingdom of God. Do you recognize anything of your own spiritual pilgrimage here?

Here is the classic story of Christian discipleship. Listen with care as faith is tested.

The disciples' faith had been tested when Jesus sent them away alone to cross the lake by night. Their hearts were filled with fear from the darkness. Do you recognize anything of your own spiritual pilgrimage here?

The disciples' belief was threatened when their boat was battered by the waves so far from land. Their imagination ran wild as the wind whipped up the storm. Do you recognize anything of your own spiritual pilgrimage here?

The disciples' souls were unsettled when the ghostly spectre walked towards them through the storm. Their commitment was undermined as panic seized their minds. Do you recognize anything of your own spiritual pilgrimage here?

Here is the classic story of Christian discipleship. Listen with care as faith is restored.

The disciples' faith is restored the moment they recognize that Jesus is travelling in the boat with them. Do you recognize anything of your own spiritual pilgrimage here?

Here is the classic story of Christian discipleship.

Feeling

There is a very clear pattern to Peter's behaviour. Get inside Peter's character and figure out that pattern.

The pattern emerges when Peter is caught out in the storm on the lake. See Peter step so fearlessly out of the boat to walk with Jesus on the waves. Feel the confidence that he has in his own strength and ability. See Peter sink lower in the water and wave his hands with all the desperation of a drowning man. Feel the confidence that he has in his strength and ability slip from his fingertips. See Jesus stretch out his hand and lead Peter safely back into the boat. Feel the new confidence that Peter has, not now in himself but in Jesus who restores him.

The pattern persists when Peter arrives at Caesarea Philippi. Hear Peter so fearlessly cry out the profession of faith, 'You are the Christ.' Feel the confidence that he has in his own insight and perception. Hear Peter challenge Jesus' path to suffering and Jesus' clear rebuke, 'Get behind me, Satan!' Feel the confidence that he has in his own insight and perception slip from his fingertips. Some days later hear Jesus call Peter to climb the mount of transfiguration with James and John as the veil between heaven and earth is lifted. Feel the new confidence that Peter has, not now in himself but in Jesus who restores him.

The pattern persists when Peter follows Jesus from the Garden of Gethsemane. See Peter walk so boldly from the garden and follow Jesus at a safe distance to the courtyard of the high priest. Feel the confidence that he has in his own commitment to the Lord. See the women come up to Peter and challenge him as a disciple. Hear Peter's oath of denial. Feel the confidence that he has in his own commitment to the Lord slip from his fingertips. Some days later hear the risen Christ commission Peter to lead the mission of his church. Feel the new confidence that Peter has, not now in himself but in Jesus who restores him.

There is a very clear pattern to Peter's behaviour. Get inside Peter's character and figure out that pattern.

Thinking

Have you thought through the theological significance of the sequence in which the events are happening?

The story begins when Jesus took those five loaves, when Jesus looked up to heaven and blessed the loaves, when Jesus broke the loaves, and when Jesus fed five thousand men. The story begins with the breaking of bread and with the feeding of people. Do you spot any connections with how Jesus made himself known to the early church through the breaking of bread?

The story tells how Jesus sent the disciples to fend for themselves, and how Jesus withdrew up the mountain away from the disciples to pray. The story tells how a great gulf felt fixed between the disciples and their master. Do you spot any connections with how the early church felt after the resurrection and when Jesus no longer walked with them on the Emmaus road?

The story tells how the disciples felt battered by the waves and how the disciples felt threatened by the wind and by the storm. The story tells how when left by themselves the disciples felt isolated and insecure. Do you spot any connections with how the early church felt in days of persecution, torment and torture?

The story tells how, when the storms were at their greatest, Jesus walked across the waves to comfort his disciples. The story tells how, when the winds were raging at their mightiest, Jesus calmed the storm. The story tells how, when Peter was at the point of drowning, Jesus stretched out his healing hand. Do you spot any connection with how the early church experienced the presence of their risen Lord at the very point when the crisis was at its worst?

Have you thought through the theological significance of the sequence in which the events are happening?

25
Matthew 15:10–28

[10]Then he called the crowd to him and said to them, 'Listen and understand: [11]it is not what goes into the mouth that defiles a person, but it is what comes out of the mouth that defiles.' [12]Then the disciples approached and said to him, 'Do you know that the Pharisees took offence when they heard what you said?' [13]He answered, 'Every plant that my heavenly Father has not planted will be uprooted. [14]Let them alone; they are blind guides of the blind. And if one blind person guides another, both will fall into a pit.' [15]But Peter said to him, 'Explain this parable to us.' [16]Then he said, 'Are you also still without understanding? [17]Do you not see that whatever goes into the mouth enters the stomach, and goes out into the sewer? [18]But what comes out of the mouth proceeds from the heart, and this is what defiles. [19]For out of the heart come evil intentions, murder, adultery, fornication, theft, false witness, slander. [20]These are what defile a person, but to eat with unwashed hands does not defile.'

[21]Jesus left that place and went away to the district of Tyre and Sidon. [22]Just then a Canaanite woman from that region came out and started shouting, 'Have mercy on me, Lord, Son of David; my daughter is tormented by a demon.' [23]But he did not answer her at all. And his disciples came and urged him, saying, 'Send her away, for she keeps shouting after us.' [24]He answered, 'I was sent only to the lost sheep of the house of Israel.' [25]But she came and knelt before him, saying, 'Lord, help me.' [26]He answered, 'It is not fair to take the children's food and throw it to the dogs.' [27]She said, 'Yes, Lord, yet even the dogs eat the crumbs that fall from their masters' table.' [28]Then Jesus answered her, 'Woman, great is your faith! Let it be done for you as you wish.' And her daughter was healed instantly.

Context

Jesus has fed five thousand people and is now reunited with the disciples after the storm. The Pharisees and scribes reappear accusing the disciples of ignoring the traditions by eating with unclean hands. This leads Jesus to teaching about defilement and to giving the children's bread to the Gentiles.

Sensing

Today you are witnessing the most extraordinary scene. Come outside and see.

Prick up your ears and listen to the voices all around. Prick up your ears and savour the strange accents. Today you have left Jewish soil. Today you stand on Gentile territory. Prick up your ears and listen to the voices.

Prick up your ears and hear the woman's voice crying in the distance, 'Have mercy on me, Lord, Son of David!' Prick up your ears and hear the woman's lament, 'My daughter is tormented, tormented by a demon. Have mercy on me, Lord, Son of David!' Prick up your ears and listen to the accent. Here is a Canaanite speaking.

Prick up your ears and hear the disciples' voices complaining, 'Send her away!' Prick up your ears and hear the disciples complaining, 'She keeps shouting after us. Send her away!' Prick up your ears and listen to the accents. Here are Galileans speaking.

Prick up your ears and hear the woman and Jesus conversing. Prick up your ears and hear Jesus proclaim, 'It is not fair to take the children's food and throw it to the dogs.' Hear the woman respond, 'Yet even the dogs eat the crumbs that fall from their master's table.' Prick up your ears and listen to the accents. Here are a Canaanite and a Galilean conversing.

Prick up your ears and hear Jesus' voice affirming, 'Woman, great is your faith!' Prick up your ears and hear Jesus affirming, 'Let it be done for you as you wish. Woman, great is your faith!' Prick up your ears and listen to the accent. Here is the Son of God speaking.

Today you are witnessing the most extraordinary scene.

Intuition

The Canaanite woman needed to be very persistent in order to claim her portion of the children's bread. I wonder if you are just as willing to be so persistent?

The Canaanite woman could have been most discouraged by all that life had thrown at her. She could have chosen to rage at Jesus for the unfair pain and torment inflicted on her family. I wonder how much you may be inclined to let life's suffering stand in the way of your faith?

The Canaanite woman could have been most discouraged by her encounter with the awesome powers of evil. She could have chosen to form an alliance with the demonic powers instead of fighting so relentlessly to gain victory over them. I wonder how much you may be tempted to concede victory to the powers of evil?

The Canaanite woman could have been most discouraged by the treatment she received at the hands of Jesus' disciples. She could have chosen to walk away offended by their dismissive attitude. I wonder how much you may be tempted to turn your back on a church weakened by imperfect disciples?

The Canaanite woman could have been most discouraged by Jesus' hesitancy and testing. She could have chosen to misread his words as racist, as sexist, or as plain discourtesy. I wonder how much you may be inclined to give up on Jesus, if Jesus first interrogates and tests the seriousness of your faith?

The Canaanite woman could have been most discouraged by the need to reflect theologically on her relationship with Jesus and on the implications of her petition. She could have chosen to insist on simple answers and to have sought faith based on experience prior to mature reflection. I wonder how much you may be inclined to grow frustrated with the rigours and demands of Christian theology and crave for instant religious experience?

The Canaanite woman needed to be very persistent in order to claim her portion of the children's bread. Pray that you may share her persistence.

Feeling

Here is the story of a remarkable woman. Put yourself in her situation and experience the depth of her despair. Here is a woman whose life had been torn apart by the torment inflicted on her daughter. Year in and year out her daughter behaved as someone possessed by the most malevolent of demons. Experience the depth of her despair.

Here is the story of a remarkable woman. Put yourself in her situation and experience the anguish of her frustration. Here is a woman driven to her wit's end by the failure of every remedy to help. Hear her desperate shout and plea for help, 'Have mercy on me, Lord, Son of David; my daughter is tormented by a demon.' Experience the anguish of her frustration.

Here is the story of a remarkable woman. Put yourself in her situation and experience the pain of her humiliation. Here is a woman driven to the margins by the disciples who appear to resent her. The words are ringing in her head, 'Send her away, for she keeps shouting after us.' Here is a woman driven to the margins by Jesus himself who appears to reject her. The words are ringing in her head, 'It is not fair to take the children's food and throw it to the dogs.' Experience the pain of her humiliation.

Here is the story of a remarkable woman. Put yourself in her situation and experience the courage of her conviction. Here is a woman who states her claim: 'Have mercy on me Lord', she cries. Here is a woman who stands her ground: 'Lord help me,' she pleads. Here is a woman who sticks to her faith: 'Even the dogs eat the crumbs that fall from their masters' table.' Experience the courage of her conviction.

Here is the story of a remarkable woman. Put yourself in her situation and experience the joy of her acceptance. Here is a woman whose persistence is affirmed. Here is a woman whose faith is rewarded. Here is a woman whose daughter is healed. Experience the joy of her acceptance.

Here is the story of a remarkable woman.

Thinking

When the five thousand people were fed from the five loaves, Jesus was making a very important statement to the Jewish people. Have you spotted its significance? When Jesus fed the five thousand, he chose a deserted place as Moses had done of old. When Jesus fed the five thousand, he reasserted God's willingness and God's ability to feed the people of God with bread that would nourish their bodies and with manna that would feed their souls.

When twelve baskets full of leftovers were collected after the feeding, Jesus was making a very important statement to the Jewish people. Have you spotted its significance? When Jesus collected the leftovers he made it clear that the food lasted into the future. When Jesus displayed the leftovers in twelve baskets he made it clear these were for the twelve tribes of Israel.

When the Pharisees criticized Jesus' disciples for eating their bread with unwashed hands, they were making a very important statement on behalf of the people of God. Have you spotted its significance? When the Pharisees criticized Jesus' disciples they were placing their ritual law above God's generous act. When the Pharisees criticized Jesus' disciples they were rejecting the bread held out to them with those unwashed hands.

When the Canaanite woman came to Jesus, shouting, 'Have mercy on me, Lord, Son of David', she was making a very important statement on behalf of the Gentile nations. Have you spotted its significance? When the Canaanite woman implored Jesus to heal her daughter, she showed real faith in Jesus' power. When the Canaanite woman stood her ground, she claimed her share in the inheritance of the children of God.

When the children's bread was taken and fed to the dogs crouching under the table, Jesus was making a very important statement to the Jewish people. Have you spotted its significance? When the twelve baskets full of bread were redistributed among the Gentile nations, the bread of the people of God was given to those who were worthy to receive it. When the table was opened up to the Gentiles the boundaries of God's grace were re-drawn.

So have you spotted the significance of all these things?

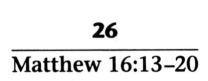

26

Matthew 16:13–20

¹³Now when Jesus came into the district of Caesarea Philippi, he asked his disciples, 'Who do people say that the Son of Man is?' ¹⁴And they said, 'Some say John the Baptist, but others Elijah, and still others Jeremiah or one of the prophets.'

¹⁵He said to them, 'But who do you say that I am?' ¹⁶Simon Peter answered, 'You are the Messiah, the Son of the living God.' ¹⁷And Jesus answered him, 'Blessed are you, Simon son of Jonah! For flesh and blood has not revealed this to you, but my Father in heaven. ¹⁸And I tell you, you are Peter, and on this rock I will build my church, and the gates of Hades will not prevail against it. ¹⁹I will give you the keys of the kingdom of heaven, and whatever you bind on earth will be bound in heaven, and whatever you loose on earth will be loosed in heaven.' ²⁰Then he sternly ordered the disciples not to tell anyone that he was the Messiah.

Context

The words and actions of Jesus had been delivered with such authority that the question of his true nature had to be clarified. The crowds and Matthew's readers would be full of speculation. The rebuilt city of Caesarea Philippi was an appropriate context for a clear answer.

Sensing

Enter the town of Caesarea Philippi, twenty miles north from the Galilean lakeside. It had been recently rebuilt by Herod's son Philip who named it Caesarea to honour the Emperor. Here is a town fit for a king. Now wait for Jesus and Peter to join you.

When Jesus enters Caesarea Philippi he is well aware that questions of authority and titles are sure to arise. Hear the rumours circulating through the crowd. Listen to the disciples speculating about Jesus' proper title and his authority. Such speculation is dangerous. The opposition is increasing. The civil and religious leaders are becoming suspicious of the claims of the crowd. Sense the anxiety in Jesus. His disciples need to know the truth, to grasp his relationship with God and his authority to act. Listen as Jesus puts the key question: 'Who do people say I am?'

When Peter enters Caesarea Philippi, he is well aware that questions about Jesus' authority and titles are sure to arise. Hear the buzz in the crowd about Jesus: 'This is John the Baptist brought back to life', 'This is Elijah, the forerunner of the Messiah', 'This is the prophet Jeremiah, preparing for the new exile.' None of these titles seems to be big enough to fit Jesus. He stands head and shoulders above John. He is not a person preparing for

a greater one to come. He does not talk about a new beginning;
he is a new beginning.

Watch Peter's face as he hears Jesus' question. The lines on it
tell of his worry, and the smile, of his conviction. There is no
other conclusion. Jesus *must* be the Messiah, God's anointed
authority. There is no other conclusion. Jesus relates so intim-
ately to God that he must be God's own Son. Listen as Peter
makes his affirmation: 'You are the Messiah, the Son of the Living
God.'

Sense the excitement and the fear in the hearts of the disciples
as they listen to Peter's answer. This is dangerous news. Share
their relief as Jesus orders silence. 'Do not tell anyone that I am
the Messiah.'

Enter the town of Caesarea Philippi. This is the proper setting
for questions of authority and titles to be answered.

Intuition

Titles, what do you make of titles? They are acknowledgements
that make someone stand out from the crowd.

Consider the title 'Teacher'. We give this title of respect to
those gifted with ability to communicate the truth, stirring the
imagination and prompting us to enlarge our vision. Teacher is a
title of respect.

Consider the title 'Prophet'. We give this title of honour to
those gifted by God to reveal the truth about the nature of God,
human nature, and the future in God's world, pointing out the
facts of the present and the consequences for the future. Prophet
is a title of honour.

Consider the title 'Son of Man'. We give this title of mystery
to one who shares the nature of being human to perfection and
carries the authority of the creator God. Son of Man is a title of
mystery and power.

Consider the title 'Messiah'. We give this title of awe to one
who exercises directly the authority of God. We bow in reverence
before the anointed of God, the one chosen and empowered to
reveal God's will to us, demonstrating God's authority over evil
and death. Messiah is a title of awe.

Consider the title 'Son of the living God'. We give this title of
worship to one who shows us an intimate relationship with God.
The Son knows the Father's will and takes the Father's place in

responsibility for the care and nurture of the world. Son of the Living God is a title of worship.

Titles, what titles do you use for Jesus? If you call Jesus 'Teacher' are you ready to obey his teaching? If you call Jesus 'Prophet' are you ready to share his vision? If you call Jesus 'Son of Man' are you ready to acknowledge him to be fully human exercising God's power? If you call Jesus 'Messiah' are you ready to honour his revelation of God? If you call Jesus 'Son of the living God' are you ready to worship Jesus as your Lord and your God? The title you use will evoke your response of faith.

Feeling

There is much to learn from the relationship between Jesus and Peter as portrayed in this passage.

Here is a relationship of trust. You can feel the interaction between the two of them. Jesus must have been anxious about raising such a difficult question, but he trusted Peter to be honest in his response. Peter must have been anxious about giving an answer which contained so many implications for Jesus and all the disciples. He must not push Jesus into the danger zone of conflict between his authority and that of the controlling human powers. Yet he trusted Jesus to receive his answer graciously, doing his best to find the right titles for such a complex character. Everything pointed to this conclusion, but he needed a steady lip and a strong heart to make such an assertion. Feel Peter's sense of honour in having a relationship as friend of such a person.

Feel the interaction between Jesus and Peter as each replies to the other's words. Peter says to Jesus, 'You are anointed by God.' Jesus says to Peter, 'You are blessed by God.' Peter says to Jesus, 'You are the Son of the Living God.' Jesus says to Peter, 'Son of Jonah, my Father has revealed this truth to you.' Feel the mutual interaction of trust and acknowledgement.

Feel the interaction as Jesus makes clear Peter's future role. Jesus, knowing full well Peter's failure through impetuosity, calls him 'Rocky'. Feel the warmth as well as the daring in these words. Peter has told Jesus that he recognizes the task God has given him to be the Messiah. Jesus has told Peter of the potential he sees in him to do the task of being the foundation stone of his new community and holder of the keys to its entry and exit. He gives Peter the responsibility of keeping its boundaries and maintaining its unity through forgiveness.

The qualities of relationship between these two friends will be the hallmarks of the relationships in the new community of the church: trust, honesty, mutual affirmation, acknowledgement, and restoration through forgiveness. Let those be the qualities found in your experience of Christ and your Christian community.

Thinking

Jesus said, 'You are Peter, and on this rock I will build my church.' Now it is hard to work out exactly what Jesus' commission to Peter really meant. Was the rock on which Jesus promised he would build his church Peter's personal authority? Was the rock the example of faith in Jesus as Messiah that Peter showed in his reply? Was the rock a type of authority which could be transferred later to Peter's replacement as leader of the disciples? What do you think 'on this rock I will build my church' means?

Jesus said, 'You are Peter, and I will give you the keys of the kingdom of heaven.' It is hard to work out exactly what Jesus' gift of 'the keys of the kingdom' really meant. Do the keys indicate that Peter should decide who should be a member of the church and who should not? Do the keys indicate that Peter should decide who should be forgiven and who should not? Do the keys indicate that Peter had authority to make all the regulations for the church? What do you think 'the keys of the kingdom' means?

For the answers to both questions it is wise to look at the record of the New Testament. There Peter is regarded as a prime leader in the early church. His name appears first in all the lists of apostles. Peter figures prominently in the record of the Acts of the Apostles, and takes the lead in preaching the gospel at Pentecost. Paul refers to Peter as the apostle to the circumcised (Galatians 2:8).

This evidence shows that Peter was a prime leader in some parts of the church. Possibly Matthew's gospel was sent to those regions. The evidence also shows Paul as a prime leader in other parts with his own authority. In other areas there are signs that John was a key apostle. Even James, the Lord's brother, was regarded as a leader. Obviously leadership was both spread and shared. Different parts of the church recognized *their* apostle as leader, and when it came to relationships between church communities the leadership was shared. How do you think this helps us to understand more fully Christ's words in Matthew's gospel?

27
Matthew 16:21–28

²¹From that time on, Jesus began to show his disciples that he must go to Jerusalem and undergo great suffering at the hands of the elders and chief priests and scribes, and be killed, and on the third day be raised. ²²And Peter took him aside and began to rebuke him, saying, 'God forbid it, Lord! This must never happen to you.' ²³But he turned and said to Peter, 'Get behind me, Satan! You are a stumbling-block to me; for you are setting your mind not on divine things but on human things.'

²⁴Then Jesus told his disciples, 'If any want to become my followers, let them deny themselves and take up their cross and follow me. ²⁵For those who want to save their life will lose it, and those who lose their life for my sake will find it. ²⁶For what will it profit them if they gain the whole world but forfeit their life? Or what will they give in return for their life?

²⁷'For the Son of Man is to come with his angels in the glory of his Father, and then he will repay everyone for what has been done. ²⁸Truly I tell you, there are some standing here who will not taste death before they see the Son of Man coming in his kingdom.'

Context

Immediately after recognition as Messiah, Jesus defines the term as the suffering leader of God's people. Obedience to God's way of love leads to the way of the cross, both for Jesus and for his disciples. Laying down life for God brings the reward of seeing the kingdom in action.

Sensing

Stand and listen as Jesus foretells his suffering. Hear Jesus say that he will be killed. Taste the sense of fear in your dry mouth. Feel cold shivers run down your spine. Moments before you had felt the joy of hearing Jesus proclaimed as Messiah. Now you hear him talk of death. Surely God will not allow it! Stand and listen as Jesus proclaims his death as God's will.

Stand and listen as Peter rebukes Jesus. Hear Peter say that this can never happen. Nod your head in agreement with Peter. Surely God would not allow the anointed one to be defeated by evil. Good must always win. God must always defend the righteous. Each hair of your head is numbered. Stand and listen as Peter echoes your thoughts: 'This must never happen to you.'

Stand and listen in amazement as Jesus flares up in anger. What has provoked such anger? Jesus looks Peter straight in the eye, but addresses his words rather than his person: 'Get behind me, Satan.' Stand in shocked silence. Peter is Satan – what a thing to say to a best friend!

Stand and listen in amazement as Jesus turns the nickname for Peter on its head. A Rock of recognition becomes a stumbling stone of rejection; insight becomes blindness; friend becomes foe; divine inspiration becomes human folly. Rock takes on a new meaning. Stones seem to be flying.

Stand and see Peter look shocked and ashamed. Watch his lips form the words, 'Sorry, sorry, I don't understand. From blessed to cursed in a few minutes, I don't understand!'

Stand there and feel the confusion. Stand there and share the shame. Take time for reflection. See why it must be this way and exercise your faith and trust in God to know the way. In hindsight you can see it from God's view, not our human point of view. Evil must be confronted even at the cost of love.

Stand there and look to the future. Observe how the pathway to Jerusalem must be strewn with crosses.

Intuition

Crosses, you see them everywhere. What does the symbol of the cross suggest to you?

The cross is the symbol of God's enduring love for humanity. Nothing will divert Jesus from the journey to Jerusalem to sacrifice life to bring life to every person. The cross is the symbol of human hatred trying to rid itself of Christ's challenge to pursue only the law of love. The cross is the symbol of the violence of envy which aims to destroy the good but cannot destroy God.

The cross is the symbol of One who embraces death so that it leads to life. Through the cross Christ shows that resurrection in God's purpose can only be found through death, not despite death. Seen from another angle the cross is the symbol of a death that humanity from its own perspective can never understand. From a human point of view death is a dead end and never a gateway to a new life.

The cross is the symbol of personal loyalty to Christ, the symbol of true discipleship. It shows that we must embrace sacrifice to be a follower of our Lord. So we wear a cross around the neck; hang it high on a wall; and hold it up as the ultimate challenge and the ultimate glory. Through these actions we obey the call, 'Take up your cross and follow me.'

In the burial ground the cross is the symbol of true dying. It is raised above the grave of the faithful disciple. It stands for the hope of resurrection and the gift of new life. It is the sign that those who have learnt to lose their life have found it in God's kingdom.

In liturgy the cross is the symbol of the coming kingdom. With the sign of the cross we bless the sick for wholeness, the missionary for service, the penitent for forgiveness, and the baptized for dedication to their Saviour. The cross symbolizes Christ's love that never lets me go and to which I will always cling.

Crosses, you see them everywhere. What does the symbol of the cross suggest to you?

Feeling

It must have been hard for Peter to be the spokesperson for the disciples. Take pity on his plight.

When Peter was asked by Jesus, 'Who do you say that I am?', he had to take the risk of faith to reply, 'You are the Messiah.' If he had got it wrong he would have been told off by Jesus and laughed at by the other disciples. When Peter protested at Jesus' statement about suffering he had to take the risk of trying to discern God's will. 'God forbid it,' he blurted out. If he had been right he would have been praised by Jesus and cheered by the other disciples. It must have been hard for Peter to be the spokesperson for the disciples. Take pity on his plight.

It must have been hard for Jesus to praise Peter for affirming him as Messiah. Peter could easily be seen as kingmaker. He could then be tempted to believe that he understood all the implications of the title Messiah. It must have been hard for Jesus to praise Peter. Take pity on his plight.

It must have been hard for Jesus to condemn Peter for trying to deny the consequences of claiming the title Christ. In condemning Peter Jesus was really condemning the temptation to forsake the pathway of the cross by avoiding clashes with the secular and religious authorities. Satan the tempter was back in the voice of Peter the disciple. It must have been hard for Jesus to condemn Peter. Take pity on his plight.

It must have been hard for the disciples to watch the interplay between Jesus and Peter. They were both caught in the trap of political circumstances. Jesus could not take up the role of Messiah without yielding to the popular expectation of a victorious king. Peter could not take up the role of true follower without being the foil for the true/false expectations of ordinary people. The disciples would have watched the drama with unease and embarrassment. Take pity on their plight.

Take pity on yourself caught in the same dilemma. You want to follow Jesus as Lord, but are frightened to lose your life to find it. Take pity on your plight.

Thinking

This passage makes you ask the question 'Why?' many times.

Why was Jesus so certain that the Messiah *must* suffer and rise again? Why did Peter say, 'It must never happen to you'? Why did Jesus accuse Peter of working things out from a human point of view? Why was Jesus so convinced that the day of divine judgement would be within the lifetime of some disciples?

For thinking types the mind seeks answers to every 'Why?' For thinking types it is not enough to exercise blind faith, and say God only knows. God is not mindless. God's purpose was revealed in Christ to make it plain for all to see.

One answer might be that Jesus was certain that the Messiah must suffer because Scripture pointed out that the true servant of God had always suffered. What was true for Amos, for Jeremiah, for the later Isaiah, was true for the whole people of God in exile. In Scripture obedience to the way of love always entailed sacrifice.

Another answer might be that Jesus was certain that the Messiah must rise again because God's gift to the faithful servant is always life. Sacrifice will bring life both to the redeemed and to the redeemer.

Peter could not see such truth. He could only see the cross as the end of life. To his mind it could never be included in the plan of the God of life. Peter still had to learn how the cross led to forgiveness and reconciliation, resurrection and eternal life. Peter could only see the cross from a human angle. Jesus had to teach him its divine dimension by costly action.

The gospels show Jesus convinced that the day of divine judgement would happen soon, in the lifetime of some of the disciples. From the cross onwards judgement was constantly being revealed by the choice of the disciples to lose life or find it by being faithful to the Messiah, whatever the cost. In this way the kingdom of God had already begun. Yet the church was always uncertain about the final consummation of this kingdom. It still is. It affirms the words of Jesus that only God knows the right time.

The question 'Why?' teases our minds and drives us to a fuller faith.

28
Matthew 17:1–9

¹Six days later, Jesus took with him Peter and James and his brother John and led them up a high mountain, by themselves. ²And he was transfigured before them, and his face shone like the sun, and his clothes became dazzling white. ³Suddenly there appeared to them Moses and Elijah, talking with him. ⁴Then Peter said to Jesus, 'Lord, it is good for us to be here; if you wish, I will make three dwellings here, one for you, one for Moses, and one for Elijah.' ⁵While he was still speaking, suddenly a bright cloud overshadowed them, and

from the cloud a voice said, 'This is my Son, the Beloved; with him I am well pleased; listen to him!' ⁶When the disciples heard this, they fell to the ground and were overcome by fear. ⁷But Jesus came and touched them, saying, 'Get up and do not be afraid.' ⁸And when they looked up, they saw no one except Jesus himself alone.

⁹As they were coming down the mountain, Jesus ordered them, 'Tell no one about the vision until after the Son of Man has been raised from the dead.'

Context

The sequence in Matthew's gospel brings together three events: Peter's affirmation of Jesus as Messiah; Jesus' warning that the Messiah must suffer; and then the revelation, to Peter, James and John, of Jesus in glory as God's beloved Son. Each provides a new insight into the truth about Jesus.

Sensing

This is a passage in which we can use our senses to become involved. Climb the mountain with Jesus and his three closest friends, Peter, James and John.

Stand on the mountain top and watch as the sun rises and shines on Jesus' face and clothes. Shield your eyes from the brightness. Hear again the words Jesus spoke six days ago: 'They will see the Son of Man coming in his kingdom.' It is true. All that Jesus said is blinding us with its reality. He really is God's Son.

Stand on the mountain top and watch as Jesus and Peter converse. Six days ago you heard Peter acknowledge Jesus as Messiah. Then you heard Jesus accuse Peter of being a stumbling block. Listen now to their dialogue of reconciliation. Note that Peter wants to hold on to this heavenly vision of truth and harmony. He wants to stay here with God's chosen, past and present.

Stand on the mountain top and watch as the misty cloud rolls in. Caught by the sun the cloud adds both to the brightness and the mystery. Both reflect God's presence. Hear the voice from the cloud reaffirm the baptismal affirmation, 'This is my Son, the Beloved.' You too are convinced about Jesus.

Drop to your knees on the mountain top. The implications of

what you have experienced are terrifying. The divine has touched the human. The Messiah is the Suffering Servant. God's glory is revealed. It is all too much to grasp in a flash.

Hear Jesus' comforting voice, 'Get up. Do not be afraid.' Feel the strength return to your body as you determine to follow this Christ, down from this mountain and into the struggle with violence, evil and destruction. Sense your heart racing. This truth is now obvious. Peter was right; this is the Messiah. Jesus was right; the Messiah must suffer. Jesus was right; God's kingdom will come. Here on the mountain top sense the mystery, and see a vision to remember and share. Brightness and mystery are the language of dreams, but these dreams give us pictures to reaffirm reality.

Intuition

Mystical experiences, what do they suggest to you?

Mystical experiences are always deeply moving. We become caught up in something greater than ourselves. They lift us to a new dimension of sight. Though we cannot 'explain' them, yet we know they are real. Recall a deep mystical experience of God. What new insights did you discover from it?

Mystical experiences are full of symbols. One object suggests another. The mountain top touches the heavens. The sun's bright light becomes the radiance of glory. Clothes define the character rather than the apparel. Figures of the past affirm the present. Clouds become the communication of the divine voice. Recall a deep mystical experience of God. In it, what did the symbols suggest to you?

Mystical experiences can be like visions in the day and dreams of the night. There we can touch the untouchable. There we can see with new eyes. There we can listen with new ears. God speaks and our hearts race in excitement and fear. Recall a deep mystical experience of God in a vision or a dream. What new message did you receive in picture language too great for words?

Mystical experiences need time to unravel and events to confirm them. It is not always wise to reveal them to others until after you see how they apply to life. People will understand better when you can connect the mystical happening to some actions in your life. Do you connect with Jesus' instruction to the disciples to wait before sharing their experience? Recall a deep mystical experience of God. Did you wait to tell others until events helped to interpret the vision? Did that anchor the mystery in reality?

Mystical experiences are a time of major affirmation of faith in God. They reassure us of God's personal relationship with us and of God's purpose for our lives. They are a time to hear again God's voice, 'You are my beloved, with whom I am well pleased.' Recall a deep mystical experience of God. How did God affirm you as a baptized disciple?

Mystical experiences, what do they suggest to you?

Feeling

Share the feelings of Peter on being invited to go up the mountain on retreat with Jesus. Share his anxiety that this might be another hurtful occasion. Peter would still be smarting from the condemnation of Jesus. Share the feelings of Peter, anxious at the prospect that something bad might happen. Would you want to accept this invitation to be with Jesus?

Share the feelings of James. Ponder with him as to why he was chosen to make this journey. He had just been warned with the other disciples that the journey with Jesus would involve loss of life to gain life. Maybe this would be one of those hurtful journeys. Share the feelings of James, anxious that something bad might happen. Would you want to accept this invitation to be with Jesus?

Share the feelings of John. Ponder with him why he should make this journey. He had been asked to leave his job and family behind to follow Jesus. Jesus had promised rewards as well as hardships to the disciples. Maybe this invitation was a reward for his deep loyalty and friendship. Share the feelings of John, excited at the prospect that something good might happen. Would you want to accept this invitation to be with Jesus?

Share the feelings of Peter on the mountain top. Peter had in faith declared that Jesus was the Messiah. Now in this vision he knows that it is true. Moses and Elijah confirm it for him. Both the Law and the Prophets point to its truth. They stand to support Jesus. Share the joy of Peter. Jesus is indeed the Messiah.

Share the feelings of James on the mountain top. You hear the voice from heaven, 'This is my beloved Son.' What Jesus told you about his baptism is true. You cast away your doubts. Share the certainty of James. Jesus is God's beloved Son.

Share the feelings of John on the mountain top. To be close to the divine is an exciting reward, but frightening. Here heaven touches the earth. The compassion and hope of Jesus give you courage to cast away your fear. Share the security of John. Jesus understands our human reactions.

Share the feelings of Peter, James and John. Such close experiences of God are the reward for faith, risk and the cross. Such close experiences of God make it worth accepting the journey to discipleship.

Thinking

The transfiguration presents a puzzle to many thinking people.

In many ways the transfiguration is more like a resurrection appearance. It seems to fit more easily into the experience of the post-resurrection period. Jesus' body is said to be 'transformed'. As in the resurrection it takes on new qualities. The affirmation that this event gives to the three disciples who shared the agony of Gethsemane would be welcome after Christ's death on the cross. Through this experience they would know for certain that Jesus was the Son of God despite his crucifixion and death.

In other ways the place that the transfiguration takes in all three synoptic gospels is perfectly logical. It comes after the claim that Jesus is the Messiah, and after Peter has been rebuked for not accepting that to be Messiah entails suffering, death and resurrection. Any doubts about Jesus and the path he has chosen must be cleared up by an experience of his true nature and his true calling. This affirmation fits well into the preparation for the Passion.

Why then did Jesus take only three of the disciples and not all twelve? The clue to the answer may well lie in the choice of the same three disciples for the task of sharing the experience of Christ in the garden of Gethsemane. In the hour of deepest affirmation and of deepest challenge Jesus calls on the most discerning of his friends to share these experiences. The sensitive nature required is gifted to only a few people. We cannot all, and need not all, share in the supreme moments of divine revelation. Most of us live off the shared insights of the few. What is theirs becomes ours through the telling.

When you think about it, we are privileged to have this shared record of their experiences both on the mountain top and in the

garden. The church was wise to treasure them. The gospel writers
were right to record them. By doing so it has become part of our
corporate experience of Christ.

How, then, does the transfiguration fit into your gospel story?

29
Matthew 18:15–20

15'If another member of the church sins against you, go and
point out the fault when the two of you are alone. If the
member listens to you, you have regained that one. 16But if
you are not listened to, take one or two others along with
you, so that every word may be confirmed by the evidence of
two or three witnesses. 17If the member refuses to listen to
them, tell it to the church; and if the offender refuses to listen
even to the church, let such a one be to you as a Gentile and
a tax-collector. 18Truly I tell you, whatever you bind on earth
will be bound in heaven, and whatever you loose on earth will
be loosed in heaven. 19Again, truly I tell you, if two of you
agree on earth about anything you ask, it will be done for you
by my Father in heaven. 20For where two or three are gathered
in my name, I am there among them.'

Context
These verses form part of Matthew's collection of teachings about
the church, and how relationships should be conducted within
it. The church is inclusive of repentant sinners, but excludes
those who will not repent.

Sensing
Take your place at the church door and note how sinners react to
one another. Watch this one scuttle off into a corner and take a
back pew, trying to appear invisible for fear of reproach. Watch
that one in brazen bravado march up the aisle and sit in a
prominent position, daring anyone to put forward a challenge.

Watch that one go into a seat and kneel in contrite confession, pouring forth sobs of sorrow.

Take your place at the church door and note how sinners react to one another. Watch this righteous group distance themselves from those they consider sinners, moving away a few seats when one of doubtful character dares to come too close for comfort. Watch that pure person march to the chosen position to sit alone in self-contentment. Watch that reconciler gently take a sinner by the hand and kneel together to seek full forgiveness.

Take your place at the church meeting and note how sinners are treated by the congregation. Listen as the resolution is formulated to dismiss the church treasurer. Observe the tone of the mover as he reads the words from his script: 'That this meeting excludes member X from its corporate life on the grounds of dishonesty in the church accounts'. Hear the storms of indignation and hurt that anyone would even consider stealing from church funds. Listen to the howls of protest as one member speaks about the need to allow for forgiveness and restitution before such a step is taken. Watch the smiles of satisfaction as the resolution is passed with only one small voice against it.

Take your place at the church meeting and prepare to address it on the subject of sin and reconciliation. Set out your advice clearly. Give them your reasons. Share the facts as you see them. You know that sin needs to be dealt with decisively but also with the aim of reconciliation where there is repentance. Set out your policy and tell them that we are all sinners too. As you address the meeting hear Christ speaking to you: 'Where two or three are gathered together in my name, I am there among them.'

Intuition

Promises, what do you make of Christ's promises in scripture?

Christ promises that decisions taken within the church community will be endorsed by God. That seems an extraordinary promise given the different decisions reached by the church over the centuries. It would seem to be dangerous to allow sinful human beings to think that God promises to be on their side in any decision which declares who is in the church and who should be excluded.

When you hear Christ's promises how do you react? Maybe

you are cautious, wanting to believe that they are true but knowing that, taken out of context, some promises would lead to extraordinary consequences. People are all too ready to accumulate power to themselves, and exercise that power by declaring people sinners. People are all too ready to let God do all the work and become over-dependent on God's promises.

When you hear Christ's promises to you individually do you take them for certain, rejoicing in their comfort and the power they give you? What would you ask of the Christ who promises to fulfil your request? Promises have no value unless we make use of them.

When you hear Christ's promises to the church as a group do you rate them uncertain, and hold back, fearing that to believe in them would give too much power to the institution? What is your reaction when the church claims fulfilment of the promises?

When you hear Christ's promises to small groups do you affirm them as being fulfilled by your own experience? How have you experienced Christ 'there among you' in the fellowship of the two or three?

Promises, what do you make of these?

> Whatever you bind or loose on earth will be bound or loosed in heaven.
> If two of you agree on earth about anything you ask, it will be done for you in heaven.
> Where two or three are gathered in my name, I am there among them.

Promises, what do you make of promises when they apply to the church; when they apply to your group; and when they apply to you personally?

Feeling

The motivation behind the teaching in this section is to gain the repentance of the sinner and the reconciliation of the community. As a feeling person you can identify with that motivation. The steps suggested for each should be able to achieve such a result.

See the process from the sinner's point of view. It is best to be confronted by the person you have hurt. If both seek reconciliation, you will become aware of the hurt you have caused. Once the offended party sees the first signs of your repentance he or she will be all the more ready to forgive you and be reconciled.

See the process from the offended person's point of view. It is best to approach the person who has sinned against you and listen to the intention rather than the hurt. You will be able to share with that person how it felt for you. You can offer the sinner the chance of forgiveness. Such a process is best both for the offended and the offender. The motivation for both is reconciliation.

As a feeling person you can see that a second step is necessary on some occasions. Two people on their own can sometimes make matters worse rather than better. They may need the help of friends to achieve repentance and reconciliation. Feeling people can often act as supporters in the process.

As a feeling person you can see that a third step in the process might be necessary in some cases. The support of the whole congregation and its leadership might be required. The hurts might need to be sorted out at that level. It may not just be an individual matter but a corporate breakdown with people taking sides. The pastoral skills of the leadership might be necessary to achieve repentance and reconciliation.

As a feeling person you can see that the ultimate step might be necessary. The offence might have begun against one member, but it may become an offence against all. Only the radical step of exclusion may shock the offender into repentance. It is extreme but it may be the only way.

As a feeling person you will have a major role to play in all the stages of this process. Practise your skills.

Thinking

Chapter 18 of Matthew's gospel appears to be a collection of teachings based on the parables and sayings of Jesus. It fits the context of a settled local church struggling to maintain unity in the face of the imperfection of Christians who go on sinning even after baptism. Similar instructions are included in the Pastoral Epistles, and in Paul's letters to the churches he founded.

The parable of the farmer and the seeds was explained in the early church to apply it to the new situation of evangelism. These sayings of Jesus about forgiveness and decision making are applied to the known church context of the readers. As we have seen this only strengthens the case to regard scripture as constantly applicable to each new situation for individuals and for the church.

In this passage the pastoral process to deal with a sinner is set out clearly. The harsh reality of the hardness of heart in a sinner is acknowledged. The final step of exclusion is logical even if it is also a possible sign of failure to achieve the goal of repentance and reconciliation. Judgement by the community is aimed at the ultimate restoration of the offender to the community. Yet at the same time it aims to safeguard the community from a breakdown of the rules and principles by which their fellowship is maintained. In the Jewish-Christian context of Matthew's gospel a Gentile is seen as one who refuses to acknowledge the true nature of God (the sin of disbelief) and the tax collector as one who undermines the welfare of the community (the sin of greed and injustice). These types of sin attack the spiritual and physical well-being of the community.

The promises of divine support for the human Christian community are vital for its self-awareness and self-confidence. It needs to be reassured that it has divine authority for the hard decisions taken in extreme cases. It needs to be aware of the guiding presence of Christ in its midst. Only so can it hold together Christ's compassion and Christ's insistence on justice.

The challenge is to act with such wisdom in our corporate life as a church assembly.

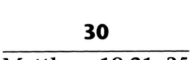

30

Matthew 18:21–35

²¹Then Peter came and said to him, 'Lord, if another member of the church sins against me, how often should I forgive? As many as seven times?' ²²Jesus said to him, 'Not seven times, but, I tell you, seventy-seven times.

²³'For this reason the kingdom of heaven may be compared to a king who wished to settle accounts with his slaves. ²⁴When he began the reckoning, one who owed him ten thousand talents was brought to him; ²⁵and, as he could not

pay, his lord ordered him to be sold, together with his wife and children and all his possessions, and payment to be made. [26]So the slave fell on his knees before him, saying, "Have patience with me, and I will pay you everything." [27]And out of pity for him, the lord of that slave released him and forgave him the debt. [28]But that same slave, as he went out, came upon one of his fellow-slaves who owed him a hundred denarii; and seizing him by the throat, he said, "Pay what you owe." [29]Then his fellow-slave fell down and pleaded with him, "Have patience with me, and I will pay you." [30]But he refused; then he went and threw him into prison until he would pay the debt. [31]When his fellow-slaves saw what had happened, they were greatly distressed, and they went and reported to their lord all that had taken place. [32]Then his lord summoned him and said to him, "You wicked slave! I forgave you all that debt because you pleaded with me. [33]Should you not have had mercy on your fellow-slave, as I had mercy on you?" [34]And in anger his lord handed him over to be tortured until he would pay his entire debt. [35]So my heavenly Father will also do to every one of you, if you do not forgive your brother or sister from your heart.'

Context

Matthew records instruction about appropriate behaviour and attitudes within the Christian community. In the previous section he gives teaching on the process required to achieve reconciliation. Here we receive instruction on the duty of the individual to be open to forgiveness to achieve the same end.

Sensing

Form a picture in your mind of a provincial governor appointed to serve a king. He has a duty to raise a large sum of taxes to contribute to the king's treasury. He fails at his job. Through greed, incompetence and sloth he cannot deliver the contribution. The annual sum is now due. Watch him receive the summons. His face shows how he fears the consequences, yet he holds out hope for understanding.

Form a picture in your mind of a king sitting at his table and calling the governors to hand over their required taxes. Watch one governor admit his failure. Hear him declare, 'I owe the whole amount of the annual tax but I cannot pay.' See how the king tries to be just and fair, but the inevitable happens. The king declares him personally bankrupt and orders everything sold, including his family, to pay the debt. Watch as the governor falls on his knees in desperation crying, 'Have patience with me. Give me another chance. I will repay you next tax day.' Watch the king dissolve in laughter. He knows that is impossible, but a governor on his knees looks so pathetic. Hear the king with pity and generosity, and at great cost to himself, declare the governor released and the debt forgiven. See the governor kiss the king's hand and rush out to share the good news with his family.

Form a picture in your mind of a court official who has borrowed three months wages to pay a gambling debt. He is required to pay it back to a governor who needs the money to get his family back home to their province. Watch him cornered by the governor as he pleads for more time to pay. Hear the governor's harsh words, 'You'll only gamble the money away. I won't give you more time, off you go to prison.'

Hold the three pictures in your mind. The actions of the governor showed that he did not really repent but took his forgiveness for granted. He failed to learn that only deep gratitude for forgiveness given to us can inspire sufficient love for us to forgive our brothers and sisters.

Intuition

It is not difficult to apply the parable to our own situations.

Consider first the size of the debt in the story. When we reckon up the sins in our own lives, we see the size of the pile. The list of what we have done wrong, and what we have failed to do right, is long. We can never accumulate enough good points to wipe out the deficit. Before God we appear bankrupt of the good works which might win us favour. When we honestly consider our sins what does the size of the debt suggest to you?

Consider the plea for forgiveness. When we fall on our knees before God and promise to do better, both we and God know that we will fail again. There is no chance of us earning our way to salvation. Before God our confident promises are laughable. When we confess our sins what does the plea for forgiveness suggest to you?

Consider the king's generous words of release. When we hear God's words of pardon, release and forgiveness, we are overwhelmed by God's generosity. We can hardly believe our good fortune. Forgiveness brings relief to our family as well. When you listen to God's absolution what do the words of release suggest to you?

Consider the governor's harsh words of retention. When others ask us to forgive them we stand on our dignity, we tally up the cost and try to get our own back. We forget God's generosity and calculate our gain from withholding forgiveness. It gives us power over the guilty. When we refuse to listen to our neighbour's cry for mercy, what do the words of retention suggest to you?

Consider the prison. If we cannot learn to forgive we will be imprisoned in bitterness, violence, jealousy and pride. We will never get out of that prison. Our souls and bodies will waste away. We will indeed be tortured until we learn to forgive. When you are chained to hatred what does the prison suggest to you?

This may be just a parable, but it is far too applicable for comfort.

Feeling

As a feeling person you can readily sympathize with Peter's question, 'Lord, how often should I forgive?'

You know that to be hurt time and time again is very destructive. The first and second time is hard enough, but when we are hurt the seventh time, the ache is too much to bear. Surely we have a right to call an end to it, even to cry out, 'Enough is enough.'

'Lord, how often should I forgive?' You can sympathize with Peter's question. He is not only thinking of himself, but also of the moral code. It is not good for the sinner to get away with it. Repeat offenders ingrain the act of sinning in their psyche. If they continue to get away with it, they will never see the error of their ways.

'Lord, how often should I forgive?' You can sympathize with Peter's question. To forgive up to seven times shows that I really am trying to be generous to the sinner. I recognize that I sin reasonably often against my neighbour. I admit that I need lots of forgiveness, and so do we all. Seven times, surely that is enough as a proper sign of true generosity.

As a feeling person you can sympathize with Jesus' answer. 'I tell you seventy-seven times (or seventy times seven).' This is the 'endless' number. Jesus tells us that is how many times we must be ready to forgive. We must accept that our sins are so many that we need endless forgiveness; and that expecting endless forgiveness in turn we must offer it equally to others.

You can sympathize with Jesus' answer. Forgiveness is endless because 'love keeps no score of wrongs' (1 Corinthians 13:5 NEB). Each time you are forgiven the record is wiped clear. Each time you are forgiven there is a new start. There is no 'last time' or 'seventh time'. Each time you forgive you wipe out the past in an act of generous love. The relationship is totally renewed as if the hurt had never happened. As a feeling person try to allow your heart to love that way.

Thinking

The parable of the accounts is unique to Matthew's gospel. It is included here to reinforce Jesus' saying about the need for endless forgiveness to be shown between one church member and another. The individual church member must not hold out on a fellow member and refuse to offer forgiveness. The church as a corporate entity might have the responsibility of excluding members who will not repent, but individual Christians must not withhold forgiveness from those who do repent. If they do, such hardness will cause divisions rather than reconciliation within the church.

At first reading, the parable Matthew uses to illustrate the point seems to highlight judgement rather than mercy. If we do not use our thinking powers we will begin to draw conclusions from parables as if they were allegories. An allegory is a story in which the characters and actions are identified with real people and happenings, and even with God and God's way of acting. If we take the story this way God becomes responsible for eternal torture, and appears cruel and *unforgiving*. Clearly the parable is told to illustrate a different point – about forgiveness. It is a wake-up call to all Christians to practise forgiveness time and time again. It does not take too much thought to see how badly the first servant acts towards the second servant. Everyone is indignant at the hardness and cruelty shown. From the parable as a whole you can quickly work out why we should forgive others: because we have experienced forgiveness on a grand scale ourselves. A little thought will help us see the connection between this parable and the line in the Lord's Prayer which in Matthew's gospel says, 'And forgive us our debts, as we also have forgiven our debtors' (Matthew 6:12).

It is true that we desperately want God to forgive us without limit. We must quickly learn to treat others in the same way. God's generosity will inspire ours. In the story, through question and answer, the point is made clear. With a little thought the application is clear. 'Endless forgiveness is necessary for imperfect humanity.' Do you think that statement sums up the point of the story?

31

Matthew 20:1–16

¹'For the kingdom of heaven is like a landowner who went out early in the morning to hire labourers for his vineyard. ²After agreeing with the labourers for the usual daily wage, he sent them into his vineyard. ³When he went out about nine o'clock, he saw others standing idle in the market-place; ⁴and he said to them, "You also go into the vineyard, and I will pay you whatever is right." So they went. ⁵When he went out again about noon and about three o'clock, he did the same. ⁶And about five o'clock he went out and found others standing around; and he said to them, "Why are you standing here idle all day?" ⁷They said to him, "Because no one has hired us." He said to them, "You also go into the vineyard." ⁸When evening came, the owner of the vineyard said to his manager, "Call the labourers and give them their pay, beginning with the last and then going to the first." ⁹When those hired about five o'clock came, each of them received the usual daily wage. ¹⁰Now when the first came, they thought they would receive more; but each of them also received the usual daily wage. ¹¹And when they received it, they grumbled against the landowner, ¹²saying, "These last worked only one hour, and you have made them equal to us who have borne the burden of the day and the scorching heat." ¹³But he replied to one of them, "Friend, I am doing you no wrong; did you not agree

with me for the usual daily wage? [14]Take what belongs to you and go; I choose to give to this last the same as I give to you. [15]Am I not allowed to do what I choose with what belongs to me? Or are you envious because I am generous?" [16]So the last will be first, and the first will be last.'

Context

Having prophesied his death in Jerusalem, Jesus leads the disciples in that direction, teaching them as they make their way. This parable emphasizes the inclusiveness of God's grace.

Sensing

Sometimes you just cannot believe your ears. Sometimes Jesus can be so provocative and so outrageous. Listen to the details of the story.

Early in the morning the landowner goes out to hire labourers for the day. The landowner strikes up a deal with them to pay a fair day's wage for a fair day's work. The labourers set to work content with the arrangement.

Not content with the progress, about nine o'clock in the morning the landowner returned to the market-place to hire more labourers. This time no deal is struck about the precise wage, but the landowner promises to be fair and just. The labourers set to work content with the arrangement.

Still not content with the progress, about noon the landowner returned to the market-place to hire yet more labourers. No clear deal is struck; no precise wage is mentioned. Again the same thing happens at three in the afternoon. Yet more labourers are busy with the harvest, content with the arrangement.

Still not content with the progress as late as five in the evening, the landowner recruited a final cohort of labourers from the market-place. By now time is so short, no negotiation takes place. The labourers are sent with urgency to join those already wearied by the toil of the day. They go content with the arrangement.

When evening came the landowner called the labourers together to receive their wage for the day. Those who were recruited at five in the afternoon received just the same as those who had been recruited at first light. All hell broke out in the workforce. Industrial relations were destroyed. But the harvest was completed.

Sometimes you just cannot believe your ears. Jesus can be so provocative and so outrageous.

Intuition

At five in the afternoon there were still people standing idle in the market-place. They had stood there idle all day long. Whose problem is that? What is your view?

At five in the afternoon there were still people standing idle in the market-place. Some would say that their problem was laziness, an unwillingness to work and to pull their weight in the national economy. How convinced are you by that analysis?

At five in the afternoon there were still people standing idle in the market-place. Some would say that they were irresponsible scroungers who could make a bigger profit by begging than by doing an honest day's work. How convinced are you by that analysis?

At five in the afternoon there were still people standing idle in the market-place. Some would say that they probably represented the long-term unemployed who had no recent experience of being in the workforce. Rehabilitation of the long-term unemployed is indeed most problematic. How convinced are you by that analysis?

At five in the afternoon there were still people standing idle in the market-place. Some would say that they probably represented the young unemployed who had no relevant work experience and no recognized skills. Preparing the young for their place in the workforce is a fundamental social challenge. How convinced are you by that analysis?

At five in the afternoon there were still people standing idle in the market-place. Some would lay the blame fairly and squarely at the feet of the landowner. Perhaps intent on maximizing profit the landowner had introduced new technology, insisted on productivity gains, and rationalized the workforce. How convinced are you by that analysis?

At five in the afternoon there were still people standing idle in the market-place. Some would lay the blame fairly and squarely at the feet of the government. Perhaps intent on lower-

ing taxes the government had privatized the vineyards and ab-
dicated responsibility for maintaining full employment within
the economy. How convinced are you by that analysis?

At five in the afternoon there were still people standing idle
in the market-place. They had stood there idle all day long.
Whose problem is that? What is your view?

Feeling

Jealousy is a very understandable human emotion, but jealousy
can be most corrosive and most destructive.

Come down to the market-place first thing in the morning
and stand there waiting to be hired for a day's work. You are
desperate for the wage. Unless you find work your family will go
hungry for yet another night. You watch the rich and powerful
landowner walk down from his vineyard. He has no need to be
anxious about feeding his family tomorrow or the day after.
Understandably enough you feel jealousy grip your heart.

Come down to the market-place first thing in the morning
and stand there waiting to be hired for a day's work. You are
desperate for the wage. Unless you find work your family will go
hungry for yet another night. You watch the rich and powerful
landowner choose the strong and healthy. You watch the deal
being struck for a fair day's wage. You watch as the chosen ones
go off to do a fair day's work. They have no need to be anxious
about feeding their families, at least for tomorrow. Understandably enough you feel jealousy grip your heart.

Come down to the market-place at nine in the morning and
stand there waiting to be hired for a part day's work. You are
desperate for the wage. Unless you find work your family will go
hungry for yet another night. You watch the rich and powerful
landowner walk in your direction, and look you in the eye. You
hear the rich and powerful landowner offer you a job for the rest
of the day. You know that you will work as hard as those who
were signed up two hours earlier, but that you will never earn a
full day's wage. Understandably enough you feel jealousy grip
your heart.

Come down to the treasury at the end of the day with all
those who have worked in the vineyard, with those who began
at first light, with those like you who began at nine in the
morning, and with those who came late at five in the after-

noon. Watch as the latecomers are paid a full day's wage for not much more than one hour's work, when you receive exactly the same. Understandably enough you feel jealousy grip your heart.

Jealousy is a very understandable human emotion, but jealousy can be most corrosive and most destructive.

Thinking

If fairness and justice really matter to you, is the kingdom of heaven the right place for you?

Jesus said that the kingdom of heaven is like a landowner who hired labourers at all odd hours of the day, from first light in the early morning until near dusk in the late afternoon. Is this really a fair and just way to run a business?

Jesus said that the kingdom of heaven is like a landowner who puts people to work in the harvest without firmly agreeing the wage that they would receive at the end of the day. Is this really a fair and just way to run a business?

Jesus said that the kingdom of heaven is like a landowner who gave precisely the same wage to those who had laboured steadily throughout the whole day and to those who had joined the workforce at the eleventh hour. Is this really a fair and just way to run a business?

If fairness and justice really matter to you, is the kingdom of heaven the right place for you?

Jesus said that the kingdom of heaven is like a landowner who really wanted to give everyone a fair chance to work on the harvest. For that reason the landowner kept returning to the market-place to recruit all who would respond. Now I call that fair and just.

Jesus said that the kingdom of heaven is like a landowner who made no false promises, no exaggerated claims to those to whom he offered work. For that reason the landowner accepted the contribution of all who came to work for him, young and old alike, able and handicapped, the early risers and the latercomers alike. Now I call that fair and just.

Jesus said that the kingdom of heaven is like a landowner who valued every individual to the same extent. For that reason the landowner paid the same wage to all who accepted his invitation to work in the vineyard, to Jew and to Gentile alike, to those who responded to the call in their youth and to those who responded in the evening of their lives. Now I call that fair and just.

If fairness and justice really matter to you, the kingdom of heaven is clearly for you.

32

Matthew 21:1–11

¹When they had come near Jerusalem and had reached Bethphage, at the Mount of Olives, Jesus sent two disciples, ²saying to them, 'Go into the village ahead of you, and immediately you will find a donkey tied, and a colt with her; untie them and bring them to me. ³If anyone says anything to you, just say this, "The Lord needs them." And he will send them immediately.' ⁴This took place to fulfil what had been spoken through the prophet, saying,

⁵'Tell the daughter of Zion,
   Look, your king is coming to you,
      humble, and mounted on a donkey,
         and on a colt, the foal of a donkey.'

⁶The disciples went and did as Jesus had directed them; ⁷they brought the donkey and the colt, and put their cloaks on them, and he sat on them. ⁸A very large crowd spread their cloaks on the road, and others cut branches from the trees and spread them on the road. ⁹The crowds that went ahead of him and that followed were shouting,

'Hosanna to the Son of David!
   Blessed is the one who comes in the name
      of the Lord!
Hosanna in the highest heaven!'

¹⁰When he entered Jerusalem, the whole city was in turmoil, asking, 'Who is this?' ¹¹The crowds were saying, 'This is the prophet Jesus from Nazareth in Galilee.'

Context

After travelling towards Jerusalem Jesus prepares to enter the city riding on a donkey. People strew Jesus' path with their cloaks and with branches cut from the trees.

Sensing

Today there is real excitement in the air. Come and experience the excitement for yourself.

Today there is real excitement in the air. Come and see what is going on. See Jesus' disciples bring a donkey and a colt. See the disciples cast their cloaks on the patient animals and then help Jesus to mount. See Jesus begin his journey towards Jerusalem, riding slowly, riding regally, riding with dignity. See the disciples escort Jesus on his journey towards the city. Come and see for yourself.

Today there is real excitement in the air. Come and hear what is going on. Hear the crowds chanting and shouting:

Hosanna to the Son of David!
Blessed is the one who comes in the name of the Lord!
Hosanna in the highest heaven!

Hear the whole city musing and puzzling:

Who is this? Who can he be?

Come and hear for yourself.

Today there is real excitement in the air. Come and feel what is going on. Feel the branches under your feet as you follow in Jesus' footsteps. Stretch out your hands and wave the branches over your head. Run to catch up with the donkey and try to touch the tails of Jesus' coat. Feel the crowds pressing all around you. Come and feel for yourself.

Today there is real excitement in the air. Come and smell what is going on. Smell the fragrance of the branches freshly torn from the trees. Smell the sweat of the people climbing their weary way up from Bethphage to Jerusalem. Smell the odour of the donkey and the colt. Smell the crowd closing in all around you. Come and smell for yourself.

Today there is real excitement in the air. Come and experience the excitement for yourself.

Intuition

The psychology of the crowd can be a puzzling business. What on earth do you make of the way in which the crowd behaves?

Take, for example, the crowd at a football match. Take the crowd united by the common scarf and the common loyalty to their team. What on earth is it that so easily unites those supporters in common hatred of the supporters of the opposite team?

Take, for example, the pupils attending their local school. Take the pupils united by the common uniform and the common loyalty to their school. What on earth is it that so easily unites those pupils in common hatred of the pupils attending the neighbouring school?

Take, for example, the gang of young people who occupy the shopping precinct throughout the evening. Take the young people united by their common dress and common loyalty to their mates. What on earth is it that so easily unites those young people to behave in anti-social ways that none of them individually would embrace?

Take, for example, the guards who ran the Nazi extermination camps. Take the ordinary decent people who constructed gas chambers and herded innocent children, women and men to their undeserved death. What on earth is it that so easily unites those ordinary decent people to commit such atrocities against humanity?

The psychology of the crowd can be a puzzling business. What on earth do you make of the way in which the crowd behaves?

Take, for example, the crowd which followed Jesus' journey into Jerusalem on that first Palm Sunday. Take the crowd which witnessed the lowly donkey transporting the Messiah. What on earth is it that so easily unites this crowd to shout in unison the cry of affirmation, 'Hosanna to the Son of David!'?

Take, for example, the crowd which followed Jesus' journey to Calvary on that first Good Friday. Take the crowd which witnessed the lowly Messiah transporting the cross. What on earth is it that so easily unites this crowd to shout in unison the cry of condemnation, 'Crucify! Crucify!'?

The psychology of the crowd can be a puzzling business.

What on earth do you make of the way in which the crowd behaves?

Feeling

This story about the entry into Jerusalem gives us a great deal of insight into the character of Jesus. It takes us right to the heart of the matter.

There at the heart of Jesus we find someone who is concerned with careful planning and detailed preparation. The entry into Jerusalem was not something left to chance, not something arranged hastily at the very last minute. Careful arrangements had been made for the donkey to be at the ready. Jesus is concerned with careful planning and detailed preparation.

There at the heart of Jesus we find someone who inspired trust and loyalty. We have no idea who owned that donkey, but we do know that the owner trusted Jesus to borrow it. We have no idea which disciples went to fetch that donkey, but we do know that they trusted Jesus' arrangements. Jesus inspired trust and loyalty.

There at the heart of Jesus we find someone who knew precisely what he was doing. As Jerusalem filled for the Passover festival, so the fervour of messianic expectation filled the air. The dramatic enactment of Zechariah's prophecy of the Messiah riding on a donkey was unmistakable. Jesus knew precisely what he was doing.

There at the heart of Jesus we find someone who was bold and totally courageous. Jesus recognized that Jerusalem had a reputation for killing God's messengers sent to her. Jesus recognized that a price was already sitting on his own head. Jesus was bold and totally courageous.

There at the heart of Jesus we find someone who won the support and affection of the common people. As he rode towards Jerusalem the crowd spread their cloaks on the road. As he approached the city the crowds shouted their acclaim, 'Hosanna to the Son of David!' Jesus won the support and affection of the common people.

This story about the entry into Jerusalem gives us a great deal of insight into the character of Jesus. It takes us right to the heart of the matter.

Thinking

Matthew is very very influenced by the claims of Jesus to fulfil Old Testament prophecies. Have you understood what is going on?

According to Matthew, the disciples go to fetch not one animal, but two. They are told to go to find a donkey tied, and a colt with her. Here is quite a challenge.

According to Matthew, the disciples brought to Jesus not one animal, but two. They brought to Jesus the donkey, and the colt as well for good measure. Here is quite a lot of transport.

According to Matthew, the disciples cast their cloaks not on one animal, but on two. They cast their cloaks on the colt as well as on the donkey. There is quite a lot of space for cloaks.

According to Matthew, Jesus sat not on one animal, but on two. Matthew's text is quite clear that Jesus came and sat on both of them, apparently at the same time. Here is quite a sight.

Matthew is very very influenced by the claims of Jesus to fulfil Old Testament prophecies. Have you understood what is going on?

In the Old Testament the prophet Zechariah delights in using a well-established literary device known as Hebrew poetic parallelism. His style is to repeat the same idea in different but parallel words. In this sense the ideas are interchangeable.

In the Old Testament Zechariah begins his prophecy with two invitations:

Rejoice greatly, O daughter of Zion!
Shout aloud, O daughter of Jerusalem!

Clearly the prophet Zechariah is not addressing two different audiences. Rather he is calling into action one community of people by two interchangeable names. Here is Hebrew poetic parallelism.

In the Old Testament, Zechariah continues his prophecy with two claims:

Your King is coming to you,
humble, and mounted on a donkey,
and on a colt, the foal of a donkey.

Clearly the prophet Zechariah is not describing two different animals. Rather he is describing one animal by two interchangeable names. Here is Hebrew poetic parallelism.

Matthew is very very influenced by the claims of Jesus to fulfil Old Testament prophecies. Have you understood what is going on?

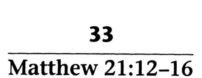

33

Matthew 21:12–16

¹²Then Jesus entered the temple and drove out all who were selling and buying in the temple, and he overturned the tables of the money-changers and the seats of those who sold doves. ¹³He said to them, 'It is written,
>   "My house shall be called a house of prayer";
>   but you are making it a den of robbers.'
¹⁴The blind and the lame came to him in the temple, and he cured them. ¹⁵But when the chief priests and the scribes saw the amazing things that he did, and heard the children crying out in the temple, 'Hosanna to the Son of David', they became angry ¹⁶and said to him, 'Do you hear what these are saying?' Jesus said to them, 'Yes; have you never read,
>   "Out of the mouths of infants and nursing
>   babies
>   you have prepared praise for yourself"?'

Context
According to Matthew, when Jesus entered Jerusalem on the donkey he proceeded directly to the temple. There he overturned the tables of the money changers and cleansed the temple.

Sensing
Today of all days is a day to avoid going up to the temple. Far too much is happening there. But if you are really curious to find out what is happening there, come and see.

Look down from the temple mount to the road leading up from Bethphage. See there a very odd sight. See Jesus of Nazareth sitting awkwardly on a donkey and on a colt, the foal of a donkey. See the crowd, wild with excitement, tearing branches from the trees and strewing them in Jesus' path. Hear the crowd, wild with excitement, chanting at the top of their voices, 'Blessed is the one who comes in the name of the Lord!' Today of all days is a day to avoid going up to the temple.

Look up into the temple. See there a very odd sight. See Jesus of Nazareth stride confidently into the holy site. See Jesus, wild with irritation, turn upside down the tables of the money changers. See Jesus drive out those who are selling doves for sacrifice. Hear Jesus, wild with irritation, shouting at the top of his voice, 'My house shall be called a house of prayer, but you are making it a den of robbers.' Today of all days is a day to avoid going up to the temple.

Look up into the temple. See there a very odd sight. See blind people grope their way to Jesus and then return home fully sighted. See lame people limp their way to Jesus and then return home fully mobile. Hear those who have been healed rejoice in their new found health, 'Hosanna to the Son of David!' Today of all days is a day to avoid going up to the temple.

Look up into the temple. See there a very odd sight. See the chief priest and the scribes look on Jesus with resentment in their eyes. Hear the chief priest and the scribes challenge Jesus with this rebuke, 'Do you hear what these people are saying?' Today of all days is a day to avoid going up to the temple.

Far too much is happening in the temple today. You must be really glad that you came out to see.

Intuition

It is very human to experience anger and foolish to deny it. The problems come when the anger builds up inside us and we just refuse to acknowledge that it is there.

It is very human to be angry with other people and foolish to deny it. Think through the past week and recall those occasions when other people were the cause of your anger. Think of those who are dearest and closest to you and recall the moments when anger is roused. Think of those with whom you work and those with whom you try to do business and recall the moments when anger is roused. The problems come when the anger builds up inside us and we just refuse to acknowledge that it is there.

It is very human to be angry with the things that frustrate us and foolish to deny it. Think through the past week and recall the occasions when things were the cause of your anger. When did you last kick your car for failing to start, thump your word processor for losing a file, or throw your tools to the ground in utter frustration? The problems come when the anger builds up inside us and we just refuse to acknowledge that it is there.

It is very human to be angry with ourselves and foolish to deny it. Think through the past week and recall those occasions when you yourself were the cause of your anger. When did you last kick yourself for getting something so simple so disastrously wrong, wish to hide under the table for doing something so embarrassingly silly, or shout aloud in utter frustration? The problems come when the anger builds up inside us and we just refuse to acknowledge that it is there.

It is very human to be angry with God and foolish to deny it. Think through the past week and recall those occasions when God was the cause of your anger. When did you last hit out at God for treating you unfairly, curse God for the pain suffered by those so close to you, or rage at God for the meaningless anguish of the world? The problems come when the anger builds up inside us and we just refuse to acknowledge that it is there.

Even Jesus experienced anger, so who are you to deny it?

Feeling

For much of the time Jesus really does seem so meek and mild. But there clearly are some things which make his blood boil.

Jesus' blood boiled when he rode into Jerusalem and found the city so unprepared for receiving God's Messiah. He came into the temple expecting to find a house of prayer. Instead he found a den of robbers. Such sacrilege made Jesus' blood boil. He overturned the tables of the money changers and sent their lucrative profits tumbling to the floor.

Jesus' blood boiled when he rode into Jerusalem and found the city so unprepared for receiving God's Messiah. He came into the temple expecting to find sanctity and holiness. Instead he found a busy market-place dealing in livestock for ritual sacrifice. Such abuse made Jesus' blood boil. He upturned the seats of those who sold doves, drove them from the temple and liberated the imprisoned birds.

Jesus' blood boiled when he rode into Jerusalem and found the city so unprepared for receiving God's Messiah. He came into the temple to set God's people free from the disabilities that held them bound. He came to open the eyes of the blind and to restore the limbs of the lame. Instead he found an atmosphere of hostility and criticism. Such deliberate misunderstanding made Jesus' blood boil. He rebuked the chief priests and the scribes who refused to hear God's good news of salvation.

Jesus' blood boiled when he rode into Jerusalem and found the city so unprepared for receiving God's Messiah. He came to the fig tree which God had planted and expected to find there figs ready for the harvest. Instead he found the outward show of leaves but never a fig in sight. Such unreadiness when God came to claim the fruit so fully deserved made Jesus' blood boil. He cursed that fig tree with an everlasting curse.

For much of the time Jesus really does seem so meek and mild. But there clearly are some things which make his blood boil.

Thinking

What do you think Jesus was up to when he rode right into Jerusalem sitting on a donkey? Are you not aware of the clear echoes of messianic prophecy resonating with Jesus' provocative action? Recall Zechariah 9:9:

> Lo, your king comes to you;
> triumphant and victorious is he,
> humble and riding on a donkey,
> on a colt, the foal of a donkey.

What do you think Jesus was up to when he entered right into the temple and asserted his presence among the people? Are you not aware of the clear echoes of messianic prophecy resonating with Jesus' provocative action? Recall Malachi 3:1:

> See I am sending my messenger to prepare the way before me; and the Lord whom you seek will suddenly come to his temple.

What do you think Jesus was up to when he drove out all who were buying and selling in the temple, and when he overturned the tables of the money changers and the seats of those who sold doves? Are you not aware of the clear echoes of messianic prophecy resonating with Jesus' provocative action? Recall Zechariah 14:21:

And there shall no longer be traders in the house of the Lord on that day.

What do you think Jesus was up to when he proclaimed the temple to be a house of prayer? Are you not aware of the clear echoes of messianic prophecy resonating with Jesus' provocative action? Recall Isaiah 56:7–8:

For my house shall be called a house of prayer for all peoples. Thus says the Lord God.

What do you think Jesus was up to when he healed the blind and the lame in the temple? Are you not aware of the clear claims of the messianic authority as Jesus overthrows David's ancient decree that the blind and the lame should not enter the temple (2 Samuel 5:8)?

What do you think Jesus was up to?

34

Matthew 21:23–32

23When he entered the temple, the chief priests and the elders of the people came to him as he was teaching, and said, 'By what authority are you doing these things, and who gave you this authority?' 24Jesus said to them, 'I will also ask you one question; if you tell me the answer, then I will also tell you by what authority I do these things. 25Did the baptism of John come from heaven, or was it of human origin?' And they argued with one another, 'If we say, "From heaven", he will say to us, "Why then did you not believe him?" 26But if we say, "Of human origin", we are afraid of the crowd; for all regard John as a prophet.' 27So they answered Jesus, 'We do not know.' And he said to them, 'Neither will I tell you by what authority I am doing these things.

28'What do you think? A man had two sons; he went to the first and said, "Son, go and work in the vineyard today." 29He answered, "I will not"; but later he changed his mind and went. ³⁰The father went to the second and said the same; and he answered, "I go, sir"; but he did not go. ³¹Which of the two did the will of his father?' They said, 'The first.' Jesus said to them, 'Truly I tell you, the tax-collectors and the prostitutes are going into the kingdom of God ahead of you. ³²For John came to you in the way of righteousness and you did not believe him, but the tax-collectors and the prostitutes believed him; and even after you saw it, you did not change your minds and believe him.

Context

Jesus has performed three unmistakably prophetic acts: entered Jerusalem on the donkey, expelled traders from the temple, and healed both the blind and the lame within the temple. This clearly raises huge questions about authority.

Sensing

You can sense the puzzlement in the air. You can sense the questions formed in people's minds. Clearly the evidence is building up, but the pieces do not quite fit together. It might be a mistake to jump to conclusions too quickly.

You can sense the puzzlement in the air. Jesus of Nazareth has ridden into the centre of Jerusalem in regal splendour, enthroned on a donkey. He has chosen to do so just before Passover when the city is filling up with pilgrims and when messianic hopes are high in everybody's mind. His followers have chanted, 'Hosanna to the son of David!' You can sense the questions forming in people's minds. Is this the moment of salvation for the people of God? Or is this the delusion of some self-appointed maniac? By what authority is Jesus of Nazareth acting?

You can sense the puzzlement in the air. Jesus of Nazareth has stormed into the temple and challenged all that was so well established there. He drove out the money changers who were fundamental for enabling pilgrims from afar to fulfil their religious obligations. He upturned the tables of those who sold doves for sacrifice. He openly reminded the onlookers of the prophecies which his actions fulfilled. You can sense the questions forming in people's minds. Is this the moment of salvation for the people of God? Or is this the delusion of some self-appointed maniac? By what authority is Jesus of Nazareth acting?

You can sense the puzzlement in the air. Jesus of Nazareth has overturned convention and disregarded tradition. He has invited into the temple the lame and the blind. Then he has sent the lame away walking; he has sent the blind away seeing. Observing what was happening, even the children have chanted, 'Hosanna to the son of David!' You can sense the questions forming in people's minds. Is this the moment of salvation for the people of God? Or is this the delusion of some self-appointed maniac? By what authority is Jesus of Nazareth acting?

Clearly the evidence is building up, but the pieces do not yet quite fit together. It might be a mistake to jump to conclusions too quickly.

Intuition

Surely you cannot really blame the chief priests and the elders of the people for doing their job and for doing it thoroughly? Their job was to guard against heresy and to warn against error. Surely they needed to check out Jesus' credentials? Surely they needed to warn the people against false teaching? Surely they needed to protect Jerusalem from false messiahs?

Surely you cannot really blame denominational leaders today for doing their job and for doing it thoroughly? Their job is to guard against heresy and to warn against error. Surely they need to check with great care changes in practice and ministry? Surely changes like the ordination of women to the priesthood or the consecration of women to the episcopacy need to be assessed with great care? Surely denominational leaders need to protect the church from false ministry?

Surely you cannot really blame denominational leaders today for doing their job and for doing it thoroughly? Their job is to guard against heresy and to warn against error. Surely they need to check with great care changes in doctrine and teaching? Surely changes in teaching about marriage, family life and same-sex relationships need to be assessed with great care? Surely denominational leaders need to protect the church from false teaching?

Surely you cannot blame local church leaders for doing their job and for doing it thoroughly? Their job is to guard against heresy and to warn against error. Surely they need to check with great care changes in practice and services? Surely changes like new forms of liturgy, new music and hymns, and inclusive language in scripture need to be assessed with great care? Surely local church leaders need to protect congregations from undesirable forms of worship?

Surely you cannot blame local church leaders for doing their job and for doing it thoroughly? Their job is to guard against heresy and to warn against error. Surely they need to check with great care reordering of buildings and changes in fabric? Surely changes like moving the altar, removing the pews and displaying work from the local school on the walls need to be assessed with great care? Surely local church leaders need to protect the congregation from undesirable changes to the building?

The chief priests and elders of the people did their job very well and crucified God's Messiah.

Feeling

Emotions were running pretty high that day in the temple. Feel what it was like on the inside.

Put yourself in the shoes of the chief priests and the elders of the people. Feel your emotions running high when you see and hear everything that Jesus has been doing to challenge the age-old faith you are commissioned to protect. Feel the satisfaction in your heart when at long last you frame a question to end all questions. 'By what authority are you doing these things and who gave you that authority?'

Put yourself in Jesus' shoes. Feel your emotions running high when you see and hear everything that the chief priests and elders of the people have been doing to challenge the gospel you are commissioned to proclaim. Feel the satisfaction in your heart when on the spur of the moment you frame the answer to end all questions. 'I will also ask you one question; if you tell me the answer then I will also tell you by what authority I do these things.'

Put yourself in the shoes of the chief priests and the elders of the people. Feel your emotions running high when you realize that Jesus has backed you into a corner. You cannot claim that John the Baptist received his authority from God without conceding that Jesus' authority has come from the same source. You cannot claim that John the Baptist lacked divine authority without infuriating the crowd. Backed into a corner you must decline to answer the question.

Put yourself in Jesus' shoes. Feel your emotions running high when you realize that the chief priests and elders of the people are refusing to come out and to fight clean. You have set them a trap and they have failed to take the bait. Running slightly scared they nonetheless remain to fight another day. But now you hit them hard with the parable of two sons. 'Truly I tell you, the tax collectors and the prostitutes are going into the kingdom of God ahead of you!'

Emotions were running pretty high that day in the temple. Feel what it was like on the inside.

Thinking

In a fair world deeds must speak louder than words. Yet deeds remain silent until someone has the courage to give them voice.

In a fair world deeds must speak louder than words. Jesus said that a certain father had two sons. To the first of them the father said, 'Son, go and work in the vineyard today.' The son spoke loudly, saying, 'Father, I go immediately according to your word.' But, having spoken, this son forgot his pious promise of obedience and did nothing in the vineyard all day long. Clearly the deeds contradicted the words.

In a fair world deeds must speak louder than words. Jesus said that a certain father had two sons. To the second of them the father said, 'Son, go and work in the vineyard today.' The son spoke loudly, saying, 'Father, I will not go at your beck and call.' But, having spoken, the son forgot his ill-mannered protest of rejection and laboured diligently in the vineyard all day long. Clearly the deeds contradicted the words.

In a fair world deeds must speak louder than words. Thinly disguised in the parable the chief priests and the elders of the people saw themselves and the whole Jewish nation as the son who had accepted so vocally the invitation to work in God's vineyard. Now they hear Jesus accuse them of failing to do as they had promised. Clearly the deeds contradicted the words.

In a fair world deeds must speak louder than words. Thinly disguised in the parable the chief priests and the elders of the people see the tax collectors and the prostitutes and the whole Gentile world as the son who had rejected so vocally the invitation to work in God's vineyard. Now they hear Jesus assure them that those who had once refused God's invitation are now the leading labourers in the kingdom. Clearly the deeds contradicted the words.

In a fair world deeds must speak louder than words. Yet deeds remain silent until someone has the courage to give them voice.

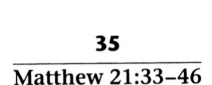

35

Matthew 21:33–46

³³'Listen to another parable. There was a landowner who planted a vineyard, put a fence around it, dug a wine press in it, and built a watch-tower. Then he leased it to tenants and went to another country. ³⁴When the harvest time had come, he sent his slaves to the tenants to collect his produce. ³⁵But the tenants seized his slaves and beat one, killed another, and stoned another. ³⁶Again he sent other slaves, more than the first; and they treated them in the same way. ³⁷Finally he sent his son to them, saying, "They will respect my son." ³⁸But when the tenants saw the son, they said to themselves, "This is the heir; come, let us kill him and get his inheritance." ³⁹So they seized him, threw him out of the vineyard, and killed him. ⁴⁰Now when the owner of the vineyard comes, what will he do to those tenants?' ⁴¹They said to him, 'He will put those wretches to a miserable death, and lease the vineyard to other tenants who will give him the produce at the harvest time.'

⁴²Jesus said to them, 'Have you never read in the scriptures:
　　"The stone that the builders rejected has
　　　　become the cornerstone;
　　this was the Lord's doing, and it is amazing in
　　　　our eyes"?
⁴³Therefore I tell you, the kingdom of God will be taken away from you and given to a people that produces the fruits of the kingdom. ⁴⁴The one who falls on this stone will be broken to pieces; and it will crush anyone on whom it falls.'
⁴⁵When the chief priests and the Pharisees heard his parables, they realized that he was speaking about them. ⁴⁶They wanted to arrest him, but they feared the crowds, because they regarded him as a prophet.

Context

Jesus has entered Jerusalem on Palm Sunday as Messiah and cleansed the temple. The chief priests and elders have challenged his authority. Now in the parable of the vineyard Jesus spells out the implications of their choices.

Sensing

Here is a well-crafted allegory, clearly shaped into four scenes.

In scene one the landowner is putting everything in place. See the landowner busy at work. See him plant a vineyard. See him construct a fence right round the vineyard perimeter. See him dig a wine press to process the grapes. See him build a tall watchtower to protect his property. Surely the vineyard is the world that sustains our life. Surely the landowner is God the creator.

In scene two the landowner has let the vineyard to his chosen tenants and patiently awaits his share of the harvest. See the landowner send his first cohort of messengers, and see each one turned away. One is beaten, one is killed and one is stoned. See the landowner send his second cohort of messengers, and see each one rejected in turn. Surely the tenants are the people of Israel. Surely the first cohort of messengers are the former prophets, from Joshua to Jeremiah. Surely the second cohort of messengers are the latter prophets from Isaiah to Malachi.

In scene three the landowner says to himself, 'I will send my son to them: they will respect my son.' See the son set out from home and arrive at last at the vineyard gate. See how the tenants seize the son. See how they throw him out of the vineyard. See how they kill him stone dead. Surely the son is Jesus himself. Surely the son's murder is the crucifixion that took place outside the city of Jerusalem.

In scene four the landowner reasserts control over the vineyard. See the landowner step in to evict those villainous tenants. See them cast out one by one. Now in their place see different faces, hear different accents. Now in their places find new tenants who will pay their rent to the landowner. Surely the tenants who are cast out are the Jewish people to whom God has entrusted his vineyard. Surely the new tenants are the Gentile disciples of Christ.

Here is a well-crafted allegory, clearly shaped into four scenes.

Intuition

There really are times when God feels just like an absentee landlord. Can you identify with such times in your life?

Those original tenants felt that they had been put in charge of the vineyard and just left there to get on with the job. They felt that they had been offered neither advice nor support. The landowner did not really seem to care.

Those original tenants felt that they would never be called to account. They felt that they could get away with whatever they wanted. The landowner seemed powerless to intervene.

That first cohort of messengers sent by the landowner to collect his share of the produce felt totally vulnerable and unprotected. Some were beaten, some were stoned, and some were killed. The landowner did not really seem to care.

That second cohort of messengers sent by the landowner to collect his share of the produce expected no better treatment than those who had been sent in the first cohort. The landowner seemed powerless to intervene.

The son who was sent by the landowner came knowing fully what to expect. He came knowing that the messengers had been beaten, stoned and killed. The landowner did not really seem to care.

The son who was sent by the landowner came fully resigned to all that awaited him. He came prepared to be seized, to be led outside the city walls, and to be crucified. The landowner seemed powerless to intervene.

There really are times when God feels just like an absentee landlord. Can you identify with such times in your life?

Feeling

Here is a story of supreme trust, a story of divine trust, a story to shape our lives.

The God in whom we believe is a God who trusts us with so much. In trust God planted the vineyard to sustain us. In trust God constructed the fence to protect us. In trust God dug the wine press to nurture us. In trust God built the tall watchtower to remind us of his ever-watchful presence. Here is a story of supreme trust, a story of divine trust, a story to shape our lives.

The God in whom we believe is a God who trusts us with the tenancy of the vineyard. In trust God gives us the responsibility to tend and to shape the vineyard as we will. In trust God leaves us in control to make our moral choices, to shape our destiny and to determine the future of the vineyard. In trust God awaits our loyalty and our service. Here is a story of supreme trust, a story of divine trust, a story to shape our lives.

The God in whom we believe is a God who trusts us with so much revelation about himself. In trust God gives us the succession of the prophets who spoke the divine word to the world. In trust God gives us the divine law of right and wrong. In trust God reveals to us the divine claim on the human heart. Here is a story of supreme trust, a story of divine trust, a story to shape our lives.

The God in whom we believe is a God who trusts us with God's only son. In trust God gives us the son who reveals the divine nature to the world. In trust God gives us the son who walked the way of the cross. In trust God gives us the son who laid down his life that we might live. Here is a story of supreme trust, a story of divine trust, a story to shape our lives.

Thinking

Skilfully placed questions can lay traps and force judgements. Both Jesus and Jesus' adversaries were skilled at that game.

Remember how the Pharisees and the Herodians laid a trap for Jesus when they asked, 'Is it lawful to pay taxes to Caesar, or not?' Jesus saw the skill in their question. One answer would alienate the Roman authorities; the other answer would alienate the Jewish loyalists. Jesus displayed good judgement by throwing the burden of the decision back onto the questioners.

Remember how the Sadducees laid a trap for Jesus when they asked about the woman who had married seven brothers, 'In the resurrection to which of the seven will she be wife?' Jesus saw the skill in their question. Accepted on its own terms any answer to that question makes an absurdity of belief in life after death. Jesus displayed good judgement by revealing how misconceived that question really was.

Remember how the Pharisees laid another trap for Jesus when they asked, 'Teacher, which is the greatest commandment in the law?' Jesus saw the skill in their question. Any direct answer would embroil Jesus in a well-worn Pharisaic debate from which no undisputed conclusion could emerge. Jesus displayed good judgement by citing and drawing together two authoritative texts from scripture concerning the love of God and the love of neighbour.

Now see the tables turned. See how Jesus laid a trap for the chief priests and for the elders of the people when he told them a deceptively simple and attractively seductive tale about a landowner who planted a vineyard. In the story rebellious tenants refused to pay their legal dues to the owner, abused the owner's representatives, and killed the owner's son. Now asked Jesus, 'When the owner of the vineyard comes, what will he do to those tenants?' The chief priests and the elders of the people failed to see the skill in his question. They displayed good judgement in recognizing that the landowner 'would put those wretches to a miserable death, and lease the vineyard to other tenants who will give him the produce of the harvest time'. And in so saying the chief priests and elders of the people stood judged by their own judgement.

Skilfully placed questions can lay traps and force judgements. Both Jesus and Jesus' adversaries were skilled at that game.

36
Matthew 22:1–14

¹Once more Jesus spoke to them in parables, saying: ²'The kingdom of heaven may be compared to a king who gave a wedding banquet for his son. ³He sent his slaves to call those who had been invited to the wedding banquet, but they would not come. ⁴Again he sent other slaves, saying, "Tell those who have been invited: Look, I have prepared my dinner, my oxen and my fat calves have been slaughtered, and everything is ready; come to the wedding banquet." ⁵But they made light of it and went away, one to his farm, another to his business, ⁶while the rest seized his slaves, mistreated them, and killed them. ⁷The king was enraged. He sent his troops, destroyed those murderers, and burned their city. ⁸Then he said to his slaves, "The wedding is ready, but those

invited were not worthy. ⁹Go therefore into the main streets, and invite everyone you find to the wedding banquet." ¹⁰Those slaves went out into the streets and gathered all whom they found, both good and bad; so the wedding hall was filled with guests.

¹¹'But when the king came in to see the guests, he noticed a man there who was not wearing a wedding robe, ¹²and he said to him, "Friend, how did you get in here without a wedding robe?" And he was speechless. ¹³Then the king said to the attendants, "Bind him hand and foot, and throw him into the outer darkness, where there will be weeping and gnashing of teeth." ¹⁴For many are called, but few are chosen.'

Context

Some parables Jesus told were greeted with applause. Some parables were greeted with rumblings of opposition. Matthew includes two parables which both focus on the wedding banquet. They run together, but should be seen as separate. Both tell of harsh words and actions from the 'king'.

Sensing

Your relative is getting married. You are invited to the wedding banquet. Look at the invitation. It does not seem too exciting. You have many things to do and the relative is not that close. Hear yourself composing an apology. 'Sorry, but this is the busiest time of the year on the farm. Sorry, I'm occupied with business. I hope you will not be too disappointed. I hope it is a happy day.' Then the wedding day comes, see all your relatives going off to the feast. How disappointing to miss a good party!

You receive an invitation at the last minute to a family wedding. Look at the card. The opportunity for a party is very exciting, but you are a stranger. You don't know any member of the wedding families. Hear yourself composing your acceptance. 'I cannot think how I deserve this honour. I do not share your race or culture. I appreciate the opportunity. I hope I can be ready. I would love to come.' Then the wedding day comes, and you arrive at the party. Enjoy the heavenly occasion.

You are invited to a wedding banquet. You received your invitation in good time, but you did not pay too much attention to it. You were busy and put it to one side. Today look at your diary and the date. Realize it is the day of the wedding. You have little time to clean up, to put on your best clothes, and to wrap the present. What a shock! You took everything for granted and now have to turn up – unprepared.

Stand waiting for your turn to congratulate the bride and groom. Try to hide your discomfort. Compare yourself with the other guests. They are a mixed bunch, but they have all tried to be at their best. Watch the bride's father approach and look you up and down. Hear him ask why you are so unprepared. Feel your heart sink as you know you have no excuse. You had the invitation. You should have been ready. You know you have missed your opportunity. You turn and leave. Outside the hall listen to the other guests having the time of their lives. This is a hell of a party.

Intuition

The first hearers of Matthew's gospel would listen to these parables and quickly make connections with the Christian story. Is it the same for you?

The invitation to join a wedding feast is like the invitation to enter the kingdom of God. What is your reaction to Christ's invitation to 'Come, follow me'? Do you make light of it? Does it have any priority for you? Does preoccupation with the cares of the world make you put it aside? How do you react?

The invitation to share in a wedding feast is sent out to a wide variety of people, both good and bad. When we accept Christ's invitation, do we expect to share the kingdom with people of many types, many cultures, many races? Are you critical of the backgrounds of many of your fellow Christians? Do you find it difficult to be in the same company as those in the church? How do you react?

To accept a wedding invitation requires preparation, a change to better clothing, and a change of attitude about people. To accept the invitation to enter the kingdom of God requires careful preparation, a change into a better character, and a change of attitude about other people. It is not enough to accept the invitation. You have to change priorities, change loyalties, change behaviour. To enter the kingdom of God you have to let the Holy Spirit change you into a new person. When you hear that part of the message, how do you react?

To find yourself outside a wedding party when you want to be inside makes you all bound up. The ache is painful and the contrasts deeply felt. To find yourself outside the kingdom of God when you want to be inside makes you all bound up. The ache is painful and the contrasts deeply felt. The opportunity to share life and joy has been missed. The terror of 'if only' is haunting. Darkness descends. How do you react?

The parable is about weddings, but you can see all too well the connection with God's kingdom.

Feeling

When you hear these stories told, you will have feelings of sympathy and feelings of confusion.

You feel for the king who gave the wedding feast for his son. It is hard when people do not want to join in a happy occasion. You feel rejected. You feel people should be ready to honour your generosity. You feel people should be glad to celebrate this beginning of new life. It is easy to feel sympathy for the king.

You feel for the servants of the king. They went out to issue a positive invitation to a wedding and people responded, 'Shoot the messenger!' These servants were mistreated and murdered. People had no right to react like this to good news. You feel sympathy for the servants of the king.

You feel for the citizens of the city where the troops of the king caused such havoc and burning. Surely all citizens do not deserve such a fate just because some people took the law into their own hands and destroyed the servants. You feel sympathy for the citizens of the city.

You feel happy for the last-minute invitees to the wedding. They were able to join in the fun, to celebrate new life, and to share the joy of the father. You feel delighted for the positive response of this varied group of people. You would like to be one of them!

You feel horrified at the offhand way one person accepted the invitation to the wedding. You feel horrified that people could be so casual, so insensitive, so ready to take without giving back in return. What a way to behave!

You feel confused at the harsh actions of the king. Fancy sending the army to destroy the city, even if it did contain some murderers. Fancy ordering such cruel treatment for the guest who could not be bothered to wear clean clothes for a wedding. What a way to behave!

Our feelings tell us much about the value we give to the kingdom of God. They remind us to grasp the opportunities for participation, and to weigh up the consequences of our actions.

Thinking

These parables, as told in Matthew's gospel, are allegories, stories used to illustrate events that happened in history. People would translate these symbols into reality. They were well aware of the inclusion of the Gentiles in the church, the destruction of Jerusalem by the Roman army, and the new character required of Christian converts.

The symbol of the wedding feast was known to represent the final judgement and joy of God. God issued the invitation to the 'chosen' to enter the kingdom. The religious leaders and ordinary people of Israel declined the invitation of the prophets, the first messengers. The old Israel failed to respond because people were too occupied with worldly things. Then God sent John the Baptist and Jesus to issue a new invitation. The secular and religious leaders and the people mistreated them and killed them both. The destruction of Jerusalem in AD 70 was seen as a punishment from God for such murderous rejection. God widened the invitation to the kingdom to people of other cultures, other races, both the good and the bad (like tax collectors and sinners). The Gentiles and all kinds of sinners saw their need for the gospel and joined the fellowship of the church.

These were the facts. The first story was another way of telling how different people in history reacted to the gospel's invitation.

The second story shows that the response to the gospel requires more than a nod and an easy come, easy go, gesture. It requires action and change. The readers would know of the power of the Holy Spirit to give them a new robe at baptism. The church taught that those who respond to the gospel must clothe themselves with compassion, kindness and humility. These are the facts, everyone knew that.

The first story includes 'punishment' for shameful action. The second story also concludes with 'punishment' for a shameful action. The facts show that there is judgement. If joy is not accepted, then anguish will be the lot we choose. On reflection it is not hard to see how facts and truth can be told in story form.

37
Matthew 22:15–22

¹⁵Then the Pharisees went and plotted to entrap him in what he said. ¹⁶So they sent their disciples to him, along with the Herodians, saying, 'Teacher, we know that you are sincere, and teach the way of God in accordance with truth, and show deference to no one; for you do not regard people with partiality. ¹⁷Tell us, then, what you think. Is it lawful to pay taxes to the emperor, or not?' ¹⁸But Jesus, aware of their malice, said, 'Why are you putting me to the test, you hypocrites? ¹⁹Show me the coin used for the tax.' And they brought him a denarius. ²⁰Then he said to them, 'Whose head is this, and whose title?' ²¹They answered, 'The emperor's.' Then he said to them, 'Give therefore to the emperor the things that are the emperor's, and to God the things that are God's.' ²²When they heard this, they were amazed; and they left him and went away.

Context

This passage begins a new series of controversies between Jesus and his opponents. The Pharisees and Herodians had contrary views about paying taxes but combined to put a trick question to Jesus. His answer pointed to much deeper issues concerning the meaning of loyalty and duty.

Sensing

Pharisees and Herodians, who held many opposing views, combined against Jesus as their common enemy.

You are a person of high moral integrity. Stand and be a Pharisee facing Jesus. Hear people admire you as the super-religious group in your society. You keep yourself apart from common trading. You believe that God will restore the kingdom to Israel. You shun the Roman authorities, whose taxes are seen as a symbol of tyranny over the land whose people should give loyalty to God alone. As a Pharisee recall how Jesus has named you a hypocrite, whose outward show hides inner corruption. He has called you whitewashed graves. Look at your proper clothing. It is as the law requires, but Jesus flouts God's law. See what ammunition you can find to have Jesus condemned by both the religious and civil authorities. Ask Jesus this trick question, 'Is it lawful to pay taxes to the emperor or not?' You seek for a weapon, not wisdom.

You are a practical person. Stand and be an Herodian facing Jesus. Hear people admire you as the cleverest business members of the community. You believe it is best to be involved in society. You collaborate with the Roman authorities. You seek their trust and their trade. You know how to wheel and deal in taxes. Count your blessings, it is a profitable business. Taxes are essential for the maintenance of good government, providing all the benefits of civilization. You tell others that paying taxes is a debt every citizen owes society. Stand and be an Herodian facing Jesus. Hear most people label you dishonest and disloyal, but Jesus has gathered some former tax collectors among his disciples. They have made substantial restoration to show their repentance. Jesus is a challenge to you. He condemns those who trust in riches. You want him destroyed so you can continue in your comfortable life. Ask Jesus the trick question, 'Is it lawful to pay taxes to the emperor or not?' You seek for a weapon, not wisdom.

Hear Jesus' answer, 'You have a duty to the emperor, and to God. Fulfil your obligations to both.' Both sides have to acknowledge the other's contribution. Your weapon has boomeranged back to you!

Intuition

Taxes, what is your attitude to paying taxes?

Do you see it as a burden which you try to avoid at all costs? Is it a symbol of civil compulsion which makes you angry? Is it a sign of the hold society has over your purse? Is it a duty you reluctantly perform if you cannot find a way out? Do you consider that the state has no right to your money? What is your attitude to paying taxes?

Do you see it as a proper contribution to the welfare of

society? Is it a symbol of your involvement in the improvements in society: health, education, research and communication? Is it the sign of your share in maintaining law and order? Is it one of the ways you express your love of neighbour? Is it a duty you gladly perform, giving you the motivation to declare your full income so that you can carry your full share of the community's responsibility?

Religious obligation, what is your attitude to fulfilling your religious obligation?

Do you see it as a burden which you try to avoid at all costs? Is it a symbol of divine compulsion which makes you rebel? Is it a sign of the hold that the church has over your time and your money? Is it a duty you reluctantly perform if you cannot find a good excuse? What is your attitude to fulfilling your religious obligation?

Do you see it as your willing response to your commitment to God and the church? Is it a symbol of your involvement in the growth of Christian society: reformed character, deeds of compassion and development of soul? Is it a sign of your share in maintaining the mission of the gospel? Is it a duty you joyfully perform so that your prayers, witness and deeds give you the motivation to carry out your religious obligations?

You can see how closely connected the attitudes to fulfilling our civil and religious duties ought to be. How do you fulfil your duty to the state and to God?

Feeling

None of us likes having to answer trick questions. Share Jesus' feelings as he finds himself subject to 'a hunting snare' in this situation. Admire his ability to leap over the top and plumb the depths of the issue. See him turning the negative attitudes into positive teaching on values.

Jesus had tried to change the hearts of those in the Pharisee party by challenging them to look at inner motives and not just outward purity. He had tried. Some no doubt responded. Others hardened their hearts. But he had tried. Now the attempt had backfired, and they were scheming to assemble evidence to condemn him. But religious people should respond to love. Share Jesus' feelings of exasperation.

Jesus had tried to change the hearts of those in the Herodian party by challenging their dishonesty, and their excuses about

accepting their religious duties. He had warned them about attach-
ment to riches. He had tried. Some had responded. Others had
tightened their pockets. But he had tried. Now the attempt had
backfired, and they were scheming to assemble evidence to condemn him. But people should use their wealth to show practical
love for their neighbours. Share Jesus' feelings of exasperation.

Share Jesus' feelings as he tries to point out that both points
of view at their best are essential for Christians. Jesus, though he
is frustrated, is pleased to see two groups with such views united
even through their negative feelings towards him. Feel with Jesus
as he longs to bring them together in positive ways. If only he
could make them relate to one another, both could contribute
their different emphasis. Duty to God includes our duty to our
neighbour. Duty to neighbour is part of our duty to God. There
is value in paying taxes to maintain the fabric of society. There is
equal value in fulfilling our duty to God to maintain the fabric of
society.

Both require wisdom and will, mind and emotion. Share
Christ's warning that taxes without divine compassion are cold
comfort. Share Christ's warning that prayers without taxes and
gifts are warm fuzzies. Share Christ's longing that the kingdom
of God might be made visible on earth.

Thinking

In most archaeological museums you can see a range of coins
uncovered from the earth. In the Roman collection the round
coin bears the portrait of the emperor of the times and an
inscription round the edge declares his name. This is often
abbreviated to allow room for the full title. When Jesus asked for
a coin to be brought forth so that he could show it to the crowd
it would have had the portrait of Tiberius on it. This emperor
held authority between AD 14 and 37. The inscription around the
rim in museum examples is worded, 'Ti [for Tiberius] Caesar Divi
Aug [for Augusti] F [for Filius] Augustus'. The titles used
demanded respect and obedience. This Tiberius, like all the earlier
Caesars, held the power of the emperor. This Tiberius claimed
almighty divinity. This Tiberius was the true son and successor of
the honoured Caesar Augustus. This emperor claimed divine right
and filial succession.

The readers of Matthew's gospel knew the titles used for Jesus
in the early church. Jesus was proclaimed Lord (a title for the

emperor), and Son of God. These titles demanded respect and obedience. The church claimed for Jesus divine right and filial succession from his heavenly Father. There was good reason for Luke and Matthew to record this incident that they found in Mark's gospel. It gave clear guidance on the principles by which Christians should live in any society. They had both civil and religious duties. They must honour both obligations. Yet it was always a struggle to know how to do this.

The principle was clear, but the application had to be worked out under the guidance of the Holy Spirit for each different situation. Jesus, by the symbolic gesture, teaches that there must be no false dichotomy between duty to God and duty to the state. Civil obligations must not be made an excuse for failing to fulfil religious obligations. Religious obligations must not be made an excuse for failing to fulfil civil obligations. Christians still have to struggle to hold these obligations together. We cannot walk away from either. Each contributes to the other.

38
Matthew 22:34–46

³⁴When the Pharisees heard that he had silenced the Sadducees, they gathered together, ³⁵and one of them, a lawyer, asked him a question to test him. ³⁶'Teacher, which commandment in the law is the greatest?' ³⁷He said to him, ' "You shall love the Lord your God with all your heart, and with all your soul, and with all your mind." ³⁸This is the greatest and first commandment. ³⁹And a second is like it: "You shall love your neighbor as yourself." ⁴⁰On these two commandments hang all the law and the prophets.'

⁴¹Now while the Pharisees were gathered together, Jesus asked them this question: ⁴²'What do you think of the Messiah? Whose son is he?' They said to him, 'The son of David.' ⁴³He said to them, 'How is it then that David by the Spirit calls him Lord, saying,

⁴⁴"The Lord said to my Lord,
      'Sit at my right hand,
      until I put your enemies under your feet' "?
⁴⁵If David thus calls him Lord, how can he be his son?' ⁴⁶No
one was able to give him an answer, nor from that day did
anyone dare to ask him any more questions.

Context

This is the last of a series of questions and answers in which Jesus
shows his superiority. He answers in turn questions from various
religious groups. In his final answer he summarizes the commandments and points to the lordship of the Messiah. All further
questions are silenced by his words.

Sensing

Many rabbis were asked to give a short memorable summary of
religious duties. We all want to know what we ought to do to
serve God. Join those who question Jesus. Enter into the debate
with this rabbi. He does not fit any of the religious labels. He
talks about life after death, so he cannot be a Sadducee. He has
attacked the Herodians. He has slandered the Pharisees. You can
see that his teaching reaches beyond all current theories and
practices in a profound way. Enter the debate and test Jesus'
ability and credibility. Push through the crowd of those around
Jesus and ask, 'Teacher, which commandment in the law is the
greatest?' Watch the ears of the crowd strain to catch his reply.

Hear yourself run through the possibilities for his answer.
What about, 'Do not murder'? If looks could kill, the Sadducees
would have him dead. If whispers could destroy, the tax collec-
tors would have their swords in him. If the holy prayers of the
Pharisees were answered, he would be struck down by lightning.
Jesus might well reply, 'Do not murder.'

Hear yourself run through the possibilities for his answer.
What about, 'Do not bear false witness'? If lies could kill, the
scribes and priests would trump up a charge to get rid of him
tomorrow. If words could be twisted, they would have him tried
for blasphemy. Jesus might well reply, 'Do not bear false witness.'

Listen in admiration to Jesus' reply, 'By your love of God and
your love of neighbour you will fulfil all the law and the demands
of the prophets.' What a challenge he has given. As a holy person

you are dedicated to your religious duties: your regular devotion to God, and your regular duty of charity to others. Jesus has spoken wisely. He has resisted all temptation to strike back at people. Instead, he has called for loyalty to God; so do you. Instead he has called for love of neighbour; so do you. Put like that there are no further questions that can be asked, only decisions to be made.

Intuition

Genealogy is a very popular pastime. We know it is important for us to have roots. We want to discover our ancestry. We like to be in touch with the past so that we can establish the present. Jesus' question, 'Whose son is he?' raises many issues.

We all ask, 'Who am I?' We find the answer both in our inner selves and in our outward circumstances. The attitude 'the person who knows me best is myself' is balanced by the statement 'I need others to reflect back to me who I am for them.' In Matthew's gospel Jesus reveals his inner experience of being God's son. It also tells us of Peter's affirmation to Jesus, 'You are the Christ, the Son of the living God.'

We also ask, 'From whom am I descended?' We want to know what combination of genes contributes to who I am. People had asked Jesus about his family. Here Jesus asks others about himself, 'The Messiah, whose son is he?' Must the Messiah be of the right line? Because of Joseph must he be of the House of David? Does what you have to say depend on your genealogy? That question by Jesus raises issues for us as well.

There is human genealogy and there is divine genealogy. Is one's divine calling more important than one's human lineage? 'If David calls him Lord, how can he be his son?' That question raises this further issue, 'Is my character shaped more by my relationship to God than by my relationship with my family and my ancestors?' For many Christians baptism creates a new person, a new relationship with God, and a new family of fellow Christians. To be a child of God defines my character even more than being a child of my human parents. Jesus by his question declares that he knows that to be the Son of God is even more important than to know he is the son of David. Divine genealogy takes precedence over human genealogy.

When Jesus talks about his genealogy what connections do you make with your own life?

Feeling

Questions and answers are often more about feelings than facts. People can ask questions to open or close relationships. People can give answers which open or close relationships. You can easily relate to that.

The lawyer's question is said to be a 'test' question. We cannot tell if his purpose behind the question was to know Jesus better or to see him exposed as a false teacher. He could have wanted to display his superior knowledge, and be seen to give his nod of approval. We need to know his feelings to see his motivation. Yet Jesus' answer has inspired Christians for generations. It has featured in the liturgy of many churches. It has highlighted the place of emotion as a stimulus to better conduct. Our actions, says Jesus, come from the heart as well as the mind. Love has become a key word in the Christian vocabulary. These verses lie at the core of much ethical teaching. The answer highlights relationship as vital to human living. Our relationship with God inspires our relationship with our neighbour. You can relate to that.

Feel for the lawyer as he hears Jesus' answer. It challenged his own conduct. As a Pharisee he was well versed in the law and the prophets. He knew key passages by heart, but did these ever touch his heart? His relationship with God should have been based on a relationship of the soul, not on knowledge of the mind. Jesus' answer shows that heart and mind and soul must together love God. You can relate to that.

Feel for the lawyer as he hears Jesus' answer. He knew well his duty to his neighbour. He was instructed on how to care for the poor and needy. But was the motivation duty or compassion? Did the heart follow the purse? To love one's neighbour means putting yourself there for that person, not just sending a cheque. You can relate to that.

Feel for the lawyer as he hears Jesus' answer. It calls for a decision about whom you value and how you will act out of love. You too can act on that.

Thinking

The reference to the Psalms by Jesus in verses 43–45 raises some issues for contemporary scholars.

First, it is now clear from textual comparisons that the Psalms are a collection of religious songs from a number of periods in the history of Israel. Some may have originated in the work of King David, but not all psalms can be attributed to him.

Second, could David in Psalm 110 be 'speaking in the spirit' in such a way that he intended to prophesy about a future Messiah? This kingship psalm may well have referred to the current ruler of God's chosen people, who with divine right accepts the place of honour while the enemies of Israel are defeated.

Third, what is the likely connection between 'my Lord' in the psalm and Jesus? Jesus has not referred to himself as 'Lord' in this dialogue.

What we do know from the New Testament is that Psalm 110 was used as a text to illustrate the lordship of Christ and his exaltation (see 1 Corinthians 15:25). It was seen as a way of explaining why the return of Christ was delayed. Jesus was exalted as Lord but, for this to be complete, the enemies of the gospel must be overcome. This psalm became a 'Messianic text'. Jesus may have been the one who first made the connection between himself and Psalm 110, or this passage may be based on teaching current in the early church in the time when Matthew wrote his gospel.

What Matthew wants to show by this section is that the Pharisees may have been expert interpreters of scripture, but that Jesus was superior in every respect. Jesus has the ability to sum up the law and the prophets in a dynamic way. He has deeper insight into the relationship between God and the Messiah. He was the Son of God whose divine wisdom showed in his teaching about scripture. When we think about it the one 'inspired by the Spirit' is Jesus rather than David. His teaching about the commandments focuses for us the will of God, and as we are obedient to it we acknowledge Jesus as Lord. Matthew's message is clear.

39

Matthew 24:1–14

[1]As Jesus came out of the temple and was going away, his disciples came to point out to him the buildings of the temple. [2]Then he asked them, 'You see all these, do you not? Truly I tell you, not one stone will be left here upon another; all will be thrown down.'

[3]When he was sitting on the Mount of Olives, the disciples came to him privately, saying, 'Tell us, when will this be, and what will be the sign of your coming and of the end of the age?' [4]Jesus answered them, 'Beware that no one leads you astray. [5]For many will come in my name, saying, "I am the Messiah!" and they will lead many astray. [6]And you will hear of wars and rumours of wars; see that you are not alarmed; for this must take place, but the end is not yet. [7]For nation will rise against nation, and kingdom against kingdom, and there will be famines and earthquakes in various places: [8]all this is but the beginning of the birth pangs.

[9]'Then they will hand you over to be tortured and will put you to death, and you will be hated by all nations because of my name. [10]Then many will fall away, and they will betray one another and hate one another. [11]And many false prophets will arise and lead many astray. [12]And because of the increase of lawlessness, the love of many will grow cold. [13]But the one who endures to the end will be saved. [14]And this good news of the kingdom will be proclaimed throughout the world, as a testimony to all the nations; and then the end will come.'

Context

Matthew includes a section of teaching on 'the last days'. The Messiah came to usher in a new age. For some this meant the destruction of the 'old age' and the obvious rule of the kingdom of God. Matthew gives instruction on how to act in these 'end times'.

Sensing

Josephus, a Jewish historian writing for the Roman authorities in the first century AD, describes the magnificence of the temple rebuilt by Herod (*Antiquities* xv, 11). The temple in Jerusalem during Jesus' time was much admired, yet it was the cause of much heartache. A glorious temple should have been the sign of God's faithful protection against the enemy. Stand on the Mount of Olives opposite the temple plateau and admire its glory. Long for God's triumph over evil. Such glory must signify God's presence.

In AD 70 this temple was destroyed by the Roman army. Constant rebellion and riots caused the foreign power to exercise its might and remove this symbol of rival loyalty and defiant opposition. Christians believed that God was right to allow this destruction because the chosen people had rejected and murdered the Messiah. They believed that Jesus had prophesied such destruction. Stand on the Mount of Olives opposite the temple plateau and marvel at the pile of stones lying in a heap around the foundation wall. Such destruction must signify God's displeasure.

Sit with Jesus on the slope of the Mount of Olives and listen to his warning, 'Beware that no one leads you astray.' Sense the confusion in your mind as you keep asking, 'Why should people want to mislead us? Why should people want to take the Messiah's place and misrepresent God's will and purpose? Why should there be so much turmoil in the world if God is in charge?' Surely for those who love God and neighbour all things should work together for good. Wrestle with your confusion.

Sit with Jesus on the slope of the Mount of Olives and listen to his encouragement, 'The one who endures to the end will be saved.' Faithfulness, endurance and ongoing love will be the qualities of true discipleship. Jesus showed these qualities as he approached his end on a cross. His disciples must show the same qualities as they take the good news to all peoples. Only then will the purpose of God be complete. We must endure the birth pangs for the new world to be born. We are all called to act as midwives for the birth of the kingdom.

Intuition

Consider a pile of stones lying in a heap. Let such stones speak to you. Such stones can be a symbol of what has been cast down or cast away.

Much in our society looks like stones that have been cast down or cast away. The fabric of settled relationships has been largely broken. Many families are in ruins. Many principles have been cast away. Law and order is violated by armed groups who rob and threaten and sometimes kill. Respect for the wisdom of elders is discarded for the latest fad. Stones can stand for society in ruins.

Much in our religion looks like stones that have been cast down or cast away. A number of Christian churches have been sold as secular buildings. Museums replace sanctuaries. Gathering places of the faithful are turned into cafés. Religious certainties have been cast away. Corporate creeds have been replaced by individual experience. The scriptures are fragmented into favourite verses. Prayer becomes a personal conversation with God rather than a joining of wills with the divine will in Christ. Stones can stand for abandoned faith.

Consider a pile of stones lying in a heap. Let such stones speak to you. Such stones can be a symbol of promise. They lie waiting to be rebuilt, the building blocks for the future.

Many in society long for firm foundations to be rebuilt. People are coming together to restore respected standards of honesty and truth, care and protection of one another. They cry, 'Enough is enough'; they form neighbourhood watch schemes; they link arms for peace; they seek reconciliation of the racial divide. They bridge the gap between the generations. Stones can stand for the building blocks of the future.

Many in the church long for firm foundations to be rebuilt. Regretting the breakdown of faith, with repentance they look for restoration. They gather in schools and homes to sing songs of worship and plumb the depths of the message of scripture hope. They open their churches to messengers of new life from other continents. They agonize in prayer and face with reality the sufferings of life, drawing on God's courage and strength. Stones can stand for the building blocks of the future.

Consider a pile of stones lying in a heap. Let the symbol of stones speak to you.

Feeling

Feel sympathy for those early Christians who were members of the church family in the first century. They were full of energy and excitement after the resurrection and the gift of the Holy Spirit. The good news of the kingdom seemed to be good indeed. They had a new faith in God's victory over death. They had a new family in their Christian brothers and sisters. They had a new freedom from the guilt of sin and the powers of darkness. They had a new future full of hope and expansion. Empathize with their energy and excitement.

But those early Christians had to face many trials. The world of their day was in turmoil. Rebellion was common and led to repression. Soldiers were trained to kill. Civil rights were possessed by few. The voices of the religious clamoured for attention and power. Natural disasters were common in the form of famine, fire and earthquake. Christians were picked on for being 'different', under suspicion of causing the gods to be angry. Christians faced many trials and were subject to many 'crosses'. Empathize with their painful sufferings.

Christ made two calls on his followers: to endure to the end, and to proclaim the good news of the kingdom throughout the world. Identify with the feelings of the early Christians as they responded to the call. *Endurance* is a gift of the heart inspired by the Holy Spirit. It is a mixture of courage and faithfulness, assurance and determination. Pray for the gift of endurance. *Proclamation* is the gift of the Spirit born out of experience. We share with others what we have ourselves received. In Christ there is a new beginning. In Christ there will be a true end, when the evil in us and in the world will be overthrown by goodness and love, when all are gathered into the unity of Christ's love and purpose. Pray for the gift of proclamation.

Let your sympathy for the first Christians inspire your faith in God for the future and your commitment, through many trials, to proclaim the Lord's death until he comes.

Thinking

This passage again raises the dilemma that Jesus and the early church seemed to believe, and stated very clearly, that the 'end of the age' was imminent. We have to ask ourselves whether they were proved wrong, and, if so, does this mean that their teaching about life was distorted.

Readers of Matthew's gospel knew that in a number of ways the end *had* come. The gift of the Spirit at Pentecost had ushered in a new era. Those baptized saw themselves as having passed from death to life. They were 'new' creatures, and the 'old' humanity had passed away. The Spirit's presence and power was their assurance of that fact in their lives.

Readers also knew that the temple had been destroyed in AD 70. What Jesus had indicated had come true. Jesus foresaw that the stubbornness of the religious leaders of his day would eventually lead to a rebellion in which they would clash directly with the might of Rome; and Rome would win. God's chosen needed a new focus for God's presence, not in the temple's stones but in hearts touched with God's love.

The readers also knew that there was a famine in the area in the middle 40s. There was a series of earthquakes in the early 60s. They knew about false prophets and many wars. All this had happened since the words of Jesus.

So what was meant by the 'end'? This was the Day of Judgement by God when all evil would be wiped out and all good treasured. This was the Day of Revelation when Christ would come in glory to possess the earth. This was the Day of New Creation when harmony in all things would be restored. What the early church discovered was that such a day came as men and women received and applied the gospel, but the gospel was still rejected by some. A final day had yet to come. We too live in such 'between times'. The new has arrived but the old is not totally destroyed. In such times we must live in the spirit of a love which 'bears all things, believes all things, hopes all things, endures all things' (1 Corinthians 13:7).

40

Matthew 24:30–35

[30]'Then the sign of the Son of Man will appear in heaven, and then all the tribes of the earth will mourn, and they will see "the Son of Man coming on the clouds of heaven" with power and great glory. [31]And he will send out his angels with a loud trumpet call, and they will gather his elect from the four winds, from one end of heaven to the other.

[32]'From the fig tree learn its lesson: as soon as its branch becomes tender and puts forth its leaves, you know that summer is near. [33]So also, when you see all these things, you know that he is near, at the very gates. [34]Truly I tell you, this generation will not pass away until all these things have taken place. [35]Heaven and earth will pass away, but my words will not pass away.'

Context

Searching for language for the 'mystery' of the triumphant return of God's representative, Matthew draws on three key passages in the First Testament, found in Daniel, Zechariah and Isaiah. A correct interpretation of scripture illuminates the present and the future, for its words do not pass away.

Sensing

A fig tree in Palestine is one of the few trees that loses its leaves in winter. Many others are evergreens, giving no sign of the changing seasons.

Stand in front of the fig tree. Examine its bare branches. All seem dead. There are no buds, no leaves. Feel the chill of the wind from the northern snows. In the sky see the storm clouds race overhead. Look over to the fields, they are brown and bare. There are no signs of life anywhere.

Stand in front of the fig tree. Examine its branches. The buds have swelled at the tips and the first leaves have pushed through. Feel the warmth of the south wind. In the sky see the clouds racing away to reveal the blue of summer. Look over to the fields, green with the first shoots of corn. There are signs of new life everywhere.

Stand in front of the fig tree. Read its signs. Buds and leaves give a promise of the harvest to come. Let your mouth water at the foretaste of future sweetness of ripe figs. See friends gathered around to share the summer feast. Read the signs of the fig tree in bud. Here is the promise of summer and harvest thanksgiving.

Stand in front of the fig tree. Read its signs. This tree has been here for generations. Each summer its buds turn to flowers and flowers into fruit. This tree has sweetened the lives of your forebears. This tree will give food and succour to your children. Read the sign of the fig tree. Here is the promise of the past. Here is the hope for the future.

Stand in front of the fig tree. Read its signs. Experience tells you when the fruit is ready for picking. Experience tells you how to preserve its fruit. Here is sustenance for those who know its secrets.

Stand in front of the bible. Touch its cover. Closed, it is lifeless and entombed. Touch its cover. Open, it reveals its message of new life. Read its words, giving thanks for its harvest of treasures, its hope for the future, and its sustenance in times of need.

Intuition

Signs, this passage is all about signs. It is not hard to see the connection between signs and what is signified.

Take the sign of clouds. What do clouds suggest to you? Clouds race across the sky, stretching between heaven and earth. Misty clouds envelop the mountain tops and give them a mysterious awe which fills us with respect. Clouds gather to themselves the power of nature, producing lightning and thunder. From their strength comes the rain, the source of new life for the plants and animals of the earth. Clouds are caught by the wind and are chased away to reveal the blue sky and the sun. The sign of the clouds; how do clouds suggest to you the revelation of God in the Son and the Spirit?

Take the sign of the angels. What do angels suggest to you? Angels are the messengers of God who tell forth great events. They are the voice of God; they are the wings of God's protection; they are the hands of God's activity. Angels fill the pages of God's holy scriptures. The sign of the angels; how do angels suggest to you the revelation of God in the Son and the Spirit?

Take the sign of the trumpet. What does a trumpet suggest to you? Trumpets sound to wake the sleeping, to rouse the slothful, to break the silence of boredom. Trumpets sound to herald the significant, to open our ears to the messenger's words, to prompt us to proclaim great events and good news. Trumpets sound to acknowledge the king, to claim our respect for those in authority, to gladden the hearts of those who wait for the victory of peace. The sign of the trumpet; how do trumpets suggest to you the revelation of God in the Son and the Spirit?

When you read in the bible of clouds, angels and trumpets, let such symbols speak to you of God's presence on earth, of God's messages of good news, of God's victory of unity and peace.

Feeling

Take a note of your feelings when you read the bible. You may experience elation or deflation, excitement or fear. You may have a sense of eager expectation or of bored resignation when you turn the pages of the bible. Sometimes you may feel the text is far too confusing because you feel that you have lost the key to its interpretation.

Our feelings are so important for us when we handle the bible. They either help us to open our ears to its message, or to shut out its truth from our minds. Unless our feelings are in the right place we will never be able to use the bible as God's communication to us.

If our feelings are negative because our previous experience is that the bible is irrelevant or too obscure, then our future reading will be prejudiced and its outcome predetermined. Before we can profit from our reading we will have to change any negative feelings.

If our feelings are positive because the words of scripture have opened windows into God's nature and purpose for us and our world, then we will always be ready to read on and search at greater depth. We will feel good about the bible and our memories will retain the phrases so the words do not pass away.

It is important that we create right feelings towards the bible. Let your positive feelings be affirmed by those who find the scriptures a source of rich inspiration for their lives and devotion. Treasure your own positive experiences of a biblical passage and build on these. Trust in Christ's promises, recorded in the gospels, that the Holy Spirit will help us discover the truth. Approach the words in the bible fully trusting that they had meaning for those who wrote them and those who first heard them. Share their confidence that these words and actions had meaning for their lives.

When scripture says, 'Truly, I tell you' feel in your heart that this word is trustworthy. Let it help you to develop a relationship with God and with your neighbour. Let it help you develop those values worth holding in life. Open your heart to this truth and approach the word with eager anticipation.

Thinking

Any description of the final appearance of the Messiah must be in symbolic language. It is impossible to find any other sort of words for an event which transcends the experience of this world and ushers in a new concept of reality. In scripture there are many attempts to find the right symbolic language, and one generation borrows from another.

Many of the phrases in verses 30 and 31 can be found in the later prophets of Israel. In verse 30 the title 'Son of Man' is a phrase from Daniel 7:13-14. There it is given to the representative of faithful humanity. On presentation to 'the Ancient One' he is given earthly authority over all peoples. In verse 30 the 'mourning of the peoples of the earth' is taken from Zechariah 12:10 where the inhabitants of Jerusalem show dismay at seeing the one whom they had pierced. In verse 31 the symbol of the trumpet call comes from Isaiah 27:13 where it is used to signify the beginning of the final judgement.

We in turn borrow words of scripture to provide the appropriate language for an event or attitude which we experience. We speak of a person acting 'like a good Samaritan', of giving someone 'a cup of cold water', of a 'lost sheep', of 'washing your hands of an affair', of being a 'Judas', of a 'kingdom divided against itself'. The knowledge of the scriptures gives us a 'common language' to share experiences or comment on the actions of others.

The loss of such common language because the reading of the bible is unfamiliar to a growing number of people is of serious detriment to any society. By using the biblical language people can share experiences with common understanding and identification. The bible is still a 'best seller' in many lands, but its reading is now mostly limited to committed Christians. One of our opportunities for evangelism is to help people read the 'signs of the times' in the light of scripture's values. The Day of Judgement is every day for the advancement of the kingdom of God. Scripture helps us make that choice with understanding.

How do you think Christians can make certain that the bible's words do not pass away?

41

Matthew 24:36–44

[36]'But about that day and hour no one knows, neither the angels of heaven, nor the Son, but only the Father. [37]For as the days of Noah were, so will be the coming of the Son of Man. [38]For as in those days before the flood they were eating and drinking, marrying and giving in marriage, until the day Noah entered the ark, [39]and they knew nothing until the flood came and swept them all away, so too will be the coming of the Son of Man. [40]Then two will be in the field; one will be taken and one will be left. [41]Two women will be grinding meal together; one will be taken and one will be left. [42]Keep awake therefore, for you do not know on what day your Lord is coming. [43]But understand this: if the owner of the house had known in what part of the night the thief was coming, he would have stayed awake and would not have let his house be broken into. [44]Therefore you also must be ready, for the Son of Man is coming at an unexpected hour.'

Context

Very early on in chapter 24 the disciples came to ask Jesus privately about when the last days would come. The present passage continues Jesus' answer.

Sensing

A lot can be learned from the old story of Noah.

Picture just how ordinary everything was the day the rain began to fall. See the women going about their daily business in the kitchen. Smell the delicious newly baked bread. Hear the stew boiling on the stove. Touch their cooking utensils. There was no reason for the women to expect that anything extraordinary was about to happen. A lot can be learned from the old story of Noah about the need to be prepared.

Picture just how ordinary everything was the day the rain began to fall. See the men going about their daily business in the fields. Smell the newly dug soil. Hear the hammering in their workshops. Touch the tools of their trade. There was no reason for the men to expect that anything extraordinary was about to happen. A lot can be learned from the old story of Noah about the need to be prepared.

Picture just how ordinary everything was the day the rain began to fall. See the children playing in the courtyards. Hear the noisy chatter of their games. Touch the toys that clutter the floor. There was no reason for the children to expect that anything extraordinary was about to happen. A lot can be learned from the old story of Noah about the need to be prepared.

Picture just how ordinary everything was the day the rain began to fall. See the animals grazing on the pasture. Hear the sheep bleating across the meadow. Touch the goats huddling by the hedge. There was no reason for the animals to expect that anything extraordinary was about to happen. A lot can be learned from the old story of Noah about the need to be prepared.

Now picture Jesus preparing the disciples for the last days. Hear Jesus say to them, 'Keep awake, for you do not know on what day your Lord is coming. For as the days of Noah were, so will be the coming of the Son of Man.' Yes, indeed, a lot can be learned from the old story of Noah.

Intuition

It is always unnerving to be taken by surprise.

Consider the motorist who knows that it is illegal to exceed the speed limit. Day in and day out that motorist travels just a little faster than he should, confident that the police have better things to do than to monitor his stretch of road. Now today the speed trap is set, the motorist is caught and the fine is imposed. It is always unnerving to be taken by surprise. Jesus said, 'Keep awake, for you do not know on what day your Lord is coming.'

Consider the traveller who knows that it is illegal to evade customs duty. Year in and year out that traveller walks unchallenged through customs check, confident that her honest face makes her an unlikely suspect. Now today the spot check takes place, the traveller is caught and the charge is made. It is always unnerving to be taken by surprise. Jesus said, 'Keep awake, for you do not know on what day your Lord is coming.'

Consider the playground bully who knows that it is against the rules to threaten fellow pupils at break time. Week in and week out that playground bully inflicts pain and instils fear, confident that the teachers have better things to do than to patrol the school perimeters. Now today the invigilation is in place, the playground bully is caught and the reprimand is delivered. It is always unnerving to be taken by surprise. Jesus said, 'Keep awake, for you do not know on what day your Lord is coming.'

Consider the workman who knows that it is against company policy not to wear protective goggles when using certain tools. Day in and day out the workman saves time by failing to put the goggles on, confident that nothing can go wrong with such a simple operation. Now today the tool slips, the sparks fly and the workman's eye is damaged. It is always unnerving to be taken by surprise. Jesus said, 'Keep awake, for you do not know on what day your Lord is coming.'

So just how seriously do you take your Lord's advice?

Feeling

Put yourself in the shoes of the burgled house owner. Feel what it is like to be the victim of crime.

Come downstairs in the morning and shiver as the chill breeze blows through the broken window. Feel your heart sink as you see the curtains torn apart, the mud-stained carpet and the ransacked room. If only you had known the time of night when the thief was coming, you would have stayed awake and fought off the intruder.

Come downstairs in the morning and shiver as the chill breeze blows through the broken window. Feel your heart sink as you see your safe door torn open, the jewel box lying empty on the floor and the precious stones removed for ever. If only you had known the time of night when the thief was coming, you would have stayed awake and fought off the intruder.

Come downstairs in the morning and shiver as the chill breeze blows through the broken window. Feel your heart sink as you gaze at the empty mantelshelf, at the gap where the precious clock had always stood, and at the spot from where the silver candlesticks had been taken. If only you had known the time of night when the thief was coming, you would have stayed awake and fought off the intruder.

Come downstairs in the morning and shiver as the chill breeze blows through the broken window. Feel your heart sink as you see the sideboard drawers stand open, emptied of your best cutlery, the silver cake slice and the engraved sugar bowl. If only you had known the time of night when the thief was coming, you would have stayed awake and fought off the intruder.

Put yourself in the shoes of the burgled house owner. Feel what it is like to be the victim of crime. Now listen again to Jesus' teaching, 'Keep awake, for you do not know on what day your Lord is coming.' Can you really afford to ignore Jesus' warning?

Thinking

Just how much do you believe in the doctrine of judgement? And is that doctrine true to what we know of the God of love and the God of mercy?

Matthew clearly proclaims a doctrine of judgement. He takes as his example the Old Testament tradition of Noah. People were going about their daily lives oblivious to God's intentions. Then the floods came bringing death and destruction to many; bringing salvation to God's chosen few. And is that doctrine of judgement true to what we know of the God of love and the God of mercy?

Matthew clearly proclaims a doctrine of judgement. He takes as his example the newspaper report of the thief who strikes at the dead of night. The owners of the house were going about their nightly slumber oblivious to the thief's intention. So the judgement of God is unexpected, unannounced and swift. And is that doctrine of judgement true to what we know of the God of love and the God of mercy?

Matthew clearly proclaims a doctrine of judgement. He takes as his example the case of two men working side by side in the fields. One will be taken into the kingdom; one will be left to face destruction. He takes as his example the case of two women working side by side grinding meal together. One will be taken into the kingdom; one will be left to face destruction. And is that doctrine of judgement true to what we know of the God of love and the God of mercy?

Just how much do you believe in the doctrine of judgement?

42

Matthew 25:1–13

¹'Then the kingdom of heaven will be like this. Ten brides-maids took their lamps and went to meet the bridegroom. ²Five of them were foolish, and five were wise. ³When the foolish took their lamps, they took no oil with them; ⁴but the wise took flasks of oil with their lamps. ⁵As the bridegroom was delayed, all of them became drowsy and slept. ⁶But at midnight there was a shout, "Look! Here is the bridegroom! Come out to meet him." ⁷Then all those bridesmaids got up and trimmed their lamps. ⁸The foolish said to the wise, "Give us some of your oil, for our lamps are going out." ⁹But the wise replied, "No! there will not be enough for you and for us; you had better go to the dealers and buy some for yourselves." ¹⁰And while they went to buy it, the bridegroom came, and those who were ready went with him into the wedding banquet; and the door was shut. ¹¹Later the other bridesmaids came also, saying, "Lord, lord, open to us." ¹²But he replied, "Truly I tell you, I do not know you." ¹³Keep awake therefore, for you know neither the day nor the hour.'

Context

The parables in Matthew 25 continue Jesus' response to the disciples' request for information about when the last days would come. It is, says Jesus, like the bridegroom who comes when he is least expected.

Sensing

Listen to the parable of the ten bridesmaids. Listen to the detail.

See there in the distance the ten women making their way towards the bride's home. See them dressed up for the occasion, smart and ready to join the celebration. See each one of them clasping her bridal lamp, ready to illuminate the bridegroom's path. See five of them encumbered with caskets of oil. See five of them travelling free and light. Listen to the parable of the ten bridesmaids. Listen to the detail.

Come into the bride's home. Hear the excited chatter. Sense the expectation. Feel the excitement in the air. No one knows when the bridegroom will arrive to claim his bride. Everyone speculates that it is unlikely to be today. It may be tomorrow, but most probably it will be the day after next. Listen to the parable of the ten bridesmaids. Listen to the detail.

Stand there at the window peering into the darkness, seeing nothing and at that precise moment expecting nothing. Hear the shout along the street proclaiming that the bridegroom is already approaching. Stand there at the window peering at the frenzied activity throughout the room. Listen to the parable of the bridesmaids. Listen to the detail.

Look carefully at those five bridesmaids who had been so encumbered with caskets of oil. See them fill their lamps, trim the wicks and light the flames. See the sense of joy in their eyes. Now look carefully at those five bridesmaids who had travelled so free and light. See them seek in desperation for oil. Hear them beg in desperation to borrow another's supply. See the sense of panic in their eyes. Listen to the parable of the bridesmaids. Listen to the detail.

Follow the five lighted lamps through the darkened street. See the lamps light up the path for the bride and the bridegroom to enter into their wedding banquet. See the owners of those lamps take their place as the banquet begins. There outside in the dark stand the five other bridesmaids, clutching empty lamps and full hearts. There, on the outside they are destined to remain. Listen to the parable of the bridesmaids. Listen to the detail.

Intuition

Clearly there are some things that other people cannot do for you. You just have to do those things for yourself.

Consider the example of the student who has to sit the exam. The student who has not attended the lectures, who has not read the books, who has not attempted the course work, may be in a very vulnerable position in the examination hall. Perhaps the student has no oil in the lamp and it is now far too late to put matters right.

Consider the example of the businessman who is seeking a responsible post in a foreign land. The businessman who has not given time to mastering the language, who has not chosen to spend holiday time in the country, who has not attended conversation classes, may be in a very vulnerable position in a job interview. Perhaps that businessman has no oil in his lamp and it is now far too late to put matters right.

Consider the example of the businesswoman who is made redundant in mid-life. The businesswoman who has built her whole life around her work, who has failed to develop recreations and personal interests, who has no close circle of friends, may be in a very vulnerable position when her work is taken from her. Perhaps the businesswoman has no oil in her lamp and it is now far too late to put matters right.

Consider the example of the committed churchgoer who is at last called to meet her Lord. The churchgoer who has failed to put faith into practice, who has resisted letting the teaching of Jesus shape her daily life, who has neglected the life of prayer, may be in a very vulnerable position before the throne of judgement. Perhaps that churchgoer has no oil in her lamp and it is far too late to put matters right.

Clearly there are some things that other people cannot do for you. You just have to do those things for yourself. So how is your supply of oil?

Feeling

The bridesmaids who failed to take the oil may have been foolish, but surely they never deserved the heartless punishment that was inflicted on them. Try to look at things from their point of view.

All five of these bridesmaids set out from home with the very best of possible intentions. They had arrived at the bride's house at the very moment when she most needed them. They were there to be with her through the anxious hours of waiting. They were there to be with her at the very moment when the bridegroom arrived. The bridesmaids who failed to take the oil may have been foolish, but surely they never deserved the heartless punishment that was inflicted on them.

All five of these bridesmaids set out from home with the very best of possible intentions. They had set aside all other commitments to be with the bride as long as they were needed. They had chosen their smartest garments for the occasion. They had taken care to bring their own lamps in case the bridegroom chose to come by night. The bridesmaids who failed to take the oil may have been foolish, but surely they never deserved the heartless punishment that was inflicted on them.

All five of these bridesmaids set out from home with the very best of possible intentions. They had brought their own lamps, and surely had every right to expect that oil would be provided with the job. They had so generously responded to the demands which the bride was placing on their time, surely they could not be expected to bear the costs of the oil as well? The bridesmaids who failed to take oil may have been foolish, but surely they never deserved the heartless punishment that was inflicted on them.

Try to look at things from the point of view of the bridesmaids who failed to take the oil.

Thinking

Sometimes it can be very very difficult to say no, but sometimes this is the best and only answer to give.

What do you think about the bridesmaids who had a supply of oil and yet refused to give some of this oil to those who had none? Do you see them as the villains of the story? Or do you see them as the heroes who had the courage to say no? Sometimes it can be very difficult to say no.

What do you think about the bridesmaids who had a supply of oil and yet refused to give some of their oil to those who had none? Do you see them as mean individuals who failed to help others when they could have done so? Or do you see them as responsible individuals who recognized that the oil which could feed five lamps throughout the whole wedding banquet could not sustain ten? Sometimes it can be very difficult to say no.

What do you think about the bridesmaids who had a supply of oil and yet refused to give some of their oil to those who had none? Do you see them as heartless women who showed absolutely no concern for their sisters in distress? Or do you see them as truly concerned women who recognized that their sisters needed to learn the lesson of responsibility from their own experience? Sometimes it can be very difficult to say no.

What do you think about the bridesmaids who had a supply of oil and yet refused to give some of their oil to those who had none? Do you see them as highly materialistic people who weighed the quantity of oil more highly than human distress? Or do you see them as highly spiritual people who interpreted the lack of oil as indicative of their sisters' fundamental lack of readiness for the wedding banquet? Sometimes it can be very difficult to say no, but sometimes this is the best and only answer to give.

What would you have done in that situation? How good are you at saying no?

43

Matthew 25:14–30

[14]"For it is as if a man, going on a journey, summoned his slaves and entrusted his property to them; [15]to one he gave five talents, to another two, to another one, to each according to his ability. Then he went away. [16]The one who had received the five talents went off at once and traded with them, and made five more talents. [17]In the same way, the one who had the two talents made two more talents. [18]But the one who had received the one talent went off and dug a hole in the ground and hid his master's money. [19]After a long time the master of those slaves came and settled accounts with them. [20]Then the one who had received the five talents came forward, bringing five more talents, saying, "Master, you handed over to me five talents; see, I have made five more talents." [21]His master said to him, "Well done, good and trustworthy slave; you have been trustworthy in a few things, I will put you in charge of many things; enter into the joy of your master." [22]And the one with the two talents also came forward, saying, "Master, you handed over to me two talents;

see, I have made two more talents." [23]His master said to him, "Well done, good and trustworthy slave; you have been trustworthy in a few things, I will put you in charge of many things; enter into the joy of your master." [24]Then the one who had received the one talent also came forward, saying, "Master, I knew that you were a harsh man, reaping where you did not sow, and gathering where you did not scatter seed; [25]so I was afraid, and I went and hid your talent in the ground. Here you have what is yours." [26]But his master replied, "You wicked and lazy slave! You knew, did you, that I reap where I did not sow, and gather where I did not scatter? [27]Then you ought to have invested my money with the bankers, and on my return I would have received what was my own with interest. [28]So take the talent from him, and give it to the one with the ten talents. [29]For to all those who have, more will be given, and they will have an abundance; but from those who have nothing, even what they have will be taken away. [30]As for this worthless slave, throw him into the outer darkness, where there will be weeping and gnashing of teeth."'

Context

The parables in Matthew 25 continue Jesus' response to the disciples' request for information about when the last days would come. It is, says Jesus, like the absentee landowner who returns when he is least expected.

Sensing

Here is a story about three first-century businessmen. Picture them in your mind. The three men differ one from another in three important ways. Explore the differences.

The three men differ one from another in terms of their basic ability, in terms of their innate intelligence. Look into their eyes one by one and see the telling difference. The first man is clearly brighter than average. The glint of intelligence is in his eye for all to see. The second man is clearly Mr Average, neither noticeably bright nor noticeably dull. The third man is clearly of a likeable but slower disposition.

The three men differ one from another in terms of the wealth that has been entrusted to them. Look at their dress and at their demeanour one by one and see the telling difference. The first man is clearly wealthier than average. The cut of his cloak is there for all to see. The second man is clearly Mr Average, neither noticeably rich nor noticeably poor. The third man is clearly of a likeable but poorer disposition.

The three men differ one from another in terms of their industry and commitment to work. Look at their activity one by one and see the telling difference. The first man is clearly more industrious than average. The single-minded commitment to work is there in his lifestyle for all to see. The second man is clearly Mr Average, neither noticeably hardworking nor noticeably idle. The third man is clearly of a likeable but lazier disposition.

The three men differ one from another in terms of the contribution they make to their employer's business. Look at their end of year appraisal one by one. The first man is clearly enhancing the firm's profitability, by making five talents. The second man is clearly pulling his weight, by making two talents. The third man is clearly an unprofitable employee, by making no talents.

Here is a story about three first-century businessmen. Picture them in your mind. Jesus wants you to learn from their example.

Intuition

Think about the talents which you have been given in life. Brainstorm a list and try to prioritize the five most important to you. For example, do you have a way with words, a natural gift for getting on with people, an ability to learn languages, an ear for music, an eye for colour, a depth of perception and understanding, a knack for sorting out problems? What talents have you been given in life?

Think about what you do to take good care of your talents, to exercise them and to sharpen them for better use. For example, if you have a gift for music, do you find time to listen and to play? If you have a depth of perception and understanding, do you train your skills to use them to good effect? How are you developing your talents?

Think about how you use your talents to nurture your personal life. For example, if you have a talent for painting, do you feed your soul by being creative? If you have a talent for cooking fine food, do you feed your soul by spending time around the stove? How are you using your talents to nurture your personal life?

Think about how you use your talents to enrich the lives of others. For example, if you have a talent for humour, do you bring laughter into the lives of others? If you have a talent for empathy, do you bring comfort into the lives of others? If you have a talent for teaching, do you bring enlightenment into the lives of others? How are you using your talents to enrich the lives of others?

Think about how you use your talents in the service of your God. For example, if you have a talent for music, how do you use this talent to enrich the worship of your church? If you have a talent for caring for people, how do you use this talent to enrich the pastoral network of your church? If you have a talent for administration, how do you use this talent to enrich the day-to-day running of your church? If you have a talent for prayer, how do you use this talent to lead others on their spiritual path? How are you using your talents in the service of God?

Feeling

It is clearly a moment of some anxiety when the master returns. Put yourself in the place of those three slaves.

Feel what it is like to be that slave to whom five talents had been entrusted. You knew from the start that a lot of wealth had been entrusted to you, more than you had ever dreamed of handling, more than most slaves ever get the opportunity of managing. You knew from the start that a lot of responsibility had been placed on your shoulders. You knew from the start that much must be expected of you. When at last the master returns, you are fearful that you have failed to satisfy a harsh man who reaps where he did not sow, who gathers where he did not scatter seed.

Feel what it is like to be that slave to whom two talents had been entrusted. You knew from the start that you had been given enough resources to prove your worth, neither too much to turn your head nor too little to be really useful. You knew from the start that the master had placed real confidence in you. You knew from the start that the master expected something worthwhile in return. When at last the master returns, you are fearful that you have failed to satisfy a harsh man who reaps where he did not sow, who gathers where he did not scatter seed.

Feel what it is like to be that slave to whom one talent had been entrusted. You knew from the start that you had been dealt a poor hand, not enough to do anything worthwhile and yet too much to ignore. You knew that with so little it would be dangerous to speculate on the property market, since you could not afford to spread the risks with a diversified portfolio. You knew that you could lose the lot overnight if you made a wrong judgement. When at last the master returns, you are fearful that you have failed to satisfy a harsh man who reaps when he did not sow, who gathers where he did not scatter seed.

It is clearly a matter of some anxiety when the master returns. Put yourself in the place of those three slaves.

Thinking

Here is a story about equal opportunities. Or is it? Begin by exploring the inequalities in the account.

Clue number one is given by that almost passing reference to the innate capabilities of those three men. The story says that the talents were distributed to 'each according to his ability'. Does this mean that some divine IQ test had been administered to the candidates one by one? Here is a story about equal opportunities. Or is it?

Clue number two is given by the opening profile of the master. He is shown to be a person of power capable of making decisions with far-reaching implications for other people's lives. The story says that the master 'summoned his slaves' and distributed property to them at will. Does this mean that the distribution of the talents may have been some form of arbitrary lottery? Here is a story about equal opportunities. Or is it?

Clue number three is given by the puzzling lack of communication among the slaves themselves. Each slave seems oblivious to the opportunities and activities of the other two. The story says nothing about the three slaves being summoned by the master at the same time. Does this mean that there was some deliberate conspiracy of silence on the part of the master? Here is a story about equal opportunities. Or is it?

Clue number four is given by the complete lack of instructions given to the slaves. The master entrusts property to them, but does not tell them what he expects them to do with it. The story says nothing about whether the talents are given to them by way of investment or by way of safe keeping. Does this mean that some kind of divine initiative test has been given to the candidates one by one? Here is a story about equal opportunities. Or is it?

So how does this story fit with your theology of the God of fairness and justice?

44
Matthew 25:31–46

³¹'When the Son of Man comes in his glory, and all the angels with him, then he will sit on the throne of his glory. ³²All the nations will be gathered before him, and he will separate people one from another as a shepherd separates the sheep from the goats, ³³and he will put the sheep at his right hand and the goats at the left. ³⁴Then the king will say to those at his right hand, "Come, you that are blessed by my Father, inherit the kingdom prepared for you from the foundation of the world; ³⁵for I was hungry and you gave me food, I was thirsty and you gave me something to drink, I was a stranger and you welcomed me, ³⁶I was naked and you gave me clothing, I was sick and you took care of me, I was in prison and you visited me." ³⁷Then the righteous will answer him, "Lord, when was it that we saw you hungry and gave you food, or thirsty and gave you something to drink? ³⁸And when was it that we saw you a stranger and welcomed you, or naked and gave you clothing? ³⁹And when was it that we saw you sick or in prison and visited you?" ⁴⁰And the king will answer them, "Truly I tell you, just as you did it to one of the least of these who are members of my family, you did it to me." ⁴¹Then he will say to those at his left hand, "You that are accursed, depart from me into the eternal fire prepared for the devil and his angels; ⁴²for I was hungry and you gave me no food, I was thirsty and you gave me nothing to drink, ⁴³I was a stranger and you did not welcome me, naked and you did not give me clothing, sick and in prison and you did not visit me." ⁴⁴Then they also will answer, 'Lord, when was it that we saw you hungry or thirsty or a stranger or naked or sick or

in prison, and did not take care of you?" ⁴⁵Then he will answer them, "Truly I tell you, just as you did not do it to one of the least of these, you did not do it to me." ⁴⁶And these will go away into eternal punishment, but the righteous into eternal life.'

Context

This teaching on the 'end times' focuses on a day of final judgement, but its message relates to current behaviour. Those who show practical love to their neighbours in distress will be rewarded with the gift of eternal life. Those who do not will be banished into eternal punishment.

Sensing

You are a Christian in the first century AD. In the late 40s you live in a land that has suffered a famine. Hunger is the lot of all. Stand in line begging for a mouthful to eat and a cup of cold water to drink. Prices have skyrocketed. Stocks have run out. Shout in dismay, 'Does Jesus care, does anyone care?' You cannot live by prayer alone.

You are a Christian in the first century AD. In the late 40s you live in a strange land. When the famine grew worse there was no other option but to join the refugees and struggle to a new land. There was food there, but also resentment. Foreigners were pushed out to a shanty town on the edge of the desert. Touch your tattered clothes. Watch your children run naked. Shout in desperation, 'Does Jesus care, does anyone care?' You cannot live by prayer alone.

You are a Christian in the first century AD. In the early 50s you fall sick. Famine has taken its toll. In a strange land you have little support. Notice the holes in your rough built shelter which cannot keep out the chill. Recall the last gasps of your dying children. None are left to look after you. Shout in despair, 'Does Jesus care, does anyone care?' You cannot recover by prayer alone.

You are a Christian in the first century AD. In the mid-60s you are imprisoned for being a Christian. Rebellion has led to repression. Jews and Christians are both under suspicion. The legion has overrun the town. Thump on your prison walls. You are weak and defenceless. There is no one to stand up in court to attest your innocence. Shout in anger, 'Why does no one care?' You cannot be freed by prayer alone.

You are a Christian in the first century AD. The Christian community, your family, wants to serve Jesus. The Christian community, your family, wants to serve you. In the end, in the 'end', there can be no difference between their desires. You and God be the judge for now and for eternity.

Intuition

Sovereigns can be purely ceremonial symbols, a dummy with a crown on, or rulers with power to promote the welfare of all their people.

There was once a sovereign who declared that all subjects in the kingdom had to pay full respect to the throne. Every citizen had to make certain that the sovereign was provided with the necessities of life. Citizens were to bring the best of food and drink, and the best clothes to wear. Whenever the sovereign was sick the best doctor had to attend. Whenever the sovereign felt lonely or isolated, citizens were to rally to pay a comforting visit. It was decreed that citizens provide all the necessities of life for the sovereign, whose duty was to make every citizen do their duty. Relate that to the task of a sovereign.

There was once a citizen who experienced every kind of trauma. This citizen had become unemployed and grew hungry. This citizen found that the water supply was cut off because the bill could not be paid. This citizen could not afford to buy new clothes. This citizen fell sick and there were no community health facilities. This citizen was imprisoned at home by poverty, illness and neglect. Surely it was the duty of the sovereign to make certain that citizens were given the necessities of life. Relate that to the task of the sovereign.

There was once a sovereign who decreed that the kingdom was made up of each person within it, where all were equal, including the sovereign. Service in this kingdom was based on the principle that what was done for the least important citizen was service to the sovereign. Such service would receive the highest honour and the greatest reward. Every member of this kingdom was to care for their neighbour as part of their duty to the sovereign. Failure to carry out the commandment of the sovereign would be punished by banishment from the kingdom. This sovereign felt duty bound to promulgate such laws and to see that they were kept. Relate that to the task of the sovereign and to your own situation.

Feeling

When asked to care for our neighbours we can respond with a variety of emotions. We may see it as a burden or a joy. We may feel obliged to help in order to prevent the breakdown of our community. When asked to give practical help to a stranger, we may protest that it is beyond the bounds of practicality. We may feel that to care for neighbours is enough; and that strangers must get help from the state. When asked to give clothes for the unemployed, we may simply search out the worn garments, and toss them in a bag. Our actions may be driven by compassion or superiority.

When asked to care for our neighbours we can respond with a variety of emotions. When asked to join a visitors' roster to the local prison, we may protest that we have nothing in common with prisoners and have nothing to say. Others may feel more supportive. When asked to help a member of our own family, we may be motivated to do whatever is necessary by the bonds of relationship, by the previous experiences of mutual love and care, by a sense that we ought to do things for them because they are kith and kin. When asked to help a member of our own church, we may be motivated to do whatever is necessary by our common loyalty to Jesus, by our experience of mutual love and care, by a sense that what we do for them we are in some way doing for the body of Christ.

See how your feelings tell you much about how you relate to other people. When we relate well to our inner selves, we will care for our needs, both physical and spiritual. When we relate well to our church community, we will care for one another with warm affectionate love, expressed by word and practical deeds. When we relate well to our wider community, we will take our share in community care and development. When we relate well to Christ, we will see Christ in the needy as well as the whole. Jesus is right, our feelings govern our actions.

Thinking

The Day of Judgement has inspired the artist's imagination over many centuries. Artists were drawn towards pictures of rewards for good and of punishment for evil. The fires of hell were vividly lit and the delights of heaven were splendidly illuminated. This account, unique to Matthew, has been a rich resource for artistic painting.

Nowadays thinking society tends to dismiss the concept as 'medieval'. We project such pictures onto the TV screen, admire them as art but distance ourselves from any reality. We declare that fear is a short-term motivation for good deeds, and that this is the world for action, not some afterlife. The whole idea of a coming Day of Judgement is seen as unrealistic and unnecessary: unrealistic, because we all fail as humans, and so a judgement day would damn us all; unnecessary, because love, not fear, is sufficient motivation for any good we may be able to do.

Yet Matthew obviously considered that this picture of Christ in his kingdom was a key image in all his teaching. In Matthew's gospel Jesus was not just a good teacher, a second Moses. Jesus was the Messiah, the anointed king of God's people. The king was responsible for setting down the proper conduct for all citizens. Jesus had summed up the old law in two phrases: love God; and love your neighbour as yourself. Jesus taught that these were so intertwined that you could not do one without the other. Love of God was shown in love of neighbour. By your love of neighbour you showed your love for God. By our obedience we would be judged worthy or unworthy to participate in the kingdom of God.

Saint Paul discovered that to persecute Christians was to persecute Christ; that the community of Christians was the body of Christ; that the Spirit of Christ remodelled lives to care for one another. Saint John likewise focused on love as the fulfilling of the law. By this we are judged as willing or unwilling to participate in the kingdom. Banishment can be our dreadful choice; incorporation our glorious reward. Such things do not change from the beginning to the end. Is this how you see it?

45

Matthew 28:1-10

¹After the sabbath, as the first day of the week was dawning, Mary Magdalene and the other Mary went to see the tomb. ²And suddenly there was a great earthquake; for an angel of the Lord, descending from heaven, came and rolled back the stone and sat on it. ³His appearance was like lightning, and his clothing white as snow. ⁴For fear of him the guards shook and became like dead men. ⁵But the angel said to the women, 'Do not be afraid; I know that you are looking for Jesus who was crucified. ⁶He is not here; for he has been raised, as he said. Come, see the place where he lay. ⁷Then go quickly and tell his disciples, "He has been raised from the dead, and indeed he is going ahead of you to Galilee; there you will see him." This is my message for you.' ⁸So they left the tomb quickly with fear and great joy, and ran to tell his disciples. ⁹Suddenly Jesus met them and said, 'Greetings!' And they came to him, took hold of his feet, and worshipped him. ¹⁰Then Jesus said to them, 'Do not be afraid; go and tell my brothers to go to Galilee; there they will see me.'

Context

As the passion ends, the stone at the tomb is sealed, and the guards are set to secure it. The resurrection story begins with the removal of the stone, and ends with the command for the disciples to meet Jesus in Galilee. Jerusalem is left for dead. Galilee's revelation is resurrected.

Sensing

Matthew gives us three pieces of data about the resurrection.

Take the place of Mary Magdalene and share her experience. Listen to the invitation of the divine messenger, 'Come, see the place where he lay.' Returning to the tomb you expect to find death sealed within. Your devotion has drawn you back to the past, hoping to relive the relationship which had come to a dead end. The upheaval of creation has shaken your expectations. See the stone rolled back. Listen to the invitation, 'Come, see the place where he lay.' Sense the loss. Touch the shroud. This is where you laid him – dead.

Take the place of Mary Magdalene and share her experience. Hear the command of the divine messenger, 'Go quickly and tell his disciples, "He has been raised from the dead. You will see him in Galilee."' The tomb is open. The future calls you on. You must return to the routine of living. Sense the fear. Sense the joy of such a prospect. Feel the strength return to your body. Run towards the future. You live because he lives.

Take the place of Mary Magdalene and share her experience. As you run, hear the greeting. Look up and freeze in your tracks. 'Shalom', it is the old familiar greeting said with new vitality. Here is the greeting of resurrected relationship. Drop to your knees in surprise and reverence. Take hold of the feet. Kiss them again though they are now marked with the nails. Hold on to the present. Recognize the divine. Enjoy the experience of worship.

Take the place of Mary Magdalene and share her experience. As you worship, hear the command of Jesus, 'Tell my brothers to go to Galilee; there they will see me.' Worship leads to mission. Your experience of worship must be shared with others so they can see him too. Rise to your feet. Rehearse the words, 'I have seen him. You will see him.' Galilee is the place of memories, the place of fishing, and the place of mission.

Off you go; you have the data; you have the message; you can share the joy of Easter.

Intuition

What does 'the first day of the week' suggest to you?

The first day of the week, is it a day for new beginnings, a day of expectation when you hope for something better to happen than in the past? Easter day was on the first day of the week because it signified a new creation, a new start when life takes on a new meaning. Is that what the first day of the week suggests to you?

The first day of the week, is it a day for worship, a day when we expect to have a new experience of God? Is it a day to pledge our loyalty and our love? Easter was the first day of the week and

Mary offered adoration and reverence to the risen Lord. Is that what the first day of the week suggests to you?

The first day of the week, is it a day of wonder when we discover a new vision of reality? Easter day gave us a new understanding of life and death. It gave us a new discovery of the presence of the living Lord, calming our fears and strengthening our resolve to follow and obey. Wonder and discovery, is that what the first day of the week suggests to you?

The first day of the week, is it a day of witness, when we are ready to share our experience of Jesus with others? Easter day became pivotal in the mission of the church. Those who had met with Jesus as the risen Lord invited others to come and meet him for themselves. News like this could not be hidden. It must be shared as the angels commanded. Witness and evangelism, is that what the first day of the week suggests to you?

The first day of the week, is it a day of Easter celebration, so that every first day of the week becomes another resurrection day: full of new life; full of renewed relationships; full of worship; full of wonder; full of mission? 'He is risen indeed', is that what every first day of the week proclaims to you?

Feeling

This Easter gospel highlights the feelings of fear and of joy. Consider these feelings.

Note how the word 'fear' keeps reoccurring in the text. The guards at the tomb were afraid of the white-robed messengers of God. They shook with fear and became as dead men. Fear deadens reaction. Fear makes us look for security. Fear imprisoned the guards and made them blind to what was happening.

Fear is a common emotion on many occasions. At a time of loss we feel afraid. When a loved one departs or dies, fear fills the heart. When the security of a relationship fails, we become nervous and afraid. When a job is lost or given up, the fear of being useless and undervalued grips our being. When the seals of security are broken, fear roams free.

The gospel tells us that the women also felt fear. They were in trepidation as they approached the tomb. Feel for them. The guards would have asked what business they had there. Their very presence would have been a threat to stability and security. Note how the divine messengers recognized the women's feelings and acknowledged their fear. Yet the messengers had startling news: 'He is not here; he has been raised.' Enter into the women's fear of the unexpected, and at the command to tell the impossible to those who had shared the loss.

This time the women had mixed emotions about the Easter message: joy and fear. Step into their shoes. The women's joy was affirmed by meeting Jesus. Here was renewed security; here was renewed relationship; here was inner peace. With Jesus alive great things would happen, and love would live again. Share the joy that makes you want to cling to the present. Feel how fear returns when you are asked to let go. Overcome your feelings of fear and step out into the future. It is there that Jesus goes ahead of us.

Easter calls us to move on to the future, motivated by our joys and with our fears overcome. Let Easter put a spring into your step.

Thinking

Matthew's gospel declares that the resurrection takes place in Jerusalem, but the birth of the church is in Galilee. Luke locates both in Jerusalem. Some take the position that this does not matter. Others look for some explanation of the differences.

Here is the first consideration. How reliable are these stories of the resurrection? If the early church wanted to make up a golden ending to the gospel, it would hardly have included variations. One version of a lie is always safer. Gospel writers all agree on two facts: the tomb was empty and the body raised; the risen Lord appeared to a variety of people in a variety of ways. However, none relate these appearances in the same place or in the same form.

Here is the second consideration. Did the church as a whole treasure different experiences of the risen Lord? The evidence seems to be that various areas in the spread of the church were loyal to different apostolic leadership. The Pauline churches saw Jerusalem as the cradle of the church. Christians influenced by their Jewish roots may have looked to Nazareth and Capernaum as the home of the gospel. All evidence points to the fact that appearances of the risen Lord were not restricted to any one location.

Here is the third consideration. Did the disciples scatter immediately after the crucifixion? Maybe those with links to Galilee headed home as the safest destination. Maybe those with family or friends in or near Jerusalem (say Bethany or Emmaus) found a safe haven nearby. It would take a few days for the news of the resurrection to reach the various locations, and then to be accepted as true. The scattered disciples would regroup to cross-check their experiences. Pentecost would give them the perfect reason for such a journey to Jerusalem, to share all their experiences of the risen Lord, and the gift of the Holy Spirit to reaffirm the continuing presence of Christ.

As we celebrate Easter we can be sure of the two 'recorded facts' of the resurrection, and gain a new experience of the risen Christ – wherever in the world we find ourselves this Easter day.

46
Matthew 28:16–20

¹⁶Now the eleven disciples went to Galilee, to the mountain to which Jesus had directed them. ¹⁷When they saw him, they worshipped him; but some doubted. ¹⁸And Jesus came and said to them, 'All authority in heaven and on earth has been given to me. ¹⁹Go therefore and make disciples of all nations, baptizing them in the name of the Father and of the Son and of the Holy Spirit, ²⁰and teaching them to obey everything that I have commanded you. And remember, I am with you always, to the end of the age.'

Context
The ending of Matthew's gospel brings together many of its key themes. Jesus is: the new Moses, teaching the disciples how to obey God; the Messiah, having full authority in heaven and earth; the head of the church, into which the disciples are baptized; and the Lord, present with all until the final day.

Sensing
Sit down with Matthew as he gathers the various threads together and weaves the gospel ending.

Look at the thread of teaching. Matthew gives teaching top priority in the work of Jesus. Discipleship is all about learning how to discover the will of God. Discipleship is putting such learning into practice. For Matthew Jesus is the new Moses giving a new law to the new Israel. Look at the thread of teaching and link it with the experience of the church.

Look at the thread of authority and worship. For Matthew this rabbi is the Messiah with the authority of the Son of the living God. In his ending Matthew restates Christ's kingship: 'All authority in heaven and on earth has been given to me.' The disciples' response to such authority is worship (verse 17) and obedience (verse 20). As he writes Matthew knows that not all have so responded. Some obey; some disobey. Look at the thread of authority and proper response, and link it with the experience of the church.

Sit down with Matthew as he draws his gospel to a close.

Look at the thread of mission. The Messiah has commanded his disciples to teach and baptize. The gospel was written to spread the good news. This mission was divinely commanded and divinely empowered. By the time that Matthew wrote, the church confessed a trinitarian faith, and Matthew's baptismal words reflect this. Look at the thread of mission and link it with the experience of the church.

Look at the thread of presence. Mission required a faith to go out into new places. Hear the disciples' voices as they ponder whether to return home often to Galilee to seek the presence of Christ, or to move out to find Jesus in new locations. Matthew had proclaimed Jesus was Emmanuel as the gospel begun (1:23). At every 'end' Jesus will be with us. Through remembrance of Christ in word, action, prayer, eucharist and fellowship, disciples will find him in every place at every time. Look at the thread of presence and link it with the experience of the church.

Watch this master craftsman weave the threads together so that the patterns shine for all to see.

Intuition

Discipleship, what does discipleship suggest to you?

Discipleship suggests learning. Every learner wants the best teacher. Learners want to be confident in the teacher's knowledge. They want to be drawn by the quality of the teaching. They want to be inspired by the depth of insight. They want vivid stories told so that they can retain what has been learnt. They will learn from life as well as lessons.

Discipleship suggests a response to good teaching. It is the responsibility of learners to work and struggle to understand the truth. Learners must strive to bring together the various parts of the programme. Learners must connect theory and practice. Learning requires a response with heart as well as mind.

Discipleship suggests commitment to learning. Disciples must be committed to be in the presence of the teacher. They must pay attention to his words. They must pledge themselves to study. They must commit themselves to putting learning into practice. They must obey as well as learn. To be a disciple is to call the teacher 'Lord'. Such commitment is expressed through baptism.

Discipleship suggests mission. What has been learnt must be shared. What has been handed on must be handed down to the next generation. Learning must be absorbed into life so that it too becomes a witness to the truth. There can be no secrets kept of what has been learnt. Life and teaching must shine forth for others to see.

Discipleship suggests community. Learning is a communal activity. When two or three are gathered together the various understandings of truth can be shared and the partial made whole. Disciples learn from one another as well as from the teacher. The Spirit of Christ inspires fellowship in which the teaching makes sense in community.

Discipleship suggests remembrance. The pupil remembers the teacher as well as the precepts taught. Disciples of Christ remember the man as well as the message. The person, the place, the story and the truth are all combined in the memory. Touch one and the others are triggered. The memory is the treasury bank of the truth.

Discipleship, there is no end to its implications.

Feeling

'And then there were eleven.' Feel for the interaction between the eleven and Jesus in this conclusion.

The eleven were back in their familiar haunts in Galilee. This was the place where they had gathered in a group around Jesus. This was the place where Jesus had tried to make them a team. This was the place where their families lived. Here they had worked and made a living. This was familiar territory. This was home. Step into the shoes of one of the eleven and share their reactions.

And then there were eleven. Once there had been twelve. Judas was dead. One of your number had totally failed. Among the eleven there were doubters too. Feel the strain of trying to last the distance. Being one of the eleven is a risky business. Share your feelings as one of the remaining eleven.

And then there were eleven. Here was a group who had discovered that the Christ who had died on the cross had risen again. It must be true, the teacher was the Son of God. We had thought that when the teacher collapsed, then the teaching would collapse, but now both seem to be resurrected. Despite some doubts we are on our knees in reverent worship. Share your feelings as one of the eleven.

And then there were eleven. Here was a group of just a few people. We are rather a shaky lot. Our faith has been tested and sometimes found wanting. We have been taught but have only partly passed the test. We are a mixed group with some jealousy and rivalry and many different ideas. Yet we are told to go 'to all nations'. This is a mighty task, and a heavy responsibility. Share your feelings as one of the eleven.

And then there were eleven. Here was a group who were promised the ongoing presence of the Master. We have seen him die. We have seen him risen. Now he promises never to leave us again. Remembrance makes him present, every place, every time, all ways. Share your feelings of assurance and anxiety as one of the eleven.

Thinking

This ending makes perfect sense as a conclusion to Matthew's gospel. It pulls together all its main themes. It looks back; it looks forward. Galilee was the site of the choice of the first disciples. Now it is the site of the commissioning of the first apostles. The mountain was the location of the first round of teaching. It is now the location for the last round of teaching. Teaching and obedience are linked together. Teaching and baptism are linked together. The authority on earth was in the hands of Emmanuel, God's incarnation disclosed in the Son. The authority in heaven was in the hands of the ascended Lord, who sits at God's right hand. The presence of God is assured by the coming of the Spirit of Christ, just as it is assured at the final coming of Christ. Yes, all the themes are carefully woven together.

The only problem on fuller examination is that the scene seems to be painted in retrospect. It seems too clever a 'rounding off'. Galilee is not the most favoured location for the final appearance of the risen Lord. The stronger tradition follows Luke's indication of Jerusalem. The 'commission' seems to ignore the struggle in the early church to decide whether the Gentiles had an equal place in the first expansion of the church. The 'trinitarian formula' at baptism seems to prejudge the gift of the Spirit at Pentecost.

What then is Matthew trying to do by putting the conclusion in this way?

Matthew links the first disciples with the present disciples. Like the first disciples they worship Jesus as Lord, though doubts remain. Like the first disciples Christ's teaching calls for the response of baptism, as they knew it then, in the name of the Trinity. Like the first disciples to remember Jesus is to be in the presence of Christ. Like the first disciples every Christian must live in the 'in-between times': Christ has died; Christ is risen; Christ will come again. Matthew sees the story of the first disciples as our story.

The gospel has no ending, until the final conclusion comes.

Further reading

The following books provide further insight into the theory of psychological type underpinning the Myers-Briggs Type Indicator and the relevance of type theory for the Christian community.

Myers-Briggs and Religion: further reading

Baab, L. M., *Personality Type in Congregations*, Washington, DC, Alban Institute, 1998.

Bayne, R., *The Myers-Briggs Type Indicator: a critical review and practical guide*, London, Chapman and Hall, 1995.

Briggs-Myers, I. and Myers, P. B., *Gifts Differing*, Palo Alto, California, Consulting Psychologists Press, 1980.

Bryant, C., *Jung and the Christian Way*, London, Darton, Longman and Todd, 1983.

Butler, A., *Personality and Communicating the Gospel*, Cambridge, Grove Books, 1999.

Davis, S. and Handschin B., *Reinventing Yourself: life planning after 50*, Palo Alto, California, Consulting Psychologists Press, 1998.

Duncan, B., *Pray Your Way: your personality and God*, London, Darton, Longman and Todd, 1993.

Dwyer, M. T., *Wake Up the Sun: an exploration of personality types and spiritual growth*, Thornbury, Victoria, Desbooks, 1988.

Dwyer, M. T., *No Light without Shadow: an exploration of personality types*, Thornbury, Australia, Desbooks, 1995.

Faucett, R. and Faucett, C. A., *Personality and Spiritual Freedom: growing in the Christian life through understanding personality type and the Myers-Briggs Type Indicator*, New York, Doubleday, 1987.

Francis, L. J., *Personality Type and Scripture: exploring Mark's gospel*, London, Mowbray, 1997.

Francis, L. J. and Atkins, P., *Exploring Luke's Gospel: a guide to the gospel readings in the Revised Common Lectionary*, London, Mowbray, 2000.

Goldsmith, M., *Knowing Me, Knowing God*, London, Triangle, 1994.

Goldsmith, M. and Wharton, M., *Knowing Me, Knowing You*, London, SPCK, 1993.

Grant, W. H., Thompson, M. and Clarke, T. E., *From Image to Likeness: a Jungian path in the gospel journey*, New York, Paulist Press, 1983.

Harbaugh, G., *God's Gifted People: discovering your personality as a gift*, Minneapolis, Augsburg Publishing House, 1990.

Hedges, P., *Understanding Your Personality: with Myers-Briggs and more*, London, Sheldon Press, 1993.

Hirsh, S. and Kummerow, J., *Life Types*, New York, Warner Books, 1989.

Innes, R., *Personality Indicators and the Spiritual Life*, Cambridge, Grove Books Ltd, 1996.

Johnson, R., *Your Personality and the Spiritual Life*, Crowbridge, Monarch, 1995.

Keating, C. J., *Who We Are is How We Pray*, Mystic, Connecticut, Twenty-Third Publications, 1987.

Keirsey, D., *Please Understand Me: 2*, Del Mar, California, Prometheus Nemesis Book Company, 1998.

Kelsey, M., *Prophetic Ministry: the psychology and spirituality of pastoral care*, Rockport, Massachusetts, Element Inc., 1991.

Kroeger, O. and Thuesen, J. M., *Type Talk*, New York, Delta, 1988.

Kroeger, O. and Thuesen, J. M., *Type Talk at Work*, New York, Delacorte Press, 1992.

Michael, C. P. and Morrisey, M. C., *Prayer and Temperament*, Charlottesville, Virginia, The Open Book Inc., 1984.

Moore, R. L. (ed.), *Carl Jung and Christian Spirituality*, Mahwah, New Jersey, Paulist Press, 1988.

Moss, S., *Jungian Typology*, Melbourne, Collins Dove, 1989.

Osborn, L. and Osborn, D., *God's Diverse People*, London, Daybreak, 1991.

Oswald, R. M. and Kroeger, O., *Personality Type and Religious Leadership*, Washington, DC, Alban Institute, 1988.

Quenk, N. L., *Beside Ourselves: our hidden personality in everyday life*, Palo Alto, California, Davies-Black, 1993.

Richardson, P. T., *Four Spiritualities: expressions of self, expressions of spirit*, Palo Alto, California, Davies-Black, 1996.

Spoto, A., *Jung's Typology in Perspective*, Boston, Massachusetts, Sigo Press, 1989.

Thorne, A. and Gough, H., *Portraits of Type*, Palo Alto, California, Consulting Psychologists Press, 1991.

Williams, I., *Prayer and My Personality*, Bramcote, Grove Books, 1987.